T0274196

Multimedia Technology and Applications

Multimedia Technology and Applications

Edited by
Olive Marsh

Larsen & Keller
www.larsen-keller.com

Multimedia Technology and Applications
Edited by Olive Marsh
ISBN: 978-1-63549-191-3 (Hardback)

© 2017 Larsen & Keller

 Larsen & Keller

Published by Larsen and Keller Education,
5 Penn Plaza,
19th Floor,
New York, NY 10001, USA

Cataloging-in-Publication Data

Multimedia technology and applications / edited by Olive Marsh.
    p. cm.
Includes bibliographical references and index.
ISBN 978-1-63549-191-3
1. Multimedia systems. 2. Multimedia communications. 3. Digital media. 4. Digital communications.
I. Marsh, Olive.
QA76.575 .M85 2017
006.7--dc23

The publisher's policy is to use permanent paper from mills that operate a sustainable forestry policy. Furthermore, the publisher ensures that the text paper and cover boards used have met acceptable environmental accreditation standards.

Printed and bound in the United States of America.

For more information regarding Larsen and Keller Education and its products, please visit the publisher's website www.larsen-keller.com

Table of Contents

Preface

This book elucidates new techniques of multimedia technology and their applications in a multidisciplinary approach. It provides thorough knowledge about the various new concepts and methods emerging in this field. Multimedia technology refers to the new age technology which combines the different media like text or print. It can be displayed, recorded, played and accessed by computer and electronic devices. A detailed explanation of the various concepts and applications of multimedia technology has been covered in this book. Some of the diverse topics covered in the book address the varied branches that fall under this category. This text is a complete source of knowledge on the present status of this important field.

A foreword of all Chapters of the book is provided below:

Chapter 1 - The chapter provides a comprehensive overview of multimedia. It helps the reader get a comprehensive understanding of multimedia and introduces the reader to the various technologies that constitute multimedia. This chapter is an overview of the subject matter incorporating all the major aspects of multimedia.; **Chapter 2** - Digital media refers to all media that is encoded in machine readable format. What is digital or digitized can only be accessed, read, modified, preserved and distributed on digital electronics devices. This chapter provides an expansive study of digital media, and the various digital media technologies in usage. It furnishes valuable information on topics like digital media player, digital video interactive (DVI), digital media among others.; **Chapter 3** - Digital image processing involves the processing of digital images using computer algorithms. Digital image processing is able to solve problems like non-linear image display and image enhancement during image processing. The chapter strategically encompasses and incorporates the major components and key concepts of digital image processing, providing a complete understanding.; **Chapter 4** - Multi-image, though now an obsolete field, was one of the pioneering techniques of digital image processing. It involves using 35mm slides projected by single or multiple slide projectors onto one or more screens in sync with an audio track or voice over. This chapter studies multi-image, slide show and their modern counterpart, the multi-dynamic image technique. This chapter is a compilation of the various branches of multi-image technologies that form an integral part of the broader subject matter.; **Chapter 5** - Art has found expression in various fields including that of the media. New media art is a genre in which art incorporates new media technologies like digital art, computer animation, computer robotics, cyborg art, interactive art etc. This chapter is dedicated to this contemporary field of artmedia and artmedia technologies and explores these topics comprehensively.; **Chapter 6** - With the fast-paced lifestyle of modern times, technology needs to accommodate changes in patterns and trends of viewership. Digitization allows for the appropriation of new media technologies for art and multimedia purposes. This chapter explores topics like non-linear media which include video on demand, hypothetical models like postliterate society, and advanced techniques like transmedia storytelling.; **Chapter 7** - The digital revolution has made the concept of new literacies possible. It is a relatively new field in the discipline of literacy studies and its definition remains open and is conceptualized in different ways by different academicians. Digital literacy refers to the knowledge and skill set based on digital devices like smartphones, laptops, PCs etc. This chapter elucidates the skills and competencies that are a result of digital and information literacy. The chapter also gives the reader material on how these literacies are changing the world of literary studies.; **Chapter 8** - An extension of the term hypertext, hypermedia refers to nonlinear media that includes things like graphics, audio, plain text and hyperlinks. The details included are hypermedia, its tools and their applications in the current scenario. This chapter discusses the methods of hypermedia in a critical manner, providing key analysis to the subject matter.; **Chapter 9** - The cellphone has made possible the mobility of media in which a consumer is able to access media on mobile devices and this has helped change the field of information and communication. This chapter explores the various technologies that have made information and media portable. The content deals extensively with topics like multimedia messaging service (MMS) and multimedia database. It will give a detailed explanation of mobile media technologies.; **Chapter 10** - The chapter explores topics like the multimedia computer, multimedia database, multimedia telephony and IP multimedia subsystem. These allied fields of multimedia have transformed media and communication strategies and techniques. Improvement of technology have bridged the gap between separate locations. This chapter provides a plethora of interdisciplinary topics for better comprehension of multimedia.; **Chapter 11** - This chapter gives a detailed account of the various kinds of software related to multimedia like mobile soft device, media player (software), 4K video downloader, multimedia framework etc. This text introduces the reader to each of these tools. This chapter is an overview of the subject matter incorporating all the major aspects of multimedia software.

I would like to thank the entire editorial team who made sincere efforts for this book and my family who supported me in my efforts of working on this book. I take this opportunity to thank all those who have been a guiding force throughout my life.

Editor

Introduction to Multimedia

The chapter provides a comprehensive overview of multimedia. It helps the reader get a comprehensive understanding of multimedia and introduces the reader to the various technologies that constitute multimedia. This chapter is an overview of the subject matter incorporating all the major aspects of multimedia.

Multimedia is content that uses a combination of different content forms such as text, audio, images, animation, video and interactive content. Multimedia contrasts with media that use only rudimentary computer displays such as text-only or traditional forms of printed or hand-produced material.

Multimedia can be recorded and played, displayed, dynamic, interacted with or accessed by information content processing devices, such as computerized and electronic devices, but can also be part of a live performance. Multimedia devices are electronic media devices used to store and experience multimedia content. Multimedia is distinguished from mixed media in fine art; by including audio, for example, it has a broader scope. The term "rich media" is synonymous for interactive multimedia. Hypermedia scales up the amount of media content in multimedia application.

Categorization

Multimedia may be broadly divided into linear and non-linear categories. Linear active content progresses often without any navigational control for the viewer such as a cinema presentation. Non-linear uses interactivity to control progress as with a video game or self-paced computer based training. Hypermedia is an example of non-linear content.

Multimedia presentations can be live or recorded. A recorded presentation may allow interactivity via a navigation system. A live multimedia presentation may allow interactivity via an interaction with the presenter or performer.

Major Characteristics

Multimedia presentations may be viewed by person on stage, projected, transmitted, or played locally with a media player. A broadcast may be a live or recorded multimedia presentation. Broadcasts and recordings can be either analog or digital electronic media technology. Digital online multimedia may be downloaded or streamed. Streaming multimedia may be live or on-demand.

Multimedia games and simulations may be used in a physical environment with special effects, with multiple users in an online network, or locally with an offline computer, game system, or simulator.

The various formats of technological or digital multimedia may be intended to enhance the users' experience, for example to make it easier and faster to convey information. Or in entertainment or art, to transcend everyday experience.

A lasershow is a live multimedia performance.

Enhanced levels of interactivity are made possible by combining multiple forms of media content. Online multimedia is increasingly becoming object-oriented and data-driven, enabling applications with collaborative end-user innovation and personalization on multiple forms of content over time. Examples of these range from multiple forms of content on Web sites like photo galleries with both images (pictures) and title (text) user-updated, to simulations whose co-efficients, events, illustrations, animations or videos are modifiable, allowing the multimedia "experience" to be altered without reprogramming. In addition to seeing and hearing, Haptic technology enables virtual objects to be felt. Emerging technology involving illusions of taste and smell may also enhance the multimedia experience.

Terminology

History of the Term

The term *multimedia* was coined by singer and artist Bob Goldstein (later 'Bobb Goldsteinn') to promote the July 1966 opening of his "LightWorks at L'Oursin" show at Southampton, Long Island. Goldstein was perhaps aware of an American artist named Dick Higgins, who had two years previously discussed a new approach to art-making he called "intermedia."

On August 10, 1966, Richard Albarino of *Variety* borrowed the terminology, reporting: "Brainchild of songscribe-comic Bob ('Washington Square') Goldstein, the 'Lightworks' is the latest *multi-media* music-cum-visuals to debut as discothèque fare." Two years later, in 1968, the term "multimedia" was re-appropriated to describe the work of a political consultant, David Sawyer, the husband of Iris Sawyer—one of Goldstein's producers at L'Oursin.

In the intervening forty years, the word has taken on different meanings. In the late 1970s, the term referred to presentations consisting of multi-projector slide shows timed to an audio track. However, by the 1990s 'multimedia' took on its current meaning.

Multimedia (multi-image) setup for the 1988 Ford New Car Announcement Show, August 1987, Detroit, MI

In the 1993 first edition of McGraw-Hill's *Multimedia: Making It Work,* Tay Vaughan declared "Multimedia is any combination of text, graphic art, sound, animation, and video that is delivered by computer. When you allow the user – the viewer of the project – to control what and when these elements are delivered, it is *interactive multimedia.* When you provide a structure of linked elements through which the user can navigate, interactive multimedia becomes *hypermedia.*"

The German language society, Gesellschaft für deutsche Sprache, decided to recognize the word's significance and ubiquitousness in the 1990s by awarding it the title of 'Word of the Year' in 1995. The institute summed up its rationale by stating "[Multimedia] has become a central word in the wonderful new media world."

In common usage, *multimedia* refers to an electronically delivered combination of media including video, still images, audio, text in such a way that can be accessed interactively. Much of the content on the web today falls within this definition as understood by millions. Some computers which were marketed in the 1990s were called "multimedia" computers because they incorporated a CD-ROM drive, which allowed for the delivery of several hundred megabytes of video, picture, and audio data. That era saw also a boost in the production of educational multimedia CD-ROMs.

Word Usage and Context

Since media is the plural of medium, the term "multimedia" is used to describe multiple occurrences of only one form of media such as a collection of audio CDs. This is why it's important that the word "multimedia" is used exclusively to describe multiple forms of media and content.

The term "multimedia" is also ambiguous. Static content (such as a paper book) may be considered multimedia if it contains both pictures and text or may be considered interactive if the user interacts by turning pages at will. Books may also be considered non-linear if the pages are accessed non-sequentially. The term "video", if not used exclusively to describe motion photography, is ambiguous in multimedia terminology. *Video* is often used to describe the file format, delivery format, or presentation format instead of *"footage"* which is used to distinguish motion photography from *"animation"* of rendered motion imagery. Multiple forms of information content are often not considered modern forms of presentation such as audio or video. Likewise, single forms of information content with single methods of information processing (e.g. non-interactive audio) are often called multimedia, perhaps to distinguish static media from active media. In the Fine arts, for example, Leda Luss Luyken's ModulArt brings two key elements of musical composition and film into the world of painting: variation of a theme and movement of and within a picture, making *ModulArt* an interactive multimedia form of art. Performing arts may also be considered multimedia considering that performers and props are multiple forms of both content and media.

The *Gesellschaft für deutsche Sprache* chose *Multimedia* as German Word of the Year 1995.

Usage/Application

A presentation using Powerpoint. Corporate presentations may combine all forms of media content.

Virtual reality uses multimedia content. Applications and delivery platforms of multimedia are virtually limitless.

VVO Multimedia-Terminal in Dresden WTC (Germany)

Multimedia finds its application in various areas including, but not limited to, advertisements, art, education, entertainment, engineering, medicine, mathematics, business, scientific research and spatial temporal applications. Several examples are as follows:

Creative Industries

Creative industries use multimedia for a variety of purposes ranging from fine arts, to entertainment, to commercial art, to journalism, to media and software services provided for any of the industries listed below. An individual multimedia designer may cover the spectrum throughout their career. Request for their skills range from technical, to analytical, to creative.

Commercial Uses

Much of the electronic old and new media used by commercial artists and graphic designers is multimedia. Exciting presentations are used to grab and keep attention in advertising. Business to business, and interoffice communications are often developed by creative services firms for advanced multimedia presentations beyond simple slide shows to sell ideas or liven-up training. Commercial multimedia developers may be hired to design for governmental services and non-profit services applications as well.

Entertainment and Fine Arts

In addition, multimedia is heavily used in the entertainment industry, especially to develop special effects in movies and animations(VFX, 3D animation, etc.). Multimedia games are a popular pastime and are software programs available either as CD-ROMs or online. Some video games also use multimedia features. Multimedia applications that allow users to actively participate instead of just sitting by as passive recipients of information are called *Interactive Multimedia*. In the Arts there are multimedia artists, whose minds are able to blend techniques using different media that in some way incorporates interaction with the viewer. One of the most relevant could be Peter Greenaway who is melding Cinema with Opera and all sorts of digital media. Another approach entails the creation of multimedia that can be displayed in a traditional fine arts arena, such as an art gallery. Although multimedia display material may be volatile, the survivability of the content is as strong as any traditional media. Digital recording material may be just as durable and infinitely reproducible with perfect copies every time.

Education

In education, multimedia is used to produce computer-based training courses (popularly called CBTs) and reference books like encyclopedia and almanacs. A CBT lets the user go through a series of presentations, text about a particular topic, and associated illustrations in various information formats. Edutainment is the combination of education with entertainment, especially multimedia entertainment.

Learning theory in the past decade has expanded dramatically because of the introduction of multimedia. Several lines of research have evolved (e.g. Cognitive load, Multimedia learning, etc.). The possibilities for learning and instruction are nearly endless.

The idea of media convergence is also becoming a major factor in education, particularly higher education. Defined as separate technologies such as voice (and telephony features), data (and productivity applications) and video that now share resources and interact with each other, media convergence is rapidly changing the curriculum in universities all over the world. Likewise, it is changing the availability, or lack thereof, of jobs requiring this savvy technological skill.

The English education in middle school in China is well invested and assisted with various equipments. In contrast, the original objective has not been achieved at the desired effect. The government, schools, families, and students spend a lot of time working on improving scores, but hardly gain practical skills. English education today has gone into the vicious circle. Educators need to consider how to perfect the education system to improve students' practical ability of English. Therefore, an efficient way should be used to make the class vivid. Multimedia teaching will bring students into a class where they can interact with the teacher and the subject. Multimedia teaching is more intuitive than old ways; teachers can simulate situations in real life. In many circumstances teachers do not have to be there, students will learn by themselves in the class. More importantly, teachers will have more approaches to stimulating students' passion of learning.

Journalism

Newspaper companies all over are also trying to embrace the new phenomenon by implementing its practices in their work. While some have been slow to come around, other major newspapers like *The New York Times, USA Today* and *The Washington Post* are setting the precedent for the positioning of the newspaper industry in a globalized world.

News reporting is not limited to traditional media outlets. Freelance journalists can make use of different new media to produce multimedia pieces for their news stories. It engages global audiences and tells stories with technology, which develops new communication techniques for both media producers and consumers. The Common Language Project, later renamed to The Seattle Globalist, is an example of this type of multimedia journalism production.

Multimedia reporters who are mobile (usually driving around a community with cameras, audio and video recorders, and laptop computers) are often referred to as mojos, from *mo*bile *jo*urnalist.

Engineering

Software engineers may use multimedia in computer simulations for anything from entertainment to training such as military or industrial training. Multimedia for software interfaces are often done as a collaboration between creative professionals and software engineers.

Industry

In the industrial sector, multimedia is used as a way to help present information to shareholders, superiors and coworkers. Multimedia is also helpful for providing employee training, advertising and selling products all over the world via virtually unlimited web-based technology.

Mathematical and Scientific Research

In mathematical and scientific research, multimedia is mainly used for modeling and simulation.

For example, a scientist can look at a molecular model of a particular substance and manipulate it to arrive at a new substance. Representative research can be found in journals such as the *Journal of Multimedia*.

Medicine

In medicine, doctors can get trained by looking at a virtual surgery or they can simulate how the human body is affected by diseases spread by viruses and bacteria and then develop techniques to prevent it. Multimedia applications such as virtual surgeries also help doctors to get practical training.

Document Imaging

Document imaging is a technique that takes hard copy of an image/document and converts it into a digital format (for example, scanners).

Disabilities

Ability Media allows those with disabilities to gain qualifications in the multimedia field so they can pursue careers that give them access to a wide array of powerful communication forms.

Miscellaneous

In Europe, the reference organisation for Multimedia industry is the European Multimedia Associations Convention (EMMAC).

Structuring Information in a Multimedia Form

Multimedia represents the convergence of text, pictures, video and sound into a single form. The power of multimedia and the Internet lies in the way in which information is linked.

Multimedia and the Internet require a completely new approach to writing. The style of writing that is appropriate for the 'on-line world' is highly optimized and designed to be able to be quickly scanned by readers.

A good site must be made with a specific purpose in mind and a site with good interactivity and new technology can also be useful for attracting visitors. The site must be attractive and innovative in its design, function in terms of its purpose, easy to navigate, frequently updated and fast to download.

When users view a page, they can only view one page at a time. As a result, multimedia users must create a "mental model" of information structure.

Conferences

There is a large number of multimedia conferences, the two main scholarly scientific conferences being:

- ACM Multimedia;
- IEEE ICME, International Conference on Multimedia & Expo.

Understanding Digital Media

Digital media refers to all media that is encoded in machine readable format. What is digital or digitized can only be accessed, read, modified, preserved and distributed on digital electronics devices. This chapter provides an expansive study of digital media, and the various digital media technologies in usage. It furnishes valuable information on topics like digital media player, digital video interactive (DVI), digital media among others.

Digital Media

Hard drives store information in binary form and so are considered a type of physical digital media.

Digital media are any media that are encoded in a machine-readable format. Digital media can be created, viewed, distributed, modified and preserved on digital electronics devices. Computer programs and software; digital imagery, digital video; video games; web pages and websites, including social media; data and databases; digital audio, such as mp3s; and e-books are examples of digital media. Digital media are frequently contrasted with print media, such as printed books, newspapers and magazines, and other traditional or analog media, such as pictures, film or audio tape.

Combined with the Internet and personal computing, digital media has caused disruption in publishing, journalism, entertainment, education, commerce and politics. Digital media has also posed new challenges to copyright and intellectual property laws, fostering an open content movement in which content creators voluntarily give up some or all of their legal rights to their work. The ubiquity of digital media and its effects on society suggest that we are at the start of a new era in industrial history, called the Information Age, perhaps leading to a paperless society in which all media are produced and consumed on computers. However, challenges to a digital transition remain, including outdated copyright laws, censorship, the digital divide, and the specter of a digital dark age, in which older media becomes inaccessible to new or upgraded information systems. Digital media has a significant, wide-ranging and complex impact on society and culture.

History

Before Electronics

Analog computers, such as Babbage's Difference Engine, use physical, i.e. tangible, parts and actions to control operations

Machine-readable media predates the Internet, modern computers and electronics. Machine-readable codes and information were first conceptualized by Charles Babbage in the early 1800s. Babbage imagined that these codes would provide instructions for his Difference Engine and Analytical Engine, machines he designed to solve the problem of error in calculations. Between 1822 and 1823, Ada Lovelace, a mathematician, wrote the first instructions for calculating numbers on Babbage's engines. Lovelace's instructions are now believed to be the first computer program.

Though the machines were designed to perform analytical tasks, Lovelace anticipated the potential social impact of computers and programming, writing, "For, in so distributing and combining the truths and the formulae of analysis, that they may become most easily and rapidly amenable to the mechanical combinations of the engine, the relations and the nature of many subjects in that science are necessarily thrown into new lights, and more profoundly investigated... there are in all extensions of human power, or additions to human knowledge, various collateral influences, besides the main and primary object attained." Other early machine-readable media include the instructions for player pianos and jacquard looms.

Digital Computers

```
01010111   01101001   01101011
01101001   01110000   01100101
01100100   01101001   01100001
```

Digital codes, like binary, can be changed without reconfiguring mechanical parts

Though they used machine-readable media, Babbage's engines, player pianos, jacquard looms and many other early calculating machines were themselves analog computers, with physical, mechanical parts. The first truly digital media came into existence with the rise of digital computers. Digital computers use binary code and Boolean logic to store and process information, allowing one machine in one configuration to perform many different tasks. The first modern, programmable, digital computers, the Manchester Mark 1 and the EDSAC, were independently invented between 1948 and 1949. Though different in many ways from modern computers, these machines had digital software controlling their logical operations. They were encoded in binary, a system of ones and zeroes that are combined to make hundreds of characters. The 1s and 0s of binary are the "digits" of digital media.

"As we may Think"

While digital media came into common use in the early 1950s, the *conceptual* foundation of digital media is traced to the work of scientist and engineer Vannevar Bush and his celebrated essay "As We May Think," published in the *Atlantic Monthly* in 1945. Bush envisioned a system of devices that could be used to help scientists, doctors, historians and others, store, analyze and communicate information. Calling this then-imaginary device a "memex", Bush wrote:

The owner of the memex, let us say, is interested in the origin and properties of the bow and arrow. Specifically he is studying why the short Turkish bow was apparently superior to the English long bow in the skirmishes of the Crusades. He has dozens of possibly pertinent books and articles in his memex. First he runs through an encyclopedia, finds an interesting but sketchy article, leaves it projected. Next, in a history, he finds another pertinent item, and ties the two together. Thus he goes, building a trail of many items. Occasionally he inserts a comment of his own, either linking it into the main trail or joining it by a side trail to a particular item. When it becomes evident that the elastic properties of available materials had a great deal to do with the bow, he branches off on a side trail which takes him through textbooks on elasticity and tables of physical constants. He inserts a page of longhand analysis of his own. Thus he builds a trail of his interest through the maze of materials available to him.

Bush hoped that the creation of this memex would be the work of scientists after World War II. Though the essay predated digital computers by several years, "As We May Think," anticipated the potential social and intellectual benefits of digital media and provided the conceptual framework for digital scholarship, the World Wide Web, wikis and even social media. It was recognized as a significant work even at the time of its publication.

Impact

The Digital Revolution

In the years since the invention of the first digital computers, computing power and storage capacity have increased exponentially. Personal computers and smartphones put the ability to access, modify, store and share digital media in the hands of billions of people. Many electronic devices, from digital cameras to drones have the ability to create, transmit and view digital media. Combined with the World Wide Web and the Internet, digital media has transformed 21st century society in a way that is frequently compared to the cultural, economic and social impact of the printing press. The change has been so rapid and so widespread that it has launched an economic transition from an industrial economy to an information-based economy, creating a new period in human history known as the Information Age or the digital revolution.

The transition has created some uncertainty about definitions. Digital media, new media, multimedia, and similar terms all have a relationship to both the engineering innovations and cultural impact of digital media. The blending of digital media with other media, and with cultural and social factors, is sometimes known as new media or "the new media." Similarly, digital media seems to demand a new set of communications skills, called transliteracy, media literacy, or digital literacy. These skills include not only the ability to read and write—traditional literacy—but the ability to navigate the Internet, evaluate sources , and create digital content. The idea that we are moving toward a fully digital, "paperless" society is accompanied by the fear that we may soon—or currently—be facing a digital dark age, in which older media are no longer accessible on modern devices or using modern methods of scholarship. Digital media has a significant, wide-ranging and complex effect on society and culture.

Disruption in Industry

Compared with print media, the mass media, and other analog technologies, digital media are easy to copy, store, share and modify. This quality of digital media has led to significant changes in many industries, especially journalism, publishing, education, entertainment, and the music business. The overall effect of these changes is so far-reaching that it is difficult to quantify. For example, in movie-making, the transition from analog film cameras to digital cameras is nearly complete. The transition has economic benefits to Hollywood, making distribution easier and making it possible to add high-quality digital effects to films. At the same time, it has affected the analog special effects, stunt, and animation industries in Hollywood. It has imposed painful costs on small movie theaters, some of which did not or will not survive the transition to digital. The effect of digital media on other media industries is similarly sweeping and complex.

In journalism, digital media and citizen journalism have led to the loss of thousands of jobs in print media and the bankruptcy of many major newspapers. But the rise of digital journalism has also created thousands of new jobs and specializations. E-books and self-publishing are changing the book industry, and digital textbooks and other media-inclusive curricula are changing primary and secondary education. In academia, digital media has led to a new form of scholarship, called digital scholarship, and new fields of study, such as digital humanities and digital history. It has changed the way libraries are used and their role in society. Every major media, communications and academic endeavor is facing a period of transition and uncertainty related to digital media.

Individual as Content Creator

Digital media has also allowed individuals to be much more active in content creation. Anyone with access to computers and the Internet can participate in social media and contribute their own writing, art, videos, photography and commentary to the Internet, as well as conduct business online. This has come to be known as citizen journalism. This spike in user created content is due to the development of the internet as well as the way in which users interact with media today. The release of technologies such mobile devices allow for easier and quicker access to all things media. Many media production tools that were once only available to a few are now free and easy to use. The cost of devices that can access the internet is dropping steadily, and now personal ownership of multiple digital devices is becoming standard. These elements have significantly affected political participation. Digital media is seen by many scholars as having a role in Arab Spring, and crackdowns on the use of digital and social media by embattled governments are increasingly common. Many governments restrict access to digital media in some way, either to prevent obscenity or in a broader form of political censorship.

User-generated content raises issues of privacy, credibility, civility and compensation for cultural, intellectual and artistic contributions. The spread of digital media, and the wide range of literacy and communications skills necessary to use it effectively, have deepened the digital divide between those who have access to digital media and those who don't.

Web Only News

As the internet becomes more and more prevalent, more companies are beginning to distribute content through internet only means. Prime time audiences have dropped 23% for News Corp, the worlds largest broadcasting channel. With the loss of viewers there is a loss of revenue but not as bad as what would be expected. While the dollar amount dropped roughly 2%, overall cable revenue was up about 5% which is slower growth than what was expected. Cisco Inc released its latest forecast and the numbers are all trending to internet news to continue to grow at a rate where it will be quadruple by 2018.

As of 2012, the worlds largest internet only media company, The Young Turks, are averaging 750,000 users per day, and are continuing to grow, currently having over 2 billion views across all The Young Turks controlled channels, which covers world news, sports, movie reviews, college focused content and a round table style discussion channel.

Copyright Challenges

Digital media pose many challenges to current copyright and intellectual property laws. The ease of creating, modifying and sharing digital media makes copyright enforcement a challenge, and copyright laws are widely seen as outdated. For example, under current copyright law, common Internet memes are probably illegal to share in many countries. Legal rights are at least unclear for many common Internet activities, such as posting a picture that belongs to someone else to a social media account, covering a popular song on a YouTube video, or writing fanfiction. Over the last decade the concept of fair use has been applied to many online medias.

To resolve some of these issues, content creators can voluntarily adopt open or copyleft licenses, giving up some of their legal rights, or they can release their work to the public domain. Among the most common open licenses are Creative Commons licenses and the GNU Free Documentation License, both of which are in use on Wikipedia. Open licenses are part of a broader open content movement that pushes for the reduction or removal of copyright restrictions from software, data and other digital media.

Additional software has been developed in order to protect digital media. Digital Rights Management (DRM) is used to digitally copyright material and allows users to use that media for specific cases. For example, DRM allows a movie producer to rent a movie at a lower price than selling the movie, restricting the movie rental license length, rather than only selling the movie at full price. Additionally, DRM can prevent unauthorized sharing or modification of media.

Digital Media is numerical, networked and interactive system of links and databases that allows us to navigate from one bit of content or webpage to another.

One form of Digital media that is becoming a phenomenon is in the form of a digital magazine. What exactly is a digital magazine? Due to the economic importance of digital magazines, the Audit Bureau of Circulations integrated the definition of this medium in its latest report (March 2011): a digital magazine involves the distribution of a magazine content by electronic means; it may be a replica. This is the out dated definition of what a digital magazine is. A digital magazine should not be, in fact, a replica of the print magazine in PDF, as was common practice in recent years. It should, rather, be a magazine that is, in essence, interactive and created from scratch to a digital platform (Internet, mobile phones, private networks, iPad or other device). The barriers for digital magazine distribution are thus decreasing. At the same time digitizing platforms are broadening the scope of where digital magazines can be published, such as within websites and on smartphones. With the improvements of tablets and digital magazines are becoming visually enticing and readable magazines with it graphic arts.

Digital Video

Digital video is a representation of moving visual images in the form of encoded digital data. This is in contrast to analog video, which represents moving visual images with analog signals.

History

Starting in the late 1970s to the early 1980s, several types of video production equipment that were digital in their internal workings were introduced, such as time base correctors (TBC) and digital video effects (DVE) units (one of the former being the Thomson-CSF 9100 Digital Video Processor, an internally all-digital full-frame TBC introduced in 1980, and two of the latter being the Ampex ADO, and the Nippon Electric Corporation (NEC) DVE). They operated by taking a standard analog composite video input and digitizing it internally. This made it easier to either correct or enhance the video signal, as in the case of a TBC, or to manipulate and add effects to the video, in the case of a DVE unit. The digitized and processed video information that was output from these units would then be converted back to standard analog video.

Later on in the 1970s, manufacturers of professional video broadcast equipment, such as Bosch (through their Fernseh division), RCA, and Ampex developed prototype digital videotape recorders (VTR) in their research and development labs. Bosch's machine used a modified 1" Type B transport, and recorded an early form of CCIR 601 digital video. Ampex's prototype digital video recorder used a modified 2" Quadruplex VTR (an Ampex AVR-3), but fitted with custom digital video electronics, and a special "octaplex" 8-head headwheel (regular analog 2" Quad machines only used 4 heads). The audio on Ampex's prototype digital machine, nicknamed by its developers as "Annie", still recorded the audio in analog as linear tracks on the tape, like 2" Quad. None of these machines from these manufacturers were ever marketed commercially, however.

Digital video was first introduced commercially in 1986 with the Sony D1 format, which recorded an uncompressed standard definition component video signal in digital form instead of the high-band analog forms that had been commonplace until then. Due to its expense, and the requirement of component video connections using 3 cables (such as YPbPr or RGB component video) to and from a D1 VTR that most television facilities were not wired for (composite NTSC or PAL video using one cable was the norm for most of them at that time), D1 was used primarily by large television networks and other component-video capable video studios.

In 1988, Sony and Ampex co-developed and released the D2 digital videocassette format, which recorded video digitally without compression in ITU-601 format, much like D1. But D2 had the major difference of encoding the video in composite form to the NTSC standard, thereby only requiring single-cable composite video connections to and from a D2 VCR, making it a perfect fit for the majority of television facilities at the time. This made D2 quite a successful format in the television broadcast industry throughout the late '80s and the '90s. D2 was also widely used in that era as the master tape format for mastering laserdiscs (prior to D2, most laserdiscs were mastered using analog 1" Type C videotape).

D1 & D2 would eventually be replaced by cheaper systems using video compression, most notably Sony's Digital Betacam (still heavily used as an electronic field production (EFP) recording format by professional television producers) that were introduced into the network's television studios. Other examples of digital video formats utilizing compression were Ampex's DCT (the first to employ such when introduced in 1992), the industry-standard DV and MiniDV (and its professional variations, Sony's DVCAM and Panasonic's DVCPRO), and Betacam SX, a lower-cost variant of Digital Betacam using MPEG-2 compression.

One of the first digital video products to run on personal computers was *PACo: The PICS Animation Compiler* from The Company of Science & Art in Providence, RI, which was developed starting in 1990 and first shipped in May 1991. PACo could stream unlimited-length video with synchronized sound from a single file (with the ".CAV" file extension) on CD-ROM. Creation required a Mac; playback was possible on Macs, PCs, and Sun Sparcstations. In 1992, Bernard Luskin, Philips Interactive Media, and Eric Doctorow, Paramount Worldwide Video, successfully put the first fifty videos in digital MPEG 1 on CD, developed the packaging and launched movies on CD, leading to advancing versions of MPEG, and to DVD.

QuickTime, Apple Computer's architecture for time-based and streaming data formats appeared in June, 1991. Initial consumer-level content creation tools were crude, requiring an analog video source to be digitized to a computer-readable format. While low-quality at first, consumer digital video increased rapidly in quality, first with the introduction of playback standards such as MPEG-1 and MPEG-2 (adopted for use in television transmission and DVD media), and then the introduction of the DV tape format allowing recordings in the format to be transferred direct to digital video files (containing the same video data recorded on the transferred DV tape) on an editing computer and simplifying the editing process, allowing non-linear editing systems (NLE) to be deployed cheaply and widely on desktop computers with no external playback/recording equipment needed, save for the computer simply requiring a FireWire port to interface to the DV-format camera or VCR. The widespread adoption of digital video has also drastically reduced the bandwidth needed for a high-definition video signal (with HDV and AVCHD, as well as several commercial variants such as DVCPRO-HD, all using less bandwidth than a standard definition analog signal) and tapeless camcorders based on flash memory and often a variant of MPEG-4.

Overview of Basic Properties

Digital video comprises a series of orthogonal bitmap digital images displayed in rapid succession at a constant rate. In the context of video these images are called frames. We measure the rate at which frames are displayed in frames per second (FPS).

Since every frame is an orthogonal bitmap digital image it comprises a raster of pixels. If it has a width of W pixels and a height of H pixels we say that the frame size is WxH.

Pixels have only one property, their color. The color of a pixel is represented by a fixed number of bits. The more bits the more subtle variations of colors can be reproduced. This is called the color depth (CD) of the video.

An example video can have a duration (T) of 1 hour (3600*sec*), a frame size of 640x480 *(WxH)* at a color depth of 24*bits* and a frame rate of 25*fps*. This example video has the following properties:

- pixels per frame = 640 * 480 = 307,200

- bits per frame = 307,200 * 24 = 7,372,800 = 7.37*Mbits*

- bit rate (BR) = 7.37 * 25 = 184.25*Mbits/sec*

- video size (VS) = 184*Mbits/sec* * 3600*sec* = 662,400*Mbits* = 82,800*Mbytes* = 82.8*Gbytes*

The most important properties are *bit rate* and *video size*. The formulas relating those two with all other properties are:

$$BR = W * H * CD * FPS$$

$$VS = BR * T = W * H * CD * FPS * T$$

(units are: BR in bit/s, W and H in pixels, CD in bits, VS in bits, T in seconds)

while some secondary formulas are:

pixels_per_frame = W * H

pixels_per_second = W * H * FPS

bits_per_frame = W * H * CD

Regarding Interlacing

In interlaced video each *frame* is composed of two *halves of an image*. The first half contains only the odd-numbered lines of a full frame. The second half contains only the even-numbered lines. Those halves are referred to individually as *fields*. Two consecutive fields compose a full frame. If an interlaced video has a frame rate of 15 frames per second the field rate is 30 fields per second. All the properties and formulas discussed here apply equally to interlaced video but one should be careful not to confuse the fields per second rate with the frames per second rate.

Properties of Compressed Video

The above are accurate for uncompressed video. Because of the relatively high bit rate of uncompressed video, video compression is extensively used. In the case of compressed video each frame requires a small percentage of the original bits. Assuming a compression algorithm that shrinks the input data by a factor of CF, the bit rate and video size would equal to:

$$BR = W * H * CD * FPS / CF$$

$$VS = BR * T / CF$$

Please note that it is not necessary that all frames are equally compressed by a factor of CF. In practice they are not, so CF is the *average* factor of compression for *all* the frames taken together.

The above equation for the bit rate can be rewritten by combining the compression factor and the color depth like this:

BR = W * H * (CD / CF) * FPS

The value (CD / CF) represents the average bits per pixel (BPP). As an example, if we have a color depth of 12bits/pixel and an algorithm that compresses at 40x, then BPP equals 0.3 (12/40). So in the case of compressed video the formula for bit rate is:

BR = W * H * BPP * FPS

In fact the same formula is valid for uncompressed video because in that case one can assume that the "compression" factor is 1 and that the average bits per pixel equal the color depth.

More on Bit Rate and BPP

As is obvious by its definition bit rate is a measure of the rate of information content of the digital video stream. In the case of uncompressed video, bit rate corresponds directly to the quality of the video (remember that bit rate is proportional to every property that affects the video quality). Bit rate is an important property when transmitting video because the transmission link must be capable of supporting that bit rate. Bit rate is also important when dealing with the storage of video because, as shown above, the video size is proportional to the bit rate and the duration. Bit rate of uncompressed video is too high for most practical applications. Video compression is used to greatly reduce the bit rate.

BPP is a measure of the efficiency of compression. A true-color video with no compression at all may have a BPP of 24 bits/pixel. Chroma subsampling can reduce the BPP to 16 or 12 bits/pixel. Applying jpeg compression on every frame can reduce the BPP to 8 or even 1 bits/pixel. Applying video compression algorithms like MPEG1, MPEG2 or MPEG4 allows for fractional BPP values.

Constant Bit Rate Versus Variable Bit Rate

As noted above BPP represents the *average* bits per pixel. There are compression algorithms that keep the BPP almost constant throughout the entire duration of the video. In this case we also get video output with a constant bit rate (CBR). This CBR video is suitable for real-time, non-buffered, fixed bandwidth video streaming (e.g. in videoconferencing).

Noting that not all frames can be compressed at the same level because quality is more severely impacted for scenes of high complexity some algorithms try to constantly adjust the BPP. They keep it high while compressing complex scenes and low for less demanding scenes. This way one gets the best quality at the smallest average bit rate (and the smallest file size accordingly). Of course when using this method the bit rate is variable because it tracks the variations of the BPP.

Technical Overview

Standard film stocks such as 16 mm and 35 mm record at 24 frames per second. For video, there are two frame rate standards: NTSC, which shoot at 30/1.001 (about 29.97) frames per second or 59.94 fields per second, and PAL, 25 frames per second or 50 fields per second.

Digital video cameras come in two different image capture formats: interlaced and deinterlaced / progressive scan.

Interlaced cameras record the image in alternating sets of lines: the odd-numbered lines are scanned, and then the even-numbered lines are scanned, then the odd-numbered lines are scanned again, and so on. One set of odd or even lines is referred to as a "field", and a consecutive pairing of two fields of opposite parity is called a *frame*. Deinterlaced cameras records each frame as distinct, with all scan lines being captured at the same moment in time. Thus, interlaced video captures samples the scene motion twice as often as progressive video does, for the same number of frames per second. Progressive-scan camcorders generally produce a slightly sharper image. However, motion may not be as smooth as interlaced video which uses 50 or 59.94 fields per second, particularly if they employ the 24 frames per second standard of film.

Digital video can be copied with no degradation in quality. No matter how many generations of a digital source is copied, it will still be as clear as the original first generation of digital footage. However a change in parameters like frame size as well as a change of the digital format can decrease the quality of the video due to new calculations that have to be made. Digital video can be manipulated and edited to follow an order or sequence on an NLE, or non-linear editing workstation, a computer-based device intended to edit video and audio. More and more, videos are edited on readily available, increasingly affordable consumer-grade computer hardware and software. However, such editing systems require ample disk space for video footage. The many video formats and parameters to be set make it quite impossible to come up with a specific number for how many minutes need how much time.

Digital video has a significantly lower cost than 35 mm film. In comparison to the high cost of film stock, the tape stock (or other electronic media used for digital video recording, such as flash memory or hard disk drive) used for recording digital video is very inexpensive. Digital video also allows footage to be viewed on location without the expensive chemical processing required by film. Also physical deliveries of tapes and broadcasts do not apply anymore. Digital television (including higher quality HDTV) started to spread in most developed countries in early 2000s. Digital video is also used in modern mobile phones and video conferencing systems. Digital video is also used for Internet distribution of media, including streaming video and peer-to-peer movie distribution. However even within Europe are lots of TV-Stations not broadcasting in HD, due to restricted budgets for new equipment for processing HD.

Many types of video compression exist for serving digital video over the internet and on optical disks. The file sizes of digital video used for professional editing are generally not practical for these purposes, and the video requires further compression with codecs such as Sorenson, H.264 and more recently Apple ProRes especially for HD. Probably the most widely used formats for delivering video over the internet are MPEG4, Quicktime, Flash and Windows Media, while MPEG2 is used almost exclusively for DVDs, providing an exceptional image in minimal size but resulting in a high level of CPU consumption to decompress.

As of 2011, the highest resolution demonstrated for digital video generation is 35 megapixels

(8192 x 4320). The highest speed is attained in industrial and scientific high speed cameras that are capable of filming 1024x1024 video at up to 1 million frames per second for brief periods of recording.

Interfaces and Cables

Many interfaces have been designed specifically to handle the requirements of uncompressed digital video (from roughly 400 Mbit/s to 10 Gbit/s):

- High-Definition Multimedia Interface
- Digital Visual Interface
- Serial Digital Interface
- DisplayPort
- Digital component video
- Unified Display Interface
- FireWire
- USB

The following interface has been designed for carrying MPEG-Transport compressed video:

- DVB-ASI

Compressed video is also carried using UDP-IP over Ethernet. Two approaches exist for this:

- Using RTP as a wrapper for video packets
- 1-7 MPEG Transport Packets are placed directly in the UDP packet

Storage Formats

Encoding

All current formats, which are listed below, are PCM based.

- CCIR 601 used for broadcast stations
- MPEG-4 good for online distribution of large videos and video recorded to flash memory
- MPEG-2 used for DVDs, Super-VCDs, and many broadcast television formats
- MPEG-1 used for video CDs
- H.261
- H.263

- H.264 also known as *MPEG-4 Part 10*, or as *AVC*, used for Blu-ray Discs and some broadcast television formats

- Theora used for video on Wikipedia

Tapes

- Betacam SX, Betacam IMX, Digital Betacam, or DigiBeta — Commercial video systems by Sony, based on original Betamax technology

- D-VHS — MPEG-2 format data recorded on a tape similar to S-VHS

- D1, D2, D3, D5, D9 (also known as Digital-S) — various SMPTE commercial digital video standards

- Digital8 — DV-format data recorded on Hi8-compatible cassettes; largely a consumer format

- DV, MiniDV — used in most of today's videotape-based consumer camcorders; designed for high quality and easy editing; can also record high-definition data (HDV) in MPEG-2 format

- DVCAM, DVCPRO — used in professional broadcast operations; similar to DV but generally considered more robust; though DV-compatible, these formats have better audio handling.

- DVCPRO50, DVCPROHD support higher bandwidths as compared to Panasonic's DVC-PRO.

- HDCAM was introduced by Sony as a high-definition alternative to DigiBeta.

- MicroMV — MPEG-2-format data recorded on a very small, matchbook-sized cassette; obsolete

- ProHD — name used by JVC for its MPEG-2-based professional camcorders

Discs

- Blu-ray Disc

- DVD

- VCD

Digital Video Interactive

Digital Video Interactive (DVI) was the first multimedia desktop video standard for IBM-compatible personal computers. It enabled full-screen, full motion video, as well as stereo audio, still images, and graphics to be presented on a DOS-based desktop computer. The scope of Digital Video Interactive encompasses a file format, including a digital container format, a number of video and audio compression formats, as well as hardware associated with the file format.

History

Development of DVI was started around 1984 by Section 17 of The David Sarnoff Research Center Labs (DSRC) then responsible for the research and development activities of RCA. When General Electric purchased RCA in 1986, GE considered the DSRC redundant with its own labs, and sought a buyer. In 1988, GE sold the DSRC to SRI International,but sold the DVI technology separately to Intel corporation.

DVI technology allowed full-screen, full motion digital video, as well as stereo audio, still images, and graphics to be presented on a DOS-based desktop computer. DVI content was usually distributed on CD-ROM discs, which in turn was decoded and displayed via specialized add-in card hardware installed in the computer. Audio and video files for DVI were among the first to use data compression, with audio content using ADPCM. DVI was the first technology of its kind for the desktop PC, and ushered in the multimedia revolution for PCs.

DVI was announced at the second annual Microsoft CD-ROM conference in Seattle to a standing ovation in 1987. The excitement at the time stemmed from the fact that a CD-ROM drive of the era had a maximum data playback rate of ~1.2 Mbit/s, thought to be insufficient for good quality motion video. However, the DSRC team was able to extract motion video, stereo audio and still images from this relatively low data rate with good quality.

Implementations

The first implementation of DVI developed in the mid-80s relied on three 16-bit ISA cards installed inside the computer, one for audio processing, another for video processing, and the last as an interface to a Sony CDU-100 CD-ROM drive. The DVI video card used a custom chipset (later known as the i80750 or i750 chipset) for decompression, one device was known as the pixel processor & the display device was called the VDP (video display processor).

Later DVI implementations used one, more highly integrated card, such as Intel's ActionMedia series (omitting the CD-ROM interface). The ActionMedia (and the later ActionMedia II) were available in both ISA and MCA-bus cards, the latter for use in MCA-bus PCs like IBM's PS/2 series.

Intel utilized the i750 technology in driving creation of the MMX instruction set. This instruction set was enabled in silicon on the original Pentium processors.

Compression

The DVI format specified two video compression schemes, Presentation Level Video or Production Level Video (PLV) and Real-Time Video (RTV) and two audio compression schemes, ADPCM and PCM8.

The original video compression scheme, called Presentation Level Video (PLV), was asymmetric in that a Digital VAX-11/750 minicomputer was used to compress the video in non-real time to 30 frames per second with a resolution of 320x240. Encoding was performed by Intel at its facilities or at licensed encoding facilities set up by Intel. Video compression involved coding both still frames and motion-compensated residuals using Vector Quantization (VQ) in dimensions 1, 2, and 4. The resulting file (in the .AVS format) was displayed in realtime on an IBM PC-AT (i286) with the add-in boards providing decompression and display functions at NTSC (30 frame/s) resolutions. The IBM PC-AT equipped with the DVI add-in boards hence had 2 monitors, the original monochrome control monitor, and a second Sony CDP1302 monitor for the color video. Stereo audio at near FM quality was also available from the system.

The Real-Time Video (RTV) format was introduced in March 1988, then called Edit-Level Video (ELV). In Fall 1992, version 2.1 of the RTV format was introduced by Intel as Indeo 2.

Legacy of DSRC

The original team from DSRC (David Sarnoff Research Center) set up an Intel operation NJ1 as the Princeton Operation. The team occupied new quarters after moving out of the DSRC in Plainsboro, New Jersey. From the original 35 researchers the Princeton Operation grew to over 200 people at its height. Andy Grove was a great supporter of the Princeton Team during its term of operation. However in 1992 Ken Fine (a vice president of Intel) decided to shutter the operation and transfer those employees willing to move to other Intel sites in Arizona and Oregon. Fine left the company shortly after he implemented this decision. Final site closure occurred almost a year later in September 1993.

Digital Media Player

The Roku XD/S digital media players works with popular streaming media sites like Amazon.com and Netflix as well as locally stored content

Digital media players (DMP) are home entertainment consumer electronics devices first introduced in 2000 that can connect to a home network to stream digital media (such as music, digital photos, or video), and are not to be confused with portable media players (also known as mobile media player). Digital media players can stream files from a personal computer and network-attached storage or from another networked media server to play back the media on a television or video projector display for home cinema. Most digital media players utilize a 10-foot user interface, and many are navigated via a remote control.

Some digital media players also have Smart TV features, like allowing users to stream media such as movies and TV shows from the Internet or streaming services and online media sites like YouTube, Vimeo, Netflix, Hulu, Spotify, and Amazon.com. Some other digital media players also allow users to play back locally stored content from a direct attached USB hard disk or even direct connect a Hard disk drive externally, or even internally in the digital media player via a Serial ATA (SATA) port. These types of digital media player are sometimes referred to as HD Media Player or HDD Media Player if they can support a Hard Disk Drive installed inside. In the 2010s, the main difference between most "digital media players" and many modern set-top boxes (also known a set-top units) is that the set-top boxes generally contain at least one TV-tuner and are as such capable of receiving broadcasting signal (cable television, satellite television, and over-the-air television, or IPTV).

Overview

In the 2010s, with the popularity of mobile digital media players and digital cameras, as well as fast Internet download speeds and relatively cheap mass storage, many people now have large collections of digital media files (songs, digital photos, movies, etc.) that cannot be played on a conventional analog HiFi without connecting a computer to an amplifier and/or television. The means to play these files on a network-connected digital media player that is permanently connected to a television and controlled by a remote is seen as a convenience. Digital media players fill this market niche.

The rapid growth in the availability of online content, including music, video, and games, has made it easier for consumers to use these devices. YouTube, for instance, is a common plug-in available on most networked devices. Netflix has also struck deals with many consumer-electronics makers to make their interface available in the device's menus, for their streaming subscribers. This symbiotic relationship between Netflix and consumer electronics makers has helped propel Netflix to become the largest subscription video service in the U.S., using up to 20% of U.S. bandwidth at peak times.

Media players are often designed for compactness and affordability, and tend to have small or non-existent hardware displays other than simple LEDvlights to indicate whether the device is powered on. Interface navigation on the television is usually performed with an infrared remote control, while more-advanced digital media players come with high-performance remote controls which allow control of the interface using integrated touch sensors. Some remotes also include accelerometers for air mouse features which allow basic motion gaming. Most digital media player devices are unable to play physical audio or video media directly, and instead require a user to convert these media into playable files using a separate computer and software. They are also usually incapable of recording audio or video. In the 2010s, it is also common to find digital media player functionality integrated into other consumer-electronics appliances, such as DVD players, set-top boxes, Smart TVs, or even video game consoles, although these devices are beyond the scope of this article.

Terminology

Digital media players are also commonly referred to as a digital media extender, digital media streamer, digital media hub, digital media adapter, or digital media receiver (which should not be confused with *AV Receiver* that are also called *Digital Media Renderer*).

Functionality and Capability

A digital media player can connect to the home network using either a wireless (IEEE 802.11a, b, g, and n) or wired Ethernet connection. Digital media players includes a user interface that allows users to navigate through their digital media library, search for, and play back media files. Some digital media players only handle music; some handle music and pictures; some handle music, pictures, and video; while others go further to allow internet browsing or controlling Live TV from a PC with a TV tuner.

Some other capabilities which are accomplished by digital media players include:

- Play, catalog, and store local hard disk, flash drive, or memory card music CDs and view CD album art, view digital photos, and watch DVD and Blu-ray or other videos.

- Stream movies, music, photos (media) over the wired or wireless network

- View digital pictures (one by one or as picture slideshows)

- Stream online video to a TV from services such as Netflix and YouTube.

- Play video games such as Angry Birds and others.

- Browse the Internet, check email and access social networking sites like Facebook, Twitter, LinkedIn on TV through downloadable applications.

- Video conference by connecting a webcam and microphone.

Hardware

In the 2010s, there are stand-alone digital media players on the market from AC Ryan, Asus, Apple (e.g., Apple TV), NetGear (e.g., NTV and NeoTV models), Dune, iOmega, Logitech, Pivos Group, Micca, Sybas (Popcorn Hour), Amkette EvoTV, D-Link, Western Digital (e.g., WD TV), EZfetch, Google TV, Pinnacle, Xtreamer, and Roku, just to name a few. The models change frequently, so it is advisable to visit their web sites for current model names.

These devices come with low power consumption processors or SoC (System on Chip) and are most commonly either based on MIPS or ARM architecture processors combined with integrated DSP GPU in a SoC (or MPSoC) package. They also include RAM-memory and some type of built-in type of non-volatile computer memory (Flash memory).

Operating System

While most media players have traditionally been running proprietary or open source software frameworks versions based Linux as their operating systems, many newer network connected media players are based on the Android platform which gives them an advantage in terms of applications and games from the Google Play store.

Even without Android some digital media players still have the ability to run applications (sometimes available via an 'app store' digital distribution platform), interactive on-demand media, personalized communications, and social networking features

Internal Harddrive Capabilities

HD media player or *HDD media player* (*HDMP*) is a generic term used for a category of consumer product that combines digital media player with a hard drive (HD) enclosure with all the hardware and software for playing audio, video and photos to a television. All these can play computer-based media files to a television without the need for a separate computer or network connection, and some can even be used as a conventional external hard drive. These types of digital media players are sometimes sold as empty shells to allow the user to fit their own choice of hard drive (some can manage unlimited hard disk capacity and other only a certain capacity, i.e. 1TB, 2TB, 3TB, or 4TB), and the same model is sometimes sold with or without an internal hard drive already fitted.

Common Connection Ports

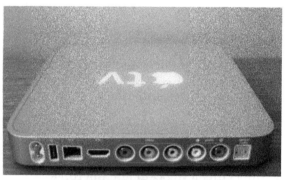

Back of 1st generation Apple TV

Back of 2nd & 3rd generation Apple TV

Television connection is usually done via; Composite, SCART, Component, HDMI video, with Optical Audio (TOSLINK/SPDIF), and connect to the local network and broadband internet using either a wired Ethernet or a wireless wifi connection, and some also have built-in Bluetooth support for remotes and game-pads or joysticks. Some players come with USB (USB 2.0 or USB 3.0) ports which allow local media content playback.

Streaming and Communication Protocols

While early digital media players used proprietary communication protocols to interface with media servers, today most digital media players either use standard-based protocols such SMB/CIFS/

SAMBA or NFS, or rely on some version of UPnP (Universal Plug and Play) and DLNA (Digital Living Network Alliance) standards. DLNA-compliant digital media players and Media Servers is meant to guarantee a minimum set of functionality and proper interoperability among digital media players and servers regardless of the manufacturer, but unfortunately not every manufacturer follows the standards perfectly which can lead to incompatibility.

Formats, Resolutions and File Systems

Digital media players can usually play H.264 (SD and HD), MPEG-4 Part 2 (SD and HD), MPEG-1, MPEG-2 .mpg, MPEG-2 .TS, VOB and ISO images video, with PCM, MP3 and AC3 audio tracks. They can also display images (such as JPEG and PNG) and play music files (such as FLAC, MP3 and Ogg).

Media Server Software

Some digital media players will only connect to specific media server software installed on a PC to stream music, pictures and recorded or live TV originating from the computer. Apple iTunes can, for example, be used this way with the Apple TV hardware that connects to a TV. Apple has developed a tightly integrated device and content management ecosystem with their iTunes Store, personal computers, iOS devices, and the AppleTV digital media receiver. The most recent version of the AppleTV, at $99, has lost the hard-drive that was included in its predecessor and fully depends on either streaming internet content, or another computer on the home network for media.

History

By November 2000, an audio-only digital media player was demonstrated by a company called SimpleDevices, which was awarded two patents covering this invention in 2006. Developed under the SimpleFi name by Motorola in late 2001, the design was based on a Cirrus Arm-7 processor and the wireless HomeRF networking standard which pre-dated 802.11b in the residential markets. Other early market entrants in 2001 included the Turtle Beach AudioTron, Rio Receiver and SliMP3 digital media players.

An early version of a video-capable digital media player was presented by F.C. Jeng et al. in the International Conf. on Consumer Electronics in 2002. It included a network interface card, a media processor for audio and video decoding, an analog video encoder (for video playback to a TV), an audio digital to analog converter for audio playback, and an IR (infrared receiver) for remote-control-interface.

A concept of a digital media player was also introduced by Intel in 2002 at the Intel Developer Forum as part of their "Extended Wireless PC Initiative." Intel's digital media player was based on an Xscale PXA210 processor and supported 802.11b wireless networking. Intel was among the first to use the Linux embedded operating system and UPnP technology for its digital media player. Networked audio and DVD players were among the first consumer devices to integrate digital media player functionality. Examples include the Philips Streamium-range of products that allowed for remote streaming of audio, the GoVideo D2730 Networked DVD player which integrated DVD playback with the capability to stream Rhapsody audio from a PC, and the Buffalo LinkTheater which combined a DVD player with a digital media player. More recently, the Xbox 360 gaming console from Microsoft was among the first gaming devices that integrated a digital media player. With the Xbox 360, Microsoft also introduced the concept of a Windows Media Center Extender, which allows users to access the Media center capabilities of a PC remotely, through a home network. More recently, Linksys, D-Link, and HP introduced the latest generation of digital media players that support 720p and 1080p high resolution video playback and may integrate both Windows Extender and traditional digital media player functionality.

Connections

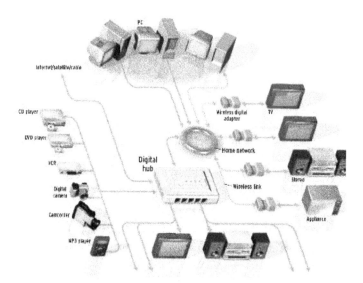

An example of a Digital media player in a network

There are two ways to connect an extender to its central media center or HTPC server - wired, or wireless.

Wireless

A wireless connection can be established between the media extender and its central media center. On the downside, interference may cause a "less than optimal" connection and cause network congestion, resulting in stuttering sound, missing frames from video, and other anomalies. It is recommended that an 802.11a or better be used, and over as short of a distance as possible.

A wireless media extender from Arctic for music streaming and multi-room entertainment

Other Names

Digital media player manufacturers use a variety of names to describe their devices. Some more commonly used alternative names include:

- Connected DVD
- Connected media player
- Digital audio receiver
- Digital media adapter
- Digital media connect
- Digital media extender
- Digital media hub
- Digital media player
- Digital media streamer
- Digital media receiver
- Digital media renderer
- Digital video receiver
- Digital video streamer
- HD Media Player
- HDD media player
- Media Extender
- Media Regulator
- Net connected media player
- Network connected media player
- Network media player
- Networked Digital Video Disc
- Networked entertainment gateway
- Smart Television media player
- Smart Television player
- Streaming media box

- Streaming media player

- Streaming video player

- Wireless Media Adapter

- OTT player

- YouTube Player Support

Market Impact on Traditional Television Services

The convergence of content, technology, and broadband access allows consumers to stream television shows and movies to their high-definition television in competition with traditional service providers (Cable TV and Satellite Television). The research company SNL Kagan expects 12 million households, roughly 10%, to go without cable, satellite or telco video service by 2015 using Over The Top services. This represents a new trend in the broadcast television industry, as the list of options for watching movies and TV over the Internet grows at a rapid pace. Research also shows that even as traditional television service providers are trimming their customer base, they are adding Broadband Internet customers. Nearly 76.6 million U.S. households get broadband from leading cable and telephone companies, although only a portion have sufficient speeds to support quality video steaming. Convergence devices for home entertainment will likely play a much larger role in the future of broadcast television, effectively shifting traditional revenue streams while providing consumers with more options.

According to a report from the researcher NPD In-Stat, only about 12 million U.S. households have their either Web-capable TVs or digital media players connected to the Internet, although In-Stat estimates about 25 million U.S. TV households own a set with the built-in network capability. Also, In-Stat predicts that 100 million homes in North America and western Europe will own digital media players and television sets that blend traditional programs with Internet content by 2016.

References

- Pavlik, John; McIntosh, Shawn. Converging Media (Fourth ed.). Oxford University Press. pp. 237–239. ISBN 978-0-19-934230-3.

- Dewar, James A. (1998). "The information age and the printing press: looking backward to see ahead". RAND Corporation. Retrieved 29 March 2014.

- Simpson, Rosemary; Allen Renear; Elli Mylonas; Andries van Dam (March 1996). "50 years after "As We May Think": the Brown/MIT Vannevar Bush symposium" (PDF). Interactions. pp. 47–67. Retrieved 29 March 2014.

- Mynatt, Elizabeth. "As we may think: the legacy of computing research and the power of human cognition". Computing Research Association. Retrieved 30 March 2014.

- Bazillion, Richard (2001). "Academic libraries in the digital revolution" (PDF). Educause Quarterly. Retrieved 31 March 2014.

- Ito, Mizuko; et al. (November 008). "Living and learning with the new media: summary of findings from the digital youth project" (PDF). Retrieved 29 March 2014. Check date values in: |date= (help)

- Cusumano, Catherine (18 March 2013). "Changeover in film technology spells end for age of analog". Brown Daily Herald. Retrieved 31 March 2014.

- Kirchhoff, Suzanne M. (9 September 2010). "The U.S. newspaper industry in transition" (PDF). Congressional Research Service. Retrieved 29 March 2014.

- Horrigan, John (May 2007). "A Typology of Information and Communication Technology Users". Pew Internet and American Life Study.

- Cohen, Cathy J.; Joseph Kahne (2012). "Participatory politics: new media and youth political action" (PDF). Retrieved 29 March 2014.

- Kelley, Peter (13 June 2013). "Philip Howard's new book explores digital media role in Arab Spring". University of Washington. Retrieved 30 March 2014.

- Rininsland, Andrew (16 April 2012). "Internet censorship listed: how does each country compare?". The Guardian. Retrieved 30 March 2014.

- Crawford, Susan P. (3 December 2011). "Internet access and the new digital divide". The New York Times. Retrieved 30 March 2014.

- Ugyer, Cenk. TYT Network Passes 2,000,000,000 Views and 3,000,000 Subscribers!. YouTube. Retrieved 22 November 2014.

- Barnett, Emma (18 May 2011). "Outdated copyright laws hinder growth says Government". The Telegraph. Retrieved 30 March 2014.

- Brunet, Maël (March 2014). "Outdated copyright laws must adapt to the new digital age". Policy Review. Retrieved 30 March 2014.

Digital Image Processing: Different Tools and Techniques

Digital image processing involves the processing of digital images using computer algorithms. Digital image processing is able to solve problems like non-linear image display and image enhancement during image processing. The chapter strategically encompasses and incorporates the major components and key concepts of digital image processing, providing a complete understanding..

Digital Image Processing

Digital image processing is the use of computer algorithms to perform image processing on digital images. As a subcategory or field of digital signal processing, digital image processing has many advantages over analog image processing. It allows a much wider range of algorithms to be applied to the input data and can avoid problems such as the build-up of noise and signal distortion during processing. Since images are defined over two dimensions (perhaps more) digital image processing may be modeled in the form of multidimensional systems.

History

Many of the techniques of digital image processing, or digital picture processing as it often was called, were developed in the 1960s at the Jet Propulsion Laboratory, Massachusetts Institute of Technology, Bell Laboratories, University of Maryland, and a few other research facilities, with application to satellite imagery, wire-photo standards conversion, medical imaging, videophone, character recognition, and photograph enhancement. The cost of processing was fairly high, however, with the computing equipment of that era. That changed in the 1970s, when digital image processing proliferated as cheaper computers and dedicated hardware became available. Images then could be processed in real time, for some dedicated problems such as television standards conversion. As general-purpose computers became faster, they started to take over the role of dedicated hardware for all but the most specialized and computer-intensive operations.

With the fast computers and signal processors available in the 2000s, digital image processing has become the most common form of image processing and generally, is used because it is not only the most versatile method, but also the cheapest.

Digital image processing technology for medical applications was inducted into the Space Foundation Space Technology Hall of Fame in 1994.

In 2002 Raanan Fattel introduced Gradient domain image processing, a new way to process images in which the differences between pixels are manipulated rather than the pixel values themselves.

Tasks

Digital image processing allows the use of much more complex algorithms, and hence, can offer both more sophisticated performance at simple tasks, and the implementation of methods which would be impossible by analog means.

In particular, digital image processing is the only practical technology for:

- Classification
- Feature extraction
- Multi-scale signal analysis
- Pattern recognition
- Projection

Some techniques which are used in digital image processing include:

- Anisotropic diffusion
- Hidden Markov models
- Image editing
- Image restoration
- Independent component analysis
- Linear filtering
- Neural networks
- Partial differential equations
- Pixelation
- Principal components analysis
- Self-organizing maps
- Wavelets

Applications

Digital Camera Images

Digital cameras generally include specialized digital image processing hardware – either dedicated chips or added circuitry on other chips – to convert the raw data from their image sensor into a color-corrected image in a standard image file format

Film

Westworld (1973) was the first feature film to use the digital image processing to pixellate photography to simulate an android's point of view.

Digitizing

Internet Archive book scanner

Digitizing or digitization is the representation of an object, image, sound, document or signal (usually an analog signal) by generating a series of numbers that describe a discrete set of its points or samples. The result is called *digital representation* or, more specifically, a *digital image*, for the object, and *digital form*, for the signal. In modern practice, the digitized data is in the form of binary numbers, which facilitate computer processing and other operations, but strictly speaking, digitizing simply means the conversion of analog source material into a numerical format; the decimal or any other number system can be used instead.

Digitization is of crucial importance to data processing, storage and transmission, because it "allows information of all kinds in all formats to be carried with the same efficiency and also intermingled". Unlike analog data, which typically suffers some loss of quality each time it is copied or transmitted, digital data can, in theory, be propagated indefinitely with absolutely no degradation. This is why it is a favored way of preserving information for many organisations around the world.

Process

The term digitization is often used when diverse forms of information, such as text, sound, image or voice, are converted into a single binary code. Digital information exists as one of two digits, either 0 or 1. These are known as bits (a contraction of *binary digits*) and the sequences of 0s and 1s that constitute information are called bytes.

Analog signals are continuously variable, both in the number of possible values of the signal *at* a given time, as well as in the number of points in the signal *in* a given period of time. However, digital signals are discrete in both of those respects – generally a finite sequence of integers – therefore a digitization can, in practical terms, only ever be an approximation of the signal it represents.

Digitization occurs in two parts:

Discretization

The reading of an analog signal *A*, and, at regular time intervals (frequency), sampling the value of the signal at the point. Each such reading is called a *sample* and may be considered to have infinite precision at this stage;

Quantization

Samples are rounded to a fixed set of numbers (such as integers), a process known as quantization.

In general, these can occur at the same time, though they are conceptually distinct.

A series of digital integers can be transformed into an analog output that approximates the original analog signal. Such a transformation is called a DA conversion. The sampling rate and the number of bits used to represent the integers combine to determine how close such an approximation to the analog signal a digitization will be.

Examples

The term is often used to describe the scanning of analog sources (such as printed photos or taped videos) into computers for editing, but it also can refer to audio (where sampling rate is often measured in kilohertz) and texture map transformations. In this last case, as in normal photos, sampling rate refers to the resolution of the image, often measured in pixels per inch.

Digitizing is the primary way of storing images in a form suitable for transmission and computer processing, whether scanned from two-dimensional analog originals or captured using an image sensor-equipped device such as a digital camera, tomographical instrument such as a CAT scanner, or acquiring precise dimensions from a real-world object, such as a car, using a 3D scanning device.

Digitizing is central to making a digital representations of geographical features, using raster or vector images, in a geographic information system, i.e., the creation of electronic maps, either from various geographical and satellite imaging (raster) or by digitizing traditional paper maps or graphs (vector).

"Digitization" is also used to describe the process of populating databases with files or data. While this usage is technically inaccurate, it originates with the previously proper use of the term to describe that part of the process involving digitization of analog sources, such as printed pictures and brochures, before uploading to target databases.

Digitizing may also used in the field of apparel, where an image may be recreated with the help of embroidery digitizing software tools and saved as embroidery machine code. This machine code is fed into an embroidery machine and applied to the fabric. The most supported format is DST file. Apparel companies also digitize clothing patterns

Analog Signals to Digital

Analog signals are continuous electrical signals; digital signals are non-continuous. Analog signal can be converted to digital signal by ADC.

Nearly all recorded music has been digitized. About 12 percent of the 500,000+ movies listed on the Internet Movie Database are digitized on DVD.

Handling of analog signal becomes easy when it is digitized because the signal is digitized before modulation and transmission. The conversion process of analog to digital consists of two processes: sampling and quantizing.

Digitization of personal multimedia such as home movies, slides, and photographs is a popular method of preserving and sharing older repositories. Slides and photographs may be scanned using an image scanner, but videos are more difficult.

Analog Texts to Digital

About 5 percent of texts have been digitized as of 2006.

Older print books are being scanned and optical character recognition technologies applied by academic and public libraries, foundations, and private companies like Google.

Unpublished text documents on paper which have some enduring historical or research value are being digitized by libraries and archives, though frequently at a much slower rate than for books. In many cases, archives have replaced microfilming with digitization as a means of preserving and providing access to unique documents.

Implications

This shift to digitization in the contemporary media world has created implications for traditional mass media products. However, these "limitations are still very unclear" (McQuail, 2000:28). The more technology advances, the more converged the realm of mass media will become with less need for traditional communication technologies. For example, the Internet has transformed many communication norms, creating more efficiency for not only individuals, but also for businesses. However, McQuail suggests traditional media have also benefited greatly from new media, allowing more effective and efficient resources available (2000:28).

Collaborative Projects

There are many collaborative digitization projects throughout the United States. Two of the earliest projects were the Collaborative Digitization Project in Colorado and NC ECHO - North Carolina Exploring Cultural Heritage Online, based at the State Library of North Carolina.

These projects establish and publish best practices for digitization and work with regional partners to digitize cultural heritage materials. Additional criteria for best practice have more recently been established in the UK, Australia and the European Union. Wisconsin Heritage Online is a collaborative digitization project modeled after the Colorado Collaborative Digitization Project. Wisconsin uses a wiki to build and distribute collaborative documentation. Georgia's collaborative digitization program, the Digital Library of Georgia, presents a seamless virtual library on the state's history and life, including more than a hundred digital collections from 60 institutions and 100 agencies of government. The Digital Library of Georgia is a GALILEO initiative based at the University of Georgia Libraries.

In South-Asia Nanakshahi trust is digitizing manuscripts of Gurmukhīscript.

In Australia specifically, there have been many collaborative projects between The National Library and Universities to improve the repository infrastructure that digitized information would be stored in. Some of these projects include, the ARROW (Australian Research Repositories Online to the World) project and the APSR (Australian Partnership for Sustainable Repository) project.

Library Preservation

Digitization at the British Library of a Dunhuang manuscript for the International Dunhuang Project

Digital preservation in its most basic form is a series of activities maintaining access to digital materials over time. Digitization in this sense is a means of creating digital surrogates of analog materials such as books, newspapers, microfilm and videotapes. Digitization can provide a means of preserving the content of the materials by creating an accessible facsimile of the object in order to put less strain on already fragile originals. For sounds, digitization of legacy analogue recordings is essential insurance against technological obsolescence.

The prevalent Brittle Books issue facing libraries across the world is being addressed with a digital solution for long term book preservation. Since the mid-1800s, books were printed on wood-pulp paper, which turns acidic as it decays. Deterioration may advance to a point where a book is completely unusable. In theory, if these widely circulated titles are not treated with de-acidification processes, the materials upon those acid pages will be lost. As digital technology evolves, it is increasingly preferred as a method of preserving these materials, mainly because it can provide easier access points and significantly reduce the need for physical storage space.

Cambridge University Library is working on the Cambridge Digital Library, which will initially contain digitised versions of many of its most important works relating to science and religion. These include examples such as Isaac Newton's personally annotated first edition of his Philosophiæ Naturalis Principia Mathematica as well as college notebooks and other papers, and some Islamic manuscripts such as a Quran from Tipoo Sahib's library.

Google, Inc. has taken steps towards attempting to digitize every title with "Google Book Search". While some academic libraries have been contracted by the service, issues of copyright law violations threaten to derail the project. However, it does provide - at the very least - an online consortium for libraries to exchange information and for researchers to search for titles as well as review the materials.

Digitization Versus Digital Preservation

There is a common misconception that to digitize something is the same as digital preservation. To digitize something is to convert something from an analog into a digital format. An example would be scanning a photograph and having a digital copy on a computer. This is essentially the first step in digital preservation. To digitally preserve something is to maintain it over a long period of time.

Digital preservation is more complicated because technology changes so quickly that a format that was used to save something years ago may become obsolete, like a 5 1/4" floppy drive. Computers are no longer made with them, and obtaining the hardware to convert a file from an obsolete format to a newer one can be expensive. As a result, the upgrading process must take place every 2 to 5 years, or as newer technology becomes affordable, but before older technology becomes unobtainable. The Library of Congress provides numerous resources and tips for individuals looking to practice digitization and digital preservation for their personal collections.

Digital preservation can also apply to born-digital material. An example of something that is born-digital is a Microsoft Word document saved as a .docx file or a post to a social media site. In contrast, digitization only applies exclusively to analog materials. Born-digital materials present a unique challenge to digital preservation not only due to technological obsolescence but also because of the inherently unstable nature of digital storage and maintenance. Most websites last between 2.5 and 5 years, depending on the purpose for which they were designed.

Many libraries, archives, and museums, as well as other institutions struggle with catching up and staying current in regards to both digitization and digital preservation. Digitization is a time-consuming process, particularly depending on the condition of the holdings prior to being digitized. Some materials are so fragile that undergoing the process of digitization could damage them irreparably; light from a scanner can damage old photographs and documents. Despite potential damage, one reason for digitizing some materials is because they are so heavily used that digitization will help to preserve the original copy long past what its life would have been as a physical holding.

Digitization can also be quite expensive. Institutions want the best image quality in digital copies so that when they are converted from one format to another over time only a high-quality copy is maintained. Smaller institutions may not be able to afford such equipment. Manpower at many facilities also limits how much material can be digitized. Archivists and librarians must have an idea of what their patrons wish to see most and try to prioritize and meet those needs digitally.

Manpower and funding also limit digital preservation in many institutions. The cost of upgrading hardware or software every few years can be prohibitively expensive. Training is another issue, since many librarians and archivists do not have a computer science background. Intellectual control of digital holdings presents yet another issue which sometimes occurs when the physical holdings have not yet been entirely processed. One suggested timeframe for completely transcribing digital holdings was every ten to twenty years, making the process an ongoing and time-consuming one.

Lean Philosophy

The broad use of internet and the increasing popularity of lean philosophy has also increased the use and meaning of "digitizing" to describe improvements in the efficiency of organizational processes. Lean philosophy refers to the approach which considers any use of time and resources, which does not lead directly to creating a product, as waste and therefore a target for elimination. This will often involve some kind of Lean process in order to simplify process activities, with the aim of implementing new "lean and mean" processes by digitizing data and activities. Digitization can help to eliminate time waste by introducing wider access to data, or by implementation of enterprise resource planning systems.

Fiction

Works of science-fiction often include the term digitize as the act of transforming people into digital signals and sending them into a computer. When that happens, the people disappear from the real world and appear in a computer world (as featured in the cult film *Tron*, the animated series *Code: Lyoko*, or the late 1980s live-action series *Captain Power and the Soldiers of the Future*). In the video game *Beyond Good & Evil*, the protagonist's holographic friend digitizes the player's inventory items.

Computer Vision

Computer vision is a field that includes methods for acquiring, processing, analyzing, and understanding images and, in general, high-dimensional data from the real world in order to produce numerical or symbolic information, *e.g.*, in the forms of decisions. A theme in the development of this field has been to duplicate the abilities of human vision by electronically perceiving and understanding an image. Understanding in this context means the transformation of visual images (the input of the retina) into descriptions of the world that can interface with other thought processes and elicit appropriate action. This image understanding can be seen as the disentangling of symbolic information from image data using models constructed with the aid of geometry, physics, statistics, and learning theory. Computer vision has also been described as the enterprise of automating and integrating a wide range of processes and representations for vision perception.

As a scientific discipline, computer vision is concerned with the theory behind artificial systems that extract information from images. The image data can take many forms, such as video sequences, views from multiple cameras, or multi-dimensional data from a medical scanner. As a technological discipline, computer vision seeks to apply its theories and models for the construction of computer vision systems.

Sub-domains of computer vision include scene reconstruction, event detection, video tracking, object recognition, object pose estimation, learning, indexing, motion estimation, and image restoration.

Related Fields

Areas of artificial intelligence deal with autonomous planning or deliberation for robotical systems to navigate through an environment. A detailed understanding of these environments is required to navigate through them. Information about the environment could be provided by a computer vision system, acting as a vision sensor and providing high-level information about the environment and the robot.

Artificial intelligence and computer vision share other topics such as pattern recognition and learning techniques. Consequently, computer vision is sometimes seen as a part of the artificial intelligence field or the computer science field in general.

Solid-state physics is another field that is closely related to computer vision. Most computer vision systems rely on image sensors, which detect electromagnetic radiation, which is typically in the form of either visible or infra-red light. The sensors are designed using quantum physics. The process by which light interacts with surfaces is explained using physics. Physics explains the behavior of optics which are a core part of most imaging systems. Sophisticated image sensors even require quantum mechanics to provide a complete understanding of the image formation process. Also, various measurement problems in physics can be addressed using computer vision, for example motion in fluids.

A third field which plays an important role is neurobiology, specifically the study of the biological vision system. Over the last century, there has been an extensive study of eyes, neurons, and the brain structures devoted to processing of visual stimuli in both humans and various animals. This has led to a coarse, yet complicated, description of how "real" vision systems operate in order to solve certain vision related tasks. These results have led to a subfield within computer vision where artificial systems are designed to mimic the processing and behavior of biological systems, at different levels of complexity. Also, some of the learning-based methods developed within computer vision (*e.g.* neural net and deep learning based image and feature analysis and classification) have their background in biology.

Some strands of computer vision research are closely related to the study of biological vision – indeed, just as many strands of AI research are closely tied with research into human consciousness, and the use of stored knowledge to interpret, integrate and utilize visual information. The field of biological vision studies and models the physiological processes behind visual perception in humans and other animals. Computer vision, on the other hand, studies and describes the processes implemented in software and hardware behind artificial vision systems. Interdisciplinary exchange between biological and computer vision has proven fruitful for both fields.

Yet another field related to computer vision is signal processing. Many methods for processing of one-variable signals, typically temporal signals, can be extended in a natural way to processing of two-variable signals or multi-variable signals in computer vision. However, because of the specific nature of images there are many methods developed within computer vision which have no counterpart in processing of one-variable signals. Together with the multi-dimensionality of the signal, this defines a subfield in signal processing as a part of computer vision.

Beside the above-mentioned views on computer vision, many of the related research topics can also be studied from a purely mathematical point of view. For example, many methods in computer vision are based on statistics, optimization or geometry. Finally, a significant part of the field is devoted to the implementation aspect of computer vision; how existing methods can be realized in various combinations of software and hardware, or how these methods can be modified in order to gain processing speed without losing too much performance.

The fields most closely related to computer vision are image processing, image analysis and machine vision. There is a significant overlap in the range of techniques and applications that these covers. This implies that the basic techniques that are used and developed in these fields are more or less identical, something which can be interpreted as there is only one field with different names. On the other hand, it appears to be necessary for research groups, scientific journals, conferences and companies to present or market themselves as belonging specifically to one of these fields and, hence, various characterizations which distinguish each of the fields from the others have been presented.

Computer vision is, in some ways, the inverse of computer graphics. While computer graphics produces image data from 3D models, computer vision often produces 3D models from image data. There is also a trend towards a combination of the two disciplines, *e.g.*, as explored in augmented reality.

The following characterizations appear relevant but should not be taken as universally accepted:

- Image processing and image analysis tend to focus on 2D images, how to transform one image to another, *e.g.*, by pixel-wise operations such as contrast enhancement, local operations such as edge extraction or noise removal, or geometrical transformations such as rotating the image. This characterization implies that image processing/analysis neither require assumptions nor produce interpretations about the image content.

- Computer vision includes 3D analysis from 2D images. This analyzes the 3D scene projected onto one or several images, *e.g.*, how to reconstruct structure or other information about the 3D scene from one or several images. Computer vision often relies on more or less complex assumptions about the scene depicted in an image.

- Machine vision is the process of applying a range of technologies & methods to provide imaging-based automatic inspection, process control and robot guidance in industrial applications. Machine vision tends to focus on applications, mainly in manufacturing, *e.g.*, vision based autonomous robots and systems for vision based inspection or measurement. This implies that image sensor technologies and control theory often are integrated with the processing of image data to control a robot and that real-time processing is emphasised by means of efficient implementations in hardware and software. It also implies that the external conditions such as lighting can be and are often more controlled in machine vision than they are in general computer vision, which can enable the use of different algorithms.

- There is also a field called imaging which primarily focus on the process of producing images, but sometimes also deals with processing and analysis of images. For example, medical imaging includes substantial work on the analysis of image data in medical applications.

- Finally, pattern recognition is a field which uses various methods to extract information from signals in general, mainly based on statistical approaches and artificial neural networks. A significant part of this field is devoted to applying these methods to image data.

Photogrammetry also overlaps with computer vision, e.g., stereophotogrammetry vs. stereo computer vision.

Applications

Applications range from tasks such as industrial machine vision systems which, say, inspect bottles speeding by on a production line, to research into artificial intelligence and computers or robots that can comprehend the world around them. The computer vision and machine vision fields have significant overlap. Computer vision covers the core technology of automated image analysis which is used in many fields. Machine vision usually refers to a process of combining automated image analysis with other methods and technologies to provide automated inspection and robot guidance in industrial applications. In many computer vision applications, the computers are pre-programmed to solve a particular task, but methods based on learning are now becoming increasingly common. Examples of applications of computer vision include systems for:

- Controlling processes, *e.g.*, an industrial robot;

- Navigation, *e.g.*, by an autonomous vehicle or mobile robot;

- Detecting events, *e.g.*, for visual surveillance or people counting;

- Organizing information, *e.g.*, for indexing databases of images and image sequences;

- Modeling objects or environments, *e.g.*, medical image analysis or topographical modeling;

- Interaction, *e.g.*, as the input to a device for computer-human interaction, and

- Automatic inspection, *e.g.*, in manufacturing applications.

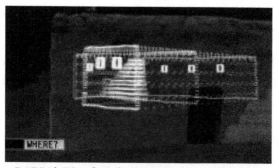

DARPA's Visual Media Reasoning concept video

One of the most prominent application fields is medical computer vision or medical image processing. This area is characterized by the extraction of information from image data for the purpose of making a medical diagnosis of a patient. Generally, image data is in the form of microscopy images, X-ray images, angiography images, ultrasonic images, and tomography images. An example of information which can be extracted from such image data is detection of tumours, arteriosclerosis or other malign changes. It can also be measurements of organ dimensions, blood flow, etc. This application area also supports medical research by providing new information, *e.g.*, about the structure of the brain, or about the quality of medical treatments. Applications of computer vision in the medical area also includes enhancement of images that are interpreted by humans, for example ultrasonic images or X-ray images, to reduce the influence of noise.

A second application area in computer vision is in industry, sometimes called machine vision, where information is extracted for the purpose of supporting a manufacturing process. One example is quality control where details or final products are being automatically inspected in order to find defects. Another example is measurement of position and orientation of details to be picked up by a robot arm. Machine vision is also heavily used in agricultural process to remove undesirable food stuff from bulk material, a process called optical sorting.

Military applications are probably one of the largest areas for computer vision. The obvious examples are detection of enemy soldiers or vehicles and missile guidance. More advanced systems for missile guidance send the missile to an area rather than a specific target, and target selection is made when the missile reaches the area based on locally acquired image data. Modern military concepts, such as "battlefield awareness", imply that various sensors, including image sensors, provide a rich set of information about a combat scene which can be used to support strategic decisions. In this case, automatic processing of the data is used to reduce complexity and to fuse information from multiple sensors to increase reliability.

Artist's Concept of Rover on Mars, an example of an unmanned land-based vehicle.
Notice the stereo cameras mounted on top of the Rover.

One of the newer application areas is autonomous vehicles, which include submersibles, land-based vehicles (small robots with wheels, cars or trucks), aerial vehicles, and unmanned aerial vehicles (UAV). The level of autonomy ranges from fully autonomous (unmanned) vehicles to vehicles where computer vision based systems support a driver or a pilot in various situations. Fully autonomous vehicles typically use computer vision for navigation, i.e. for knowing where it is, or for producing a map of its environment (SLAM) and for detecting obstacles. It can also be used for detecting certain task specific events, e.g., a UAV looking for forest fires. Examples of supporting systems are obstacle warning systems in cars, and systems for autonomous landing of aircraft. Several car manufacturers have demonstrated systems for autonomous driving of cars, but this technology has still not reached a level where it can be put on the market. There are ample examples of military autonomous vehicles ranging from advanced missiles, to UAVs for recon missions or missile guidance. Space exploration is already being made with autonomous vehicles using computer vision, e.g., NASA's Mars Exploration Rover and ESA's ExoMars Rover.

Other application areas include:

- Support of visual effects creation for cinema and broadcast, e.g., camera tracking (matchmoving).

- Surveillance.

Representational and Control Requirements

Image-understanding systems (IUS) include three levels of abstraction as follows: Low level includes image primitives such as edges, texture elements, or regions; intermediate level includes boundaries, surfaces and volumes; and high level includes objects, scenes, or events. Many of these requirements are really topics for further research.

The representational requirements in the designing of IUS for these levels are: representation of prototypical concepts, concept organization, spatial knowledge, temporal knowledge, scaling, and description by comparison and differentiation.

While inference refers to the process of deriving new, not explicitly represented facts from currently known facts, control refers to the process that selects which of the many inference, search, and matching techniques should be applied at a particular stage of processing. Inference and control requirements for IUS are: search and hypothesis activation, matching and hypothesis testing, generation and use of expectations, change and focus of attention, certainty and strength of belief, inference and goal satisfaction.

Typical Tasks

Each of the application areas described above employ a range of computer vision tasks; more or less well-defined measurement problems or processing problems, which can be solved using a variety of methods. Some examples of typical computer vision tasks are presented below.

Recognition

The classical problem in computer vision, image processing, and machine vision is that of determining whether or not the image data contains some specific object, feature, or activity. Different varieties of the recognition problem are described in the literature:

- Object recognition (also called object classification) – one or several pre-specified or learned objects or object classes can be recognized, usually together with their 2D positions in the image or 3D poses in the scene. Blippar, Google Goggles and LikeThat provide stand-alone programs that illustrate this functionality.

- Identification – an individual instance of an object is recognized. Examples include identification of a specific person's face or fingerprint, identification of handwritten digits, or identification of a specific vehicle.

- Detection – the image data are scanned for a specific condition. Examples include detection of possible abnormal cells or tissues in medical images or detection of a vehicle in an automatic road toll system. Detection based on relatively simple and fast computations is sometimes used for finding smaller regions of interesting image data which can be further analyzed by more computationally demanding techniques to produce a correct interpretation.

Currently, the best algorithms for such tasks are based on convolutional neural networks. An illustration of their capabilities is given by the ImageNet Large Scale Visual Recognition Challenge;

this is a benchmark in object classification and detection, with millions of images and hundreds of object classes. Performance of convolutional neural networks, on the ImageNet tests, is now close to that of humans. The best algorithms still struggle with objects that are small or thin, such as a small ant on a stem of a flower or a person holding a quill in their hand. They also have trouble with images that have been distorted with filters (an increasingly common phenomenon with modern digital cameras). By contrast, those kinds of images rarely trouble humans. Humans, however, tend to have trouble with other issues. For example, they are not good at classifying objects into fine-grained classes, such as the particular breed of dog or species of bird, whereas convolutional neural networks handle this with ease.

Several specialized tasks based on recognition exist, such as:

- Content-based image retrieval – finding all images in a larger set of images which have a specific content. The content can be specified in different ways, for example in terms of similarity relative a target image (give me all images similar to image X), or in terms of high-level search criteria given as text input (give me all images which contains many houses, are taken during winter, and have no cars in them).

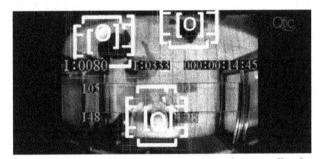
Computer vision for people counter purposes in public places, malls, shopping centres

- Pose estimation – estimating the position or orientation of a specific object relative to the camera. An example application for this technique would be assisting a robot arm in retrieving objects from a conveyor belt in an assembly line situation or picking parts from a bin.

- Optical character recognition (OCR) – identifying characters in images of printed or handwritten text, usually with a view to encoding the text in a format more amenable to editing or indexing (*e.g.* ASCII).

- 2D Code reading Reading of 2D codes such as data matrix and QR codes.

- Facial recognition

- Shape Recognition Technology (SRT) in people counter systems differentiating human beings (head and shoulder patterns) from objects

Motion Analysis

Several tasks relate to motion estimation where an image sequence is processed to produce an estimate of the velocity either at each points in the image or in the 3D scene, or even of the camera that produces the images . Examples of such tasks are:

- Egomotion – determining the 3D rigid motion (rotation and translation) of the camera from an image sequence produced by the camera.

- Tracking – following the movements of a (usually) smaller set of interest points or objects (*e.g.*, vehicles or humans) in the image sequence.

- Optical flow – to determine, for each point in the image, how that point is moving relative to the image plane, i.e., its apparent motion. This motion is a result both of how the corresponding 3D point is moving in the scene and how the camera is moving relative to the scene.

Scene Reconstruction

Given one or (typically) more images of a scene, or a video, scene reconstruction aims at computing a 3D model of the scene. In the simplest case the model can be a set of 3D points. More sophisticated methods produce a complete 3D surface model. The advent of 3D imaging not requiring motion or scanning, and related processing algorithms is enabling rapid advances in this field. Grid-based 3D sensing can be used to acquire 3D images from multiple angles. Algorithms are now available to stitch multiple 3D images together into point clouds and 3D models.

Image Restoration

The aim of image restoration is the removal of noise (sensor noise, motion blur, etc.) from images. The simplest possible approach for noise removal is various types of filters such as low-pass filters or median filters. More sophisticated methods assume a model of how the local image structures look like, a model which distinguishes them from the noise. By first analysing the image data in terms of the local image structures, such as lines or edges, and then controlling the filtering based on local information from the analysis step, a better level of noise removal is usually obtained compared to the simpler approaches.

An example in this field is inpainting.

System Methods

The organization of a computer vision system is highly application dependent. Some systems are stand-alone applications which solve a specific measurement or detection problem, while others constitute a sub-system of a larger design which, for example, also contains sub-systems for control of mechanical actuators, planning, information databases, man-machine interfaces, etc. The specific implementation of a computer vision system also depends on if its functionality is pre-specified or if some part of it can be learned or modified during operation. Many functions are unique to the application. There are, however, typical functions which are found in many computer vision systems.

- Image acquisition – A digital image is produced by one or several image sensors, which, besides various types of light-sensitive cameras, include range sensors, tomography devices, radar, ultra-sonic cameras, etc. Depending on the type of sensor, the resulting image data is an ordinary 2D image, a 3D volume, or an image sequence. The pixel values typically correspond to light intensity in one or several spectral bands (gray images or colour images), but can also be related to various physical measures, such as depth, absorption or reflectance of sonic or electromagnetic waves, or nuclear magnetic resonance.

- Pre-processing – Before a computer vision method can be applied to image data in order to extract some specific piece of information, it is usually necessary to process the data in order to assure that it satisfies certain assumptions implied by the method. Examples are

  o Re-sampling in order to assure that the image coordinate system is correct.

  o Noise reduction in order to assure that sensor noise does not introduce false information.

  o Contrast enhancement to assure that relevant information can be detected.

  o Scale space representation to enhance image structures at locally appropriate scales.

- Feature extraction – Image features at various levels of complexity are extracted from the image data. Typical examples of such features are

  o Lines, edges and ridges.

  o Localized interest points such as corners, blobs or points.

More complex features may be related to texture, shape or motion.

- Detection/segmentation – At some point in the processing a decision is made about which image points or regions of the image are relevant for further processing. Examples are

  o Selection of a specific set of interest points

  o Segmentation of one or multiple image regions which contain a specific object of interest.

  o Segmentation of image into nested scene architecture comprised foreground, object groups, single objects or salient object parts (also referred to as spatial-taxon scene hierarchy)

- High-level processing – At this step the input is typically a small set of data, for example a set of points or an image region which is assumed to contain a specific object. The remaining processing deals with, for example:

  o Verification that the data satisfy model-based and application specific assumptions.

  o Estimation of application specific parameters, such as object pose or object size.

  o Image recognition – classifying a detected object into different categories.

  o Image registration – comparing and combining two different views of the same object.

- Decision making Making the final decision required for the application, for example:

- o   Pass/fail on automatic inspection applications

- o   Match / no-match in recognition applications

- o   Flag for further human review in medical, military, security and recognition applications

Hardware

There are many kinds of computer vision systems, nevertheless all of them contain these basic elements: a power source, at least one image acquisition device (i.e. camera, ccd, etc.), a processor as well as control and communication cables or some kind of wireless interconnection mechanism. In addition, a practical vision system contains software, as well as a display in order to monitor the system. Vision systems for inner spaces, as most industrial ones, contain an illumination system and may be placed in a controlled environment. Furthermore, a completed system includes many accessories like camera supports, cables and connectors.

While traditional broadcast and consumer video systems operate at a rate of 30 frames per second, advances in digital signal processing and consumer graphics hardware has made high-speed image acquisition, processing, and display possible for real-time systems on the order of hundreds to thousands of frames per second. For applications in robotics, fast, real-time video systems are critically important and often can simplify the processing needed for certain algorithms. When combined with a high-speed projector, fast image acquisition allows 3D measurement and feature tracking to be realised.

As of 2016, vision processing units are emerging as a new class of processor, to complement CPUs and GPUs in this role.

CVIPtools

CVIPtools (Computer Vision and Image Processing Tools) is an Open Source image processing software. It is free for use with Windows, and previous versions are available for UNIX. It is an interactive program for image processing and computer vision.

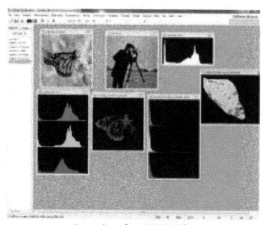

Running the CVIPtools

About CVIPtools

CVIPtools is a Windows-based software (previous versions for various flavors of UNIX are also available) for computer vision and image processing developed at the Computer Vision and Image Processing Laboratory at Southern Illinois University at Edwardsville. CVIPtools 5.6j is implemented in four layers: the algorithms code layer, the Common Object Module (COM) interface layer, the CvipOp layer, and the Graphical user interface (GUI). The algorithms code layer is based primarily on previous versions of CVIPtools, consists of all image and data-processing procedures and functions, and is written in standard C. The COM interface layer is written in C++ and links the CVIPtools C functions to the GUI through the CVIPimage Class. The CvipOp layer provides an object-oriented paradigm by using the Class CVIPimage to consolidate data safety and memory management. The GUI layer, written in C#, implements the image queue, viewer, and manages user input and output. For development, CVIPtools5.x includes the CVIPlab environment and the CVIPtools libraries. In addition to the standard C libraries, a dynamically linked library (cviptools.dll) is provided that contains all the COM versions of these functions.

Features

CVIPtools can read many image formats including TIFF, PNG, GIF, JPEG, BMP, as well as raw formats. CVIPtools supports standard image processing functions such as image compression, image restoration, logical and arithmetical operations between images, contrast manipulation, image sharpening, Frequency transform, edge detection, segmentation and geometric transformations.

CVIPtools5.x also contains two powerful development tools that allow for batch processing and automatic algorithm analysis and development. The CVIP-ATAT, Algorithm Test and Analysis Tool, can be used to test all combinations and values of parameters to speed front-end algorithm development. The CVIP-FEPC, Feature Extraction and Pattern Classification, will allow for batch processing and test all combinations of features and pattern classification techniques. These are described in more detail, along with application examples, in the new edition of the textbook Digital Image Processing and Analysis: Human and Computer Vision Applications with CVIPtools, Second Edition.

CVIP-ATAT

The Computer Vision and Image Processing Algorithm Test and Analysis Tool, CVIP-ATAT, was created to facilitate the development of both human and computer vision applications. The primary function of this tool is to allow the user to explore many more algorithmic possibilities than can be considered by processing one image at a time with CVIPtools. It allows for the automatic processing of large image sets with many different algorithmic and parameter variations. We call this the "front-end" tool because its primary purpose is to find the best algorithm to preprocess, segment and post-process a set of images for a particular application in order to best separate the most important regions of interest within the image.

It has a GUI which allows the user to enter multi-stage algorithms for testing and analysis. At each stage the user can specify a number of different processes to test and a range for the processes' parameters. The user also specifies a set of images to process and a set of "ideal" output images which will be used to determine the success for each algorithm. Note that one algorithm is defined as a specific set of processes and a specific set of parameter values.

The tool will then automatically perform algorithms which consist of all the permutations of the values for each of the parameters for each process and all the processes for each stage. Next, the user can compare the various algorithm results to determine the best set of processes and parameters for the particular application. The tool is useful for application development where the ideal image results are available, or can be created. Additionally, it can serve as a front end development tool for image analysis to find the optimal set of processes and parameters for extracting regions of interest for further processing.

CVIP-FEPC

The Computer Vision and Image Processing Feature Extraction and Pattern Classification Tool, CVIP-FEPC, was created to facilitate the development of both human and computer vision applications. The primary application area is computer vision, but it can be used, for example, as an aid in the development of image compression schemes for human vision applications. This can be done by helping to determine salient image features that must be retained for a given compression scheme. Conversely, computer vision applications are essentially deployed image analysis systems for a specific application, so the feature extraction and pattern classification is an integral part of all computer vision systems.

The primary function of this tool is to explore feature extraction and pattern classification and allow the user to perform batch processing with large image sets and is thus much more efficient than processing one image at a time with CVIPtools. It allows the user to select the features and pattern classification parameters for the automatic processing of these large image sets. CVIP-FEPC enables the user to easily specify the training and test sets and run multiple experiments in an efficient manner. Its primary purpose is to find the best parameters for a particular application in order to best classify the image objects of interest.

This tool is designed to work with a set of images that have binary masks that have been created for the objects of interest – one object per image. These masks can be created manually with CVIPtools, or, many image database applications will have the masks available. In general, the user will load the images, specify the classes, select the features, select the test set, choose the pattern classification parameters and then let the program process the entire image set. An output file will be created with the results for the experiment..

Homomorphic Filtering

Homomorphic filtering is a generalized technique for signal and image processing, involving a nonlinear mapping to a different domain in which linear filter techniques are applied, followed by mapping back to the original domain. This concept was developed in the 1960s by Thomas Stockham, Alan V. Oppenheim, and Ronald W. Schafer at MIT.

Image Enhancement

Homomorphic filter is sometimes used for image enhancement. It simultaneously normalizes the brightness across an image and increases contrast. Here homomorphic filtering is used to remove multiplicative noise. Illumination and reflectance are not separable, but their approximate locations in the frequency domain may be located. Since illumination and reflectance combine multiplicatively, the components are made additive by taking the logarithm of the image intensity, so that these multiplicative components of the image can be separated linearly in the frequency domain. Illumination variations can be thought of as a multiplicative noise, and can be reduced by filtering in the log domain.

To make the illumination of an image more even, the high-frequency components are increased and low-frequency components are decreased, because the high-frequency components are assumed to represent mostly the reflectance in the scene (the amount of light reflected off the object in the scene), whereas the low-frequency components are assumed to represent mostly the illumination in the scene. That is, high-pass filtering is used to suppress low frequencies and amplify high frequencies, in the log-intensity domain.

Audio and Speech Analysis

Homomorphic filtering is used in the log-spectral domain to separate filter effects from excitation effects, for example in the computation of the cepstrum as a sound representation; enhancements in the log spectral domain can improve sound intelligibility, for example in hearing aids.

Image Analysis

Image analysis is the extraction of meaningful information from images; mainly from digital images by means of digital image processing techniques. Image analysis tasks can be as simple as reading bar coded tags or as sophisticated as identifying a person from their face.

Computers are indispensable for the analysis of large amounts of data, for tasks that require complex computation, or for the extraction of quantitative information. On the other hand, the human visual cortex is an excellent image analysis apparatus, especially for extracting higher-level information, and for many applications — including medicine, security, and remote sensing — human analysts still cannot be replaced by computers. For this reason, many important image analysis tools such as edge detectors and neural networks are inspired by human visual perception models.

Computer Image Analysis

Computer Image Analysis largely contains the fields of computer or machine vision, and medical imaging, and makes heavy use of pattern recognition, digital geometry, and signal processing. This field of computer science developed in the 1950s at academic institutions such as the MIT A.I. Lab, originally as a branch of artificial intelligence and robotics.

It is the quantitative or qualitative characterization of two-dimensional (2D) or three-dimensional (3D) digital images. 2D images are, for example, to be analyzed in computer vision, and 3D images in medical imaging. The field was established in the 1950s–1970s, for example with pioneering contributions by Azriel Rosenfeld, Herbert Freeman, Jack E. Bresenham, or King-Sun Fu.

Techniques

There are many different techniques used in automatically analysing images. Each technique may be useful for a small range of tasks, however there still aren't any known methods of image analysis that are generic enough for wide ranges of tasks, compared to the abilities of a human's image analysing capabilities. Examples of image analysis techniques in different fields include:

- 2D and 3D object recognition,
- image segmentation,
- motion detection e.g. Single particle tracking,
- video tracking,
- optical flow,
- medical scan analysis,
- 3D Pose Estimation,
- automatic number plate recognition.

Digital Image Analysis

Digital Image Analysis is when a computer or electrical device automatically studies an image to obtain useful information from it. Note that the device is often a computer but may also be an electrical circuit, a digital camera or a mobile phone. The applications of digital image analysis are continuously expanding through all areas of science and industry, including:

- assay micro plate reading, such as detecting where a chemical was manufactured.
- astronomy, such as calculating the size of a planet.
- defense
- filtering
- machine vision, such as to automatically count items in a factory conveyor belt.
- materials science, such as determining if a metal weld has cracks.
- medicine, such as detecting cancer in a mammography scan.
- metallography, such as determining the mineral content of a rock sample.
- microscopy, such as counting the germs in a swab.
- optical character recognition, such as automatic license plate detection.
- remote sensing, such as detecting intruders in a house, and producing land cover/land use maps.

- robotics, such as to avoid steering into an obstacle.

- security, such as detecting a person's eye color or hair color.

Object-based Image Analysis

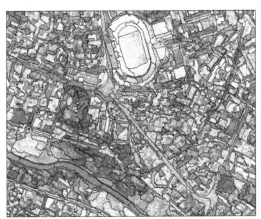

Image segmentation during the object base image analysis

Object-Based Image Analysis (OBIA) employs two main processes, segmentation and classification. Traditional image segmentation is on a per-pixel basis. However, OBIA groups pixels into homogeneous objects. These objects can have different shapes and scale. Objects also have statistics associated with them which can be used to classify objects. Statistics can include geometry, context and texture of image objects. The analyst defines statistics in the classification process to generate land cover. The technique is implemented in software such as eCognition.

When applied to earth images, OBIA is known as *Geographic Object-Based Image Analysis* (GEOBIA), defined as "a sub-discipline of geoinformation science devoted to (...) partitioning remote sensing (RS) imagery into meaningful image-objects, and assessing their characteristics through spatial, spectral and temporal scale". The international GEOBIA conference has been held biannually since 2006.

Land Cover Mapping

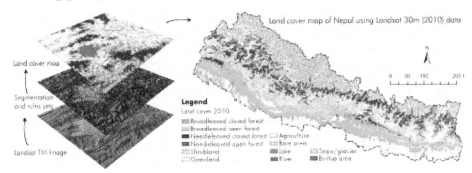

Process of land cover mapping using TM images

Land cover and land use change detection using remote sensing and geospatial data provides baseline information for assessing the climate change impacts on habitats and biodiversity, as well as natural resources, in the target areas.

Application of land cover mapping

- Local and regional planning

- Disaster management

- Vulnerability and Risk Assessments

- Ecological management

- Monitoring the effects of climate change

- Wildlife management.

- Alternative landscape futures and conservation

- Environmental forecasting

- Environmental impact assessment

- Policy development

Super-resolution Imaging

An example of geometrical superresolution processing, using noise reduction by image averaging. The left half shows the original image, the right half the result (at native resolution) when the software combines seven images.

Super-resolution imaging (SR) is a class of techniques that enhance the resolution of an imaging system. In some SR techniques—termed *optical* SR—the diffraction limit of systems is transcended, while in others—*geometrical* SR—the resolution of digital imaging sensors is enhanced.

Super-resolution imaging techniques are used in general image processing and in super-resolution microscopy.

Basic Concepts

Because some of the ideas surrounding superresolution raise fundamental issues, there is need at the outset to examine the relevant physical and information-theoretical principles.

Diffraction Limit The detail of a physical object that an optical instrument can reproduce in an image has limits that are mandated by laws of physics, whether formulated by the diffraction equations in the wave theory of light or the Uncertainty Principle for photons in quantum mechanics. Information transfer can never be increased beyond this boundary, but packets outside the limits can be cleverly swapped for (or multiplexed with) some inside it. One does not so much "break" as "run around" the diffraction limit. New procedures probing electro-magnetic disturbances at the molecular level (in the so-called near field) remain fully consistent with Maxwell's equations.

A succinct expression of the diffraction limit is given in the spatial-frequency domain. In Fourier optics light distributions are expressed as superpositions of a series of grating light patterns in a range of fringe widths, technically spatial frequencies. It is generally taught that diffraction theory stipulates an upper limit, the cut-off spatial-frequency, beyond which pattern elements fail to be transferred into the optical image, i.e., are not resolved. But in fact what is set by diffraction theory is the width of the passband, not a fixed upper limit. No laws of physics are broken when a spatial frequency band beyond the cut-off spatial frequency is swapped for one inside it: this has long been implemented in dark-field microscopy. Nor are information-theoretical rules broken when superimposing several bands, disentangling them in the received image needs assumptions of object invariance during multiple exposures, i.e., the substitution of one kind of uncertainty for another.

Information When the term superresolution is used in techniques of inferring object details from statistical treatment of the image within standard resolution limits, for example, averaging multiple exposures, it involves an exchange of one kind of information (extracting signal from noise) for another (the assumption that the target has remained invariant).

Resolution and localization True resolution involves the distinction of whether a target, e.g. a star or a spectral line, is single or double, ordinarily requiring separable peaks in the image. When a target is known to be single, its location can be determined with higher precision than the image width by finding the centroid (center of gravity) of its image light distribution. The word *ultra-resolution* had been proposed for this process but it did not catch on, and the high-precision localization procedure is typically referred to as superresolution.

In summary: The technical achievements of enhancing the performance of imaging-forming and – sensing devices now classified as superresolution utilize to the fullest but always stay within the bounds imposed by the laws of physics and information theory.

Techniques to which the Term "Superresolution" has been Applied

Optical or Diffractive Superresolution

Substituting spatial-frequency bands. Though the bandwidth allowable by diffraction is fixed, it can be positioned anywhere in the spatial-frequency spectrum. Dark-field illumination in microscopy is an example.

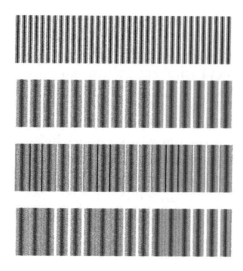

The "structured illumination" technique of superresolution is related to moiré patterns. The target, a band of fine fringes (top row), is beyond the diffraction limit. When a band of somewhat coarser resolvable fringes (second row) is artificially superimposed, the combination (third row) features moiré components that are within the diffraction limit and hence contained in the image (bottom row) allowing the presence of the fine fringes to be inferred even though they are not themselves represented in the image.

Multiplexing spatial-frequency bands such as structured illumination

An image is formed using the normal passband of the optical device. Then some known light structure, for example a set of light fringes that is also within the passband, is superimposed on the target. The image now contains components resulting from the combination of the target and the superimposed light structure, e.g. moiré fringes, and carries information about target detail which simple, unstructured illumination does not. The "superresolved" components, however, need disentangling to be revealed.

Multiple parameter use within traditional diffraction limit

If a target has no special polarization or wavelength properties, two polarization states or non-overlapping wavelength regions can be used to encode target details, one in a spatial-frequency band inside the cut-off limit the other beyond it. Both would utilize normal passband transmission but are then separately decoded to reconstitute target structure with extended resolution.

Probing near-field electromagnetic disturbance

The usual discussion of superresolution involved conventional imagery of an object by an optical system. But modern technology allows probing the electromagnetic disturbance within molecular distances of the source which has superior resolution properties, evanescent waves and the development of the new Super lens.

Geometrical or Image-processing Superresolution

Multi-exposure image noise reduction

When an image is degraded by noise, there can be more detail in the average of many exposures, even within the diffraction limit.

Compared to a single image marred by noise during its acquisition or transmission (left), the signal-to-noise ratio is improved by suitable combination of several separately-obtained images (right). This can be achieved only within the intrinsic resolution capability of the imaging process for revealing such detail.

Single-frame deblurring

Known defects in a given imaging situation, such as defocus or aberrations, can sometimes be mitigated in whole or in part by suitable spatial-frequency filtering of even a single image. Such procedures all stay within the diffraction-mandated passband, and do not extend it.

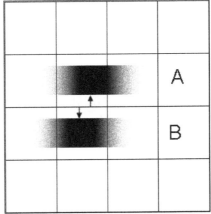

Both features extend over 3 pixels but in different amounts, enabling them to be localized with precision superior to pixel dimension.

Sub-pixel image localization

The location of a single source can be determined by computing the "center of gravity" (centroid) of the light distribution extending over several adjacent pixels. Provided that there is enough light, this can be achieved with arbitrary precision, very much better than pixel width of the detecting apparatus and the resolution limit for the decision of whether the source is single or double. This technique, which requires the presupposition that all the light comes from a single source, is at the basis of what has becomes known as superresolution microscopy, e.g. STORM, where fluorescent probes attached to molecules give nanoscale distance information. It is also the mechanism underlying visual hyperacuity.

Bayesian induction beyond traditional diffraction limit

Some object features, though beyond the diffraction limit, may be known to be associated with other object features that are within the limits and hence contained in the image. Then conclusions can be drawn, using statistical methods, from the available image data about the presence of the full object. The classical example is Toraldo di Francia's proposition of judging whether an image is that of a single or double star by determining whether its width exceeds the spread from a single star. This can be achieved at separations well below the classical resolution bounds, and requires the prior limitation to the choice "single or double?"

The approach can take the form of extrapolating the image in the frequency domain, by assuming that the object is an analytic function, and that we can exactly know the function values in some interval. This method is severely limited by the ever-present noise in digital imaging systems, but it can work for radar, astronomy, microscopy or magnetic resonance imaging. More recently, a fast single image super-resolution algorithm based on a closed-form solution to $\ell_2 - \ell_2$ problems has been proposed and demonstrated to accelerate most of the existing Bayesian super-resolution methods significantly.

Aliasing

Geometrical SR reconstruction algorithms are possible if and only if the input low resolution images have been under-sampled and therefore contain aliasing. Because of this aliasing, the high-frequency content of the desired reconstruction image is embedded in the low-frequency content of each of the observed images. Given a sufficient number of observation images, and if the set of observations vary in their phase (i.e. if the images of the scene are shifted by a sub-pixel amount), then the phase information can be used to separate the aliased high-frequency content from the true low-frequency content, and the full-resolution image can be accurately reconstructed.

In practice, this frequency-based approach is not used for reconstruction, but even in the case of spatial approaches (e.g. shift-add fusion), the presence of aliasing is still a necessary condition for SR reconstruction.

Technical Implementations

There are both single-frame and multiple-frame variants of SR. Multiple-frame SR uses the sub-pixel shifts between multiple low resolution images of the same scene. It creates an improved resolution image fusing information from all low resolution images, and the created higher resolution images are better descriptions of the scene. Single-frame SR methods attempt to magnify the image without introducing blur. These methods use other parts of the low resolution images, or other unrelated images, to *guess* what the high-resolution image should look like. Algorithms can also be divided by their domain: frequency or space domain. Originally, super-resolution methods worked well only on grayscale images, but researchers have found methods to adapt them to color camera images. Recently, the use of super-resolution for 3D data has also been shown.

Research

There is promising research on using deep convolutional networks to perform super-resolution.

References

- Bernd Jähne; Horst Haußecker (2000). Computer Vision and Applications, A Guide for Students and Practitioners. Academic Press. ISBN 0-13-085198-1.

- Milan Sonka; Vaclav Hlavac; Roger Boyle (2008). Image Processing, Analysis, and Machine Vision. Thomson. ISBN 0-495-08252-X.

- Steger, Carsten; Markus Ulrich & Christian Wiedemann (2008). Machine Vision Algorithms and Applications. Weinheim: Wiley-VCH. p. 1. ISBN 978-3-527-40734-7. Retrieved 2010-11-05.

- Shapiro, Stuart C. (1992). Encyclopedia of Artificial Intelligence, Volume 1. New York: John WIley & Sons, Inc. pp. 643–646. ISBN 0-471-50306-1.

- Umbaugh, Scott E (2011). Digital image processing and analysis : human and computer vision applications with CVIPtools (2nd ed.). Boca Raton, FL: CRC Press. ISBN 9-7814-3980-2052.

- Solomon, C.J., Breckon, T.P. (2010). Fundamentals of Digital Image Processing: A Practical Approach with Examples in Matlab. Wiley-Blackwell. doi:10.1002/9780470689776. ISBN 0470844736.

- Kagami, Shingo (2010). "High-speed vision systems and projectors for real-time perception of the world". IEEE Computer Society Conference on Computer Vision and Pattern Recognition - Workshops 2010: 100–107. doi:10.1109/CVPRW.2010.5543776. Retrieved 2 May 2016.

- Barghout, Lauren. "Visual Taxometric Approach to Image Segmentation Using Fuzzy-Spatial Taxon Cut Yields Contextually Relevant Regions." Information Processing and Management of Uncertainty in Knowledge-Based Systems. Springer International Publishing, 2014.

- D. Poot, B. Jeurissen, Y. Bastiaensen, J. Veraart, W. Van Hecke, P. M. Parizel, and J. Sijbers, "Super-Resolution for Multislice Diffusion Tensor Imaging", Magnetic Resonance in Medicine, (2012)

- J. Simpkins, R.L. Stevenson, "An Introduction to Super-Resolution Imaging." Mathematical Optics: Classical, Quantum, and Computational Methods, Ed. V. Lakshminarayanan, M. Calvo, and T. Alieva. CRC Press, 2012. 539-564.

- Newton, Isaac. "Philosophiæ Naturalis Principia Mathematica". Cambridge University Digital Library. Retrieved 10 January 2012.

- Bhat, Pravin, et al. "Gradientshop: A gradient-domain optimization framework for image and video filtering." ACM Transactions on Graphics 29.2 (2010).

4

Various Technologies of Multi-Image

Multi-image, though now an obsolete field, was one of the pioneering techniques of digital image processing. It involves using 35mm slides projected by single or multiple slide projectors onto one or more screens in sync with an audio track or voice over. This chapter studies multi-image, slide show and their modern counterpart, the multi-dynamic image technique. This chapter is a compilation of the various branches of multi-image technologies that form an integral part of the broader subject matter.

Multi-image

Multi-image is the now largely obsolete practice and business of using 35 mm slides (diapositives) projected by single or multiple slide projectors onto one or more screens in synchronization with an audio voice-over or music track. Multi-image productions are also known as multi-image slide presentations, slide shows and diaporamas and are a specific form of multimedia or audio-visual production.

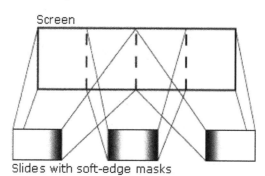

One of the hallmarks of multi-image was the use of the wide screen panorama. Precisely overlapping slides were placed in slide mounts with soft-edge density masks; when the resulting images were projected, the images would blend seamlessly on the screen to create the panorama. By cutting and dissolving between images in the projectors, animation effects were created in the panorama format.

The term *multi-image* is sometimes used to describe digital photo image computer programs that combine or change images on-screen, for photo montages, and image stitching.

Description

Multi-image presentations were a unique form of communication to audiences of various sizes, to meet a variety of communication and entertainment needs. The use of projected photographic images such as lantern slides for entertainment and instruction dates to the early 1800s. Others, such as L. Frank Baum had a traveling show (1908) that included slides, film, and actors describing the land of Oz. Throughout the years improvements in technology took place and applications for multi-image continued to expand. During the 1960s, automated synchronized audio and slides modules became more common and found use in instructional environments.

In general, multi-image can be defined as being:

- Based largely on analog production tools and technologies including art and audio production and film-based photography. 35mm slide film has high resolution and color range and are based on grain and dye clouds rather than on a fixed raster pattern, which when projected often is perceived as being more realistic, uniform, and detailed than digital images.

- Multi-disciplinary in terms of the types of skills required to create and stage multi-image presentations.

- Venue driven; multi-image presentations had specific requirements for the equipment and spaces they were intended for and presented in.

Multi-image Business

Multi-image as a business thrived during the 1970s and 1980s. Multi-image presentations ranged from single projector shows run by projector-viewer to large events for business meetings and conventions where multiple shows would be presented and often were rear-projected by 24 or more projectors.

Creating and presenting multi-image productions involved a relatively large number of specialized skills, equipment, and facilities to produce. During the height of multi-image, a number of types of businesses were directly engaged in the industry which employed thousands of specialists that ranged from producers and designers, writers, artists, typesetters, photographers, photo lab technicians, audio technicians, programmers, staging specialists as well as others associated with these disciplines.

AMI Gold Tour promotion.

A professional organization, the Association for Multi-image International (AMI), was created and had numerous active chapters around the world. The AMI held an annual convention and multi-image competition. Local chapters of AMI in various cities also held regional competitions.

An entire industry grew around supplying the tools and equipment needed to supply and support multi-image production.

- Corporations who manufactured and sold basic equipment and materials used in the production of multi-image, such as 35mm slide projectors, film, slide mounts, soft-edge masks and other items. The list of suppliers for the multi-image industry was extensive with a number of companies attaining international importance for the products they produced, including Eastman Kodak, Wess Slide Mounts, Chief Manufacturing, Navitar and Schneider Optics.

- Manufacturers of highly specialized multi-image equipment such as optical slide cameras and slide projector programming hardware. Precise camera systems were developed for the multi-image market featuring pin-registered film movements capable of making multiple exposures, controlled backlit color light sources, motorized multi-axis compounds for precise positioning of artwork, and long-roll film loads. Slide projector programming computers and dissolve equipment and software was developed to synchronize the slides with the audio by providing precise time control over slide tray positioning and lamp fade rates needed to create multi-image animation. Programmer and camera manufacturers included Audio Visual Labs, Electrosonic, Clearlight Inc. Spindler & Sauppe, Marron Carrel and Forox.

Driven by changes in technology and by economic considerations, multi-image has almost entirely been replaced by video presentations and by readily available computer based technologies such as laptop computers running PowerPoint and projecting through digital projectors. Visual presentation and photo and graphics editing software programs have allowed a wider range of communicators quick, flexible, and easy access to the tools and technologies needed to create presentations. Digital photography has reduced the need for laboratory services and complex equipment. The expansion and ease of use of desktop computing brought a close to the multi-image industry.

Multi-image Production Technologies

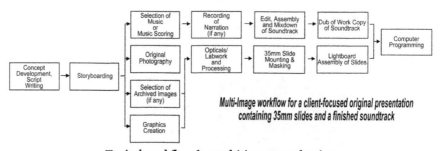

Typical workflow for multi-image production

The art and business of multi-image drew from many older existing technologies. When a multi-image project was initiated, various overall management roles were required to provide direction, planning, and project management. These roles generally involved the activities similar to those found in other media industries, such as creative, visual, and technical directors, producers, production managers, and writers.

Often individuals with the various production skills would fill these roles as well as performing their production roles. Multi-image productions in general were deadline driven and it was common that the production process would be non-linear, allowing for multiple activities to take place with overlapping roles.

Art and Design

The visual quality of a presentation was based on using photographs or artwork created for use in the presentation as source material. 35mm slides could be used directly as they were originally taken. Often the original photographs were masked or duplicated for positioning and sizing. In some instances, 35mm cameras modified for pin-registration were used to create animated sequences.

Through the use of multiple projectors set up to project onto a screen area, over-projected images could be designed as animations. Typical multi-image animation effects included fading from one photograph or graphic to another, progressively building text to form a completed statement, inserting images or graphics into frames or windows on screen, step by step movement of images across the screen area, and superimposing text or images onto a background. The visual effects were synchronized to music or voice and based on the capabilities and limitations of the slide projectors and dissolve units.

Artwork produced for multi-image presentations in general was based on one of two forms of top-lit reflective copy artwork:

1. Materials that were produced and copied as flat art directly to slides to be used in the production, or

2. Color- or image separated and layered photomechanical art that would be copied to high-contrast masks which were then used to create slides. This second process was called optical slide printing and was based on many of the basic principles from photomechanical prepress art used in offset printing, silk-screen printing, and cel animation.

Flat art was created by using a variety of standard graphic illustration techniques, using pen and ink, airbrush, paints, from clip art, colored paper, transfer lettering such as Letraset, and by copying from existing materials on a copy stand or on optical slide camera. Cel art, such as found in cel animation, was also used.

Art used in optical slide printing was based on the use of high-contrast photomechanical materials such as photomechanical transfers, black and white type, rubylith and other materials. Phototypesetting was done by a variety of means including the Visual Graphics Corporation PhotoTypositor and the Compugraphic EditWriter at companies that specialized in providing typography. When making artwork for multi-image presentations, photographs, transparencies, and film images or continuous tone film or airbrushed masks could also be used as part of the camera-ready artwork.

The color or image separated layers of artwork were pin-registered using a variety of standard pin systems including 1/4-inch, Oxberry, and Acme. The artwork was created on a light table or animation disc to provide back lighting.

Often the art was created based on a grid system. A copy of the optical slide camera grid or reticle was used to align the artwork elements. The use of the grid for alignment could be used to accurately position images and art elements throughout the process from the creation of the artwork to the final projected images. This process also allowed layers of the artwork to be interchangeable from slide to slide, images or graphic elements could be carefully placed on the screen relative to other images, and for combining parts of images or graphics by separate slides as in an animated sequence.

Audio Production

The audio track of a multi-image show provided a framework for the timing of the presentation and for the sequencing and animations of the slides. These were produced generally on 1/4-inch audio tape on multi-track tape recorders such as models by Tascam, TEAC, Sony, Fostex and Crown, which allowed for having two tracks or channels for stereo sound and one for the synchronization or click track which was used to encode and playback the signals for the dissolve units. The audio and synchronization tracks were normally separated by a blank track to prevent any carryover of the synchronization cues into the audio playback. Audio editing of the music or voice-over was done manually to create a scratch track, usually with a cutting block and tape. Once the audio edits were completed, the final version would be copied onto another tape; either to 1/4 inch, cassette or other format so that there tape used to run the presentation would be a fresh uncut tape.

As productions became more sophisticated, 16 and 24-track recording processes were used to create elaborate soundtracks and 4-channel surround sound for large business theatre environments. In productions such as the Maritz-produced car announcement shows for GM and Ford Motor Company, 16-track recorders were used for playback onsite. These 2-inch showtapes would contain extra tracks to support the vocals for a live cast onstage, as well as additional string-section support for the live orchestra and a click track to cue the conductor, in order to maintain synchronization between the cast, orchestra and on-screen visuals.

Printing with Light

Completed artwork was copied under top lights on a pin-registered camera on a high contrast film such as Kodaline or Kodalith to create 35mm mattes used in the optical slide printing process. When needed, pin-registered positive mattes known as countermattes were made by contact printing from the mattes. When a set of mattes and countermates were completed, the optical slide camera was used to assemble the separate images onto a single frame of film by making multiple exposures through the mattes. Accuracy in positioning the separate elements of the slide is made possible by the film sprockets, which were also used to position the finished color slides and masks in the slide mounts.

Maron 1600 camera table, large format 12-field compound, and colorhead.

Copy cameras and optical slide cameras usually had motorized movement of the camera on the column toward and away from the table to allow for resizing the image on the camera on the Z-axis.

Fully functional optical slide cameras had compounds for positioning both artwork and the mattes relative to the lens and camera head. A compound could move left to right (horizontal) X-axis and top to bottom (vertical) Y-axis movement as well as rotate (theta-axis). Compounds were often motorized with micro-stepping motors to allow for smooth programmable and repeatable positioning. Higher end optical slide cameras had the ability to create and save programs.

Light sources for copying artwork generally were quartz halogen lights. Backlighting was generally provided by the use a darkroom photographic enlarger colorhead modified for use with the camera. This form of controlled light provide colored light balanced for the color sensitivity of the film used and provided color light for the separate exposures that are made through the mattes.

The optical slide camera could be used to create a number of types of slides and special effects commonly used in multi-image presentations:

- Duplicates: copies of transparencies

- Copy slides: slides made by top-light copying of artwork or illustrations

- Title burns: made by making multiple exposures through a series of mattes, such as text slides

- Color on color slides: Similar to burn slides but with a color background, often requiring countermattes

- Step and repeat: Using a compound, making a series of exposures where the compound is moved between each exposure

- Movements: long exposures made from a backlit matte, the shutter is open while the compound and the camera move the matte creating a streaking effect

- Glow effects: using a light diffusing material while exposing the backlight through a matte to create soft edges around the image on the matte

- Filter effects: using color, star and other types of camera filters for special effects

- Image effects: by either manipulating the mattes and countermattes of by positioning transparencies while duplicating them; posterizations, inserts, split frames, and panoramas

- Camera effects: Some optical slide cameras have the capabilities for in-camera mattes, bi-packing, and rotoscoping

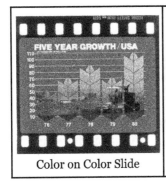			
Color on Color Slide	Step and Repeat Slide	Movement Slide	Glow Slide

Slides created by these methods and combinations of these methods were made to align and animate when projected, creating what was considered the visual multi-image experience.

Film Processing

Film processing requires specific facilities, equipment, and skill needed to maintain consistent results. Film processors for developing transparency film require maintaining processing control which was based on good practices in chemical mixing and storage, accurate time, temperature and agitation during the process and the use of control strips. Control strips were run with the film and read on a densitometer to determine their variation from a standard so that corrections could be made

Computer Graphics

The use of computer graphics replaced much of the manual activity in creating the artwork and converting the art into slides. Service bureaus offering production work from large workstations such as Dicomed and Genigraphics dominated larger markets. Smaller producers using desktop software such as Photoshop, Persuasion, Harvard Graphics and PowerPoint allowed many slide producers to quickly create slides which were imaged on film recorders such as Management Graphics, Lasergraphics, Polaroid, Celco, and CCG.

Assembly and Programming

Completed slides were mounted into pin-registered slide mounts. Three or more pieces of film could be mounted into a slide mount which allowed slides to contain the image film chip and masks to allow for inserting and over-projecting. Slides were edited and arranged for programming on light tables.

Multi-image programming setup for the 1988 Ford Division New Car Announcement Show. AVL Eagle Genesis computers in foreground; background, from left: Brad Smith (art director), Sung Lee (producer/art director), Bob Kassal (executive producer), Paul 'PJ' Jackson (producer/programmer). Produced by Maritz Communications, 1987, Detroit, MI

Programming of multi-projector multi-image shows was generally done on one of several systems such as Arion, Audio-Visual Laboratories (AVL), Electrosonic, Clearlight, Dataton, UAV, Spindler-Sauppe and Multivision. Slides were placed in projector trays, projectors were set up on a "grid" so that alignment was made of the projectors onto the screen area. The programming itself was done on a system that allowed for input by the programmer and dissolve units which were attached to the projectors and controlled the functions of the projectors based on the programming instructions. Programming could also be used to control room lights, rewind of the audio tape and resetting of the projectors, and to trigger other effects that might be used in the presentation, such as a strobe light.

There were two basic slide projector programming controls: a set of instructions to position the slide in the projector and a set of instructions for the slide projector lamp. These controls would be used to define the cues. The cues would often designate an action for more than one projector such as with a dissolve between two slides which would require simultaneously fading up on one lamp and fading down another lamp. Similar commands were used to control motion-picture projectors, as well as auxiliary controls for lighting and effects, etc.

Slide tray	Multi-image programming timing based on slide positioning
Forward	Lifts the current slide from the projector gate into the slide tray, rotates the tray one position and drops the next slide into the gate. During this process a shutter at the slide gate in the projector is used prevent projecting while the lamp remains lit. The average time to cycle from slide to slide varies from 0.9 to 1.5 seconds, depending on the projector.
No movement	The slide projector is instructed to make no tray move during a cue or series of cues. On AVL systems, this is termed an "alt", and embedded into a lamp command.
Reverse	Lifts the current slide from the projector gate into the slide tray, rotates the tray one position in reverse and drops the previous slide into the gate. During the cycle the shutter will close and open in the same manner as a forward movement.
Use of shutter	The slide projector shutter can be controlled to block light without controlling voltage to the lamp. The shutter cycle time varies from projector to projector, averaging at about 0.2 seconds to cycle from open to closed.

Projector Lamp	Multi-image programming effects based on lamp intensity
Lamp on and off	The projector lamp can be instructed to turn on and off. When programmed one or more projectors, can be made to produce several basic effects including: • Cut – Lamp is turned on or off quickly. When two projectors are involved, the lamp in one projector is turned off while the lamp in a second is turned, made to appear that these two actions are made at the same time. A cue based on a cut will include a slide tray advance, unless designated an "alt". • Hard Cut – By first using the slide projector shutter, the transition between two projectors can be made faster than by controlling the lamp on and off. A visible "shutter chop" can be seen, depending on the shutter speed of the projector involved. • Soft Cut – Usually a term applied to a fast dissolve that takes place in less than a second. • Alternate – Appears as a cut, but with no slide tray advance. • Fast Alternate – As above, but allowing the programmer to create flickering effects while the lamp intensity fades up or down.
Lamp Fade	• Fade – A timed, controlled operation where the projector lamp is either turned on or off over a set period of time, producing the effect of the slide image slowly appearing or disappearing on the screen. • Dissolve – A timed crossfading of two or more projectors. Dissolves can be programmed to occur as quickly as one second, or as slow as 32 seconds. • Freeze – During a fade process, the intensity or light output of the lamp in any projector can be stopped in time at a given light intensity for a given period of time. This capability can be used to produce complex multi-projector dissolves. Also, it allows for a projected background to be "faded back" while a brighter image is superimposed.

Other Commands	
Timing	• Wait X – Add timing to a sequence during programming either to add padding to a programmed effect or as a temporary timing pad that will be resolved as the programming is completed. The 'X' represents a time value, expressed in seconds and hundredths of seconds. • Time X – Instructing a programmed event or sequence of events to begin at the time read from the timecode track of a prerecorded tape. The 'X' represents a time value, expressed in hours, minutes, seconds and hundredths of seconds, or hours, minutes, seconds and SMPTE video frames. During programming, the computer reads the incoming timecode. With the program list resting at a Time X cue, a snapshot of the incoming timecode is recorded when the Enter key is struck.
Other effects	• Loop Load/Loop Go/Loop Stop – Loads a sequence of commands to be repeated continuously until instructed to stop. During a Loop sequence, the programming computer is freed-up to control other projectors. • Blink Alt/Blink Load/Blink Go/Blink Stop – Loads a sequence of blink commands to be repeated continuously until instructed to stop. A series of projectors can be included, with lamp fade up/down options available, with the ability to preprogram cycle-animation into a Blink sequence. During a Blink sequence, the programming computer is freed-up to control other projectors.

Through synchronizing the audio and the visual effects and combining visual slide effects, the programming process could create a single continuous show that was saved to memory. Once the programming was completed, the most common way to preserve the programming information was to record the programming cues onto the audio track so that the show could be run synchronized with the audio playback. In some situations, data would be contained in the programming computer (stored either on an internal hard disk drive or a floppy disk), and the events would be triggered by a timecode track on the audio tape.

As multi-image programming devices progressed to digital computers and became more sophisticated in the late 1970s, more programming features were added. Complex looping effects, independent cycling allowing background animation over foreground effects, comprehensive control of motion picture projectors, control of (and by) video devices and other peripheral devices, and the use of SMPTE timecode for synchronization became commonplace. Multiply-exposed optical effects and the use of computer-generated imagery allowed the medium to emerge, briefly, as an art form. The use of multitrack audio playback enhanced the experience and provided for surround sound.

On the Road

Completed multi-image productions were presented in a variety of venues ranging from temporary one-on-one settings to semi-permanent world's fair pavilions and museum exhibitions. Large multi-projector multi-image presentations required adequate projection space which was often from behind the screen for rear-screen projection. Setting up large show required control over the room lighting and often involved drapes and scaffolds.

The actual presentations often were considered to be business theater, incorporating special effects such as pyrotechnics, breakaway screens, live entertainment, even breakaway screens such as having a vehicle crash through the screen to introduce a new model truck.

Slide Show

A slide show

A slide show is a presentation of a series of still images on a projection screen or electronic display device, typically in a prearranged sequence. The changes may be automatic and at regular intervals or they may be manually controlled by a presenter or the viewer. Slide shows originally consisted of a series of individual photographic slides projected onto a screen with a slide projector. When referring to the video or computer-based visual equivalent, in which the slides are not individual physical objects, the term is often written as one word, slideshow.

A slide show may be a presentation of images purely for their own visual interest or artistic value, sometimes unaccompanied by description or text, or it may be used to clarify or reinforce information, ideas, comments, solutions or suggestions which are presented verbally. Slide shows are sometimes still conducted by a presenter using an apparatus such as a carousel slide projector or an overhead projector, but now the use of an electronic video display device and a computer running presentation software is typical.

History

Slide shows had their beginnings in the 1600s, when hand-painted images on glass were first projected onto a wall with a "magic lantern". By the late 1700s, showmen were using magic lanterns to thrill audiences with seemingly supernatural apparitions in a popular form of entertainment called a phantasmagoria. Sunlight, candles and oil lamps were the only available light sources. The development of new, much brighter artificial light sources opened up a world of practical applications for image projection. In the early 1800s, a series of hand-painted glass "lantern slides" was sometimes projected to illustrate story-telling or a lecture. Widespread and varied uses for amusement and education evolved throughout the century. By 1900, photographic images on glass had replaced hand-painted images, but the black-and-white photographs were sometimes hand-colored with transparent dyes. The production of lantern slides had become a considerable industry, with dimensions standardized at 3.25 inches high by 4 inches wide in the US and 3.25 inches square in the UK and much of Europe.

"Magic lantern shows" also served as a form of home entertainment and were especially popular with children. They continued to have a place among commercial public amusements even after the coming of projected "moving pictures". Between films, early movie theaters often featured "illustrated songs", which were community sing-alongs with the lyrics and illustrations provided by a series of projected lantern slides. Theaters also used their lanterns to project advertising slides and messages such as "Ladies, kindly remove your hats".

After 35 mm Kodachrome color film was introduced in 1936, a new standard 2x2 inch (5x5 cm) miniature lantern slide format was created to better suit the very small transparencies the film produced. In advertising, the antique "magic lantern" terminology was streamlined, so that the framed pieces of film were simply "slides" and the lantern used to project them was a "slide projector". The old-fashioned magic lantern show became an up-to-date "slide show".

Home slide shows were a relatively common phenomenon in middle-class American homes during the 1950s and 1960s. If there was an enthusiast in the family, any visit from relatives or the arrival of a new batch of Kodachrome slides from the film processing service provided an excuse to bring out the entire collection of 35 mm slides, set up the slide projector and the screen, turn out the lights, then test the endurance of the assembled audience with a marathon of old vacation photos and pictures taken at weddings, birthdays and other family events, all accompanied by live commentary.

An image on 35 mm film mounted in a 2x2 inch (5x5 cm) metal, card or plastic frame is still by far the most common photographic slide format.

Uses

A well-organized slide show allows a presenter to fit visual images to an oral presentation. The old adage "A picture is worth a thousand words" holds true, in that a single image can save a presenter from speaking a paragraph of descriptive details. As with any public speaking or lecturing, a certain amount of talent, experience, and rehearsal is required to make a successful slide show presentation.

Presentation software is most commonly used in the business world, where millions of presentations are created daily. Another very important area where it is used is for instructional purposes, usually with the intention of creating a dynamic, audiovisual presentation. The relevant points to the entire presentation are put on slides, and accompany a spoken monologue.

Slide shows have artistic uses as well, such as being used as a screensaver, or to provide dynamic imagery for a museum presentation, for example, or in installation art. David Byrne, among others, has created *PowerPoint* art.

Slide Show in Art

Since the late 1960s, visual artists have used slide shows in museums and galleries as a device, either for presenting specific information about an action or research or as a phenomenological form in itself. According to the introduction of *Slide Show*, an exhibition organized at the Baltimore Museum of Art: "Through the simple technology of the slide projector and 35 mm color transparency, artists discovered a tool that enabled the transformation of space through the magnification of projected pictures, texts, and images." Although some artists have not necessarily used 35 mm or color slides, and some, such as Robert Barry, have even abandoned images for texts, 35 mm color film slides are most commonly used. The images are sometimes accompanied by written text, either in the same slide or as an intertitle. Some artists, such as James Coleman and Robert Smithson, have used a voice-over with their slide presentations.

Slide shows have also been used by artists who use other media such as painting and sculpture to present their work publicly. In recent years there has been a growing use of the slide show by a younger generation of artists. The non-profit organization Slideluck Potshow holds slide show events globally, featuring works by amateur and professional artists, photographers, and gallerists. Participants in the event bring food, potluck style, and have a social dinner before the slide show begins.

Other known artists who have used slide shows in their work include Bas Jan Ader, Francis Alys, Jan Dibbets, Dan Graham, Rodney Graham, Nan Goldin, Louise Lawler, Ana Mendieta, Jonathan Monk, Dennis Oppenheim, Allan Sekula, Carey Young and Krzysztof Wodiczko.

Digital "Slideshows"

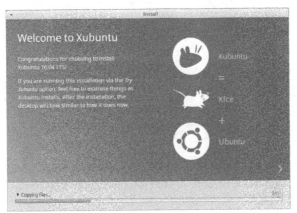

Slide show in Xubuntu 16.04

Digital photo slideshows can be custom-made for clients from their photos, music, wedding invitations, birth announcements, or virtually any other scannable documents. Some producers call the resulting DVDs the new photomontage. Slideshows can be created not only on DVD, but also in HD video formats and as executable computer files. Photo slideshow software has made it easy to create electronic digital slideshows, eliminating the need for expensive color reversal film and requiring only a digital camera and computer.

Photo slideshow software often provides more options than simply showing the pictures. It is possible to add transitions, pan and zoom effects, video clips, background music, narration, captions, etc. By using computer software one therefore has the ability to enhance the presentation in a way that is not otherwise practical. The finished slideshow can then be burned to a DVD, for use as a gift or for archiving, and later viewed using an ordinary DVD player.

Multi-dynamic Image Technique

Multi-dynamic image technique is a name given by its Canadian creator Christopher Chapman (b. January 24, 1927, d. October 24, 2015) to a film innovation which shows several images shifting simultaneously on panes, some panes containing a single image and others forming part of an image completed by other panes. The process was first used in his film *A Place to Stand*, produced for the Ontario pavilion at Expo 67, held in Montreal, Canada.

Background

The 1956 Associated British-Pathe fantasy/science fiction release *The Door in the Wall* (dir. Glenn Alvey, screenplay by Alvey and H.G. Wells) can be seen as a primitive forerunner of Chapman's technique. Utilizing what it announced as "The Dynamic Frame - in which the shape and size of the picture change according to the dramatic needs of the story", the film displayed however neither movement of image panels nor multiplicity or division of images. Chapman felt "it was clear that its failure was creative, not technical" and decided against advice to employ this matting technique when making a film for the Telephone Association Pavilion at Expo 67.

Scene from Christopher Chapman's *A Place to Stand* (1967) premiering the multi-dynamic image technique

Chapman initially had great difficulties with the technical aspects of his expanded concept for *A Place to Stand* and almost gave up on the idea as a result; in his own words, he "had nothing to read about how to do it." Working from 350 pages of notes, he was limited to editing on a 2-picture-head moviola, so that only two images could be viewed simultaneously; he "could never 'see' the film develop."

Shots were viewed "with an eye to vertical frames and horizontal frames, odd frames, small frames and large frames." It was important to also shoot material that would be of limited interest, so as not to confuse the viewer with too many visual stimuli. Editing required close attention to where the various images would direct the viewer's gaze.

The technique as employed in *A Place to Stand* displayed as many as 15 images at a time. In this way, the under-18-minute film contained an actual hour-and-a-half of footage. The dimensions of the original screen used were 66 feet or 20.12 m (wide) by 30 feet or 9.14 m (high). Unlike other multi-image films, it did not require special equipment or a special theatre.

Response

The film and its innovative technique enjoyed great immediate popularity. It was seen by an estimated two million at Expo 67 and was later distributed to theatres, ultimately reaching an audience of an estimated 100 million in North America and Europe.

A Place to Stand was nominated in two categories at the 1967 40th Academy Awards presented on April 10, 1968, Best Documentary Short Subject and Best Live Action Short Subject, winning in the latter. It also won Chapman the Canadian Film Award (later to become the Genie Awards) for Film of the Year (and additionally won for Best Non-Feature Sound-Editing). Chapman himself was ultimately appointed to the Order of Canada in 1987.

Influence

Scene from *The Thomas Crown Affair* (1968) demonstrating one example of the multi-dynamic image technique

Prints of Chapman's film were purchased for viewing by executives, producers and directors by almost all of the major studios in Hollywood. The technique has inspired many films and television series, most notably Norman Jewison's 1968 film *The Thomas Crown Affair*. Steve McQueen, star of the film, was on hand for the premiere screening of *A Place to Stand* at the Todd-AO studios in Hollywood and personally told an unsure Chapman (who "thought it was a failure") that he was highly impressed; the following year, Norman Jewison had incorporated the technique into the film, inserting the scenes into the already finished product. (Chapman later dissuaded a "very disappointed" McQueen from using the technique in his 1971 vehicle *Le Mans*, claiming "it was much too big a film, with too many writers; it wouldn't work that way." He has stated that "many filmmakers then adopted multi-dynamic image even though few understood it.")

The Boston Strangler, also from 1968 (dir. Richard Fleischer), has several long multi-frame sequences clearly based on Chapman's original in terms of arrangement and rhythm; here, however, the panes remain static and do not show identical images in simultaneous multiplicity. Fleischer used the technique again, this time with subdivided images and moving panes closer to Chapman's original, in the title sequence to his 1973 film *Soylent Green*.

Chapman's innovation found quick favour in late 1960s and 1970s television, notably in title sequences. *Mannix, Barnaby Jones, Kojak, Medical Center, Dallas, The Brady Bunch* and *The Bob Newhart Show* (beginning with the fifth season in 1976-77) are all examples of the technique being used in opening credits to some extent, whether approximately as in *A Place to Stand* or combined with regular film sequences (as with the latter). Indeed, the multi-dynamic image technique has been referred to in the press as the "Brady Bunch effect." The contemporary TV series *24* also utilizes the technique.

More broadly, the multi-dynamic image technique has been credited with laying the groundwork for the IMAX format.

References

- Kenny, Michael F.; Schmitt, Raymond F. (1983). Images, Images, Images: The Book of Programmed Multi-Image Production. New York: Eastman Kodak. ISBN 978-0-87985-327-3.

- The Personal Vision of Christopher Chapman, CM, RCA, CSC, CFE, Ontario Film Institute; 1989 interview published March, 2010.

5

Artmedia: Study of New Technologies

Art has found expression in various fields including that of the media. New media art is a genre in which art incorporates new media technologies like digital art, computer animation, computer robotics, cyborg art, interactive art etc. This chapter is dedicated to this contemporary field of artmedia and artmedia technologies and explores these topics comprehensively.

Artmedia

Artmedia, *Seminar and Laboratory of the Aesthetics of Media and Communication*, was one of the first scientific projects concerning the relationship between art, technology, philosophy and aesthetics. It was founded in 1985 at the University of Salerno. For over two decades, until 2009, dozens of projects, studies, exhibitions and conferences on new technologies made Artmedia a reference point for many internationally renowned scholars and artists, and contributed to the growing cultural interest in the aesthetics of media, the aesthetics of networks, and their ethical and anthropological implications.

Beginnings and International Events

Since the late 1970s, a permanent *Seminar of the Aesthetics of Media and Communication* has been directed by its founder Mario Costa at the University of Salerno. The basic principles of the aesthetics of technological communication were identified and conceptualized in 1983. A conference on "Technological Imaginary", held in 1984 at the Museo del Sannio in Benevento, discussed the issue of the new relationship between art and technology and the consequent need to re-evaluate aesthetics, warning that "all our future existence will be played at the crossroads between technology and imaginary".

The comprehensive relationship between art and technoscience, technology, and philosophy has also been the theoretical subject of the ten international "Artmedia" conferences which were held in Salerno and Paris between 1985 and 2008. Particularly relevant were conferences held in Paris between 2002 and 2008, which took place at the Ecole Normale Supérieure, the Bibliotheque Nationale de France (BNF) and the Institut National d'Histoire de l'Art (INHA), with the partnership of the Société Française d'Esthétique, the Université du Québec à Montréal, the University of Toronto, the Universidade de São Paulo, the Université de Paris 1 Sorbonne, and the U.S. magazine Leonardo.

Continuous Debate Between Artists and Theorists

Artmedia wanted to gather theorists and artists from all over the world and encourage both joint and complementary work, beginning with the need to give attention to theoretical and artistic practices and developing both together. These also contributed towards spreading the spirit of the project, both in a number of festivals and shows, and through their own artworks and research.

Derrick de Kerckhove, René Berger and Mario Costa, Artmedia IV (1992)

Maurizio Bolognini, Richard Kriesche, Mario Costa and Eduardo Kac, Artmedia VII (1999)

Theorists who worked with Artmedia and participated in its activities included Bernard Stiegler, René Berger, Abraham Moles, Derrick De Kerckhove, Pierre Levy, Gillo Dorfles, Paul Virilio, Frank Popper, Roger Malina, Daniel Charles, José Jiménez, Anne Cauquelin, Edgar Morin, Thierry de Duve, Catherine Millet, Filiberto Menna, Andreas Broeckmann, Rudolf zur Lippe, Edmond Couchot, Dominique Chateau, Yannick Geffroy, Philippe Queau, Arlindo Machado, Tetsuo Kogawa, and Bernard Teyssedre.

Artists included Fred Forest, Roy Ascott, Takahiko Iimura, Maurizio Bolognini, Tom Klinkowstein, Tom Sherman, Eduardo Kac, Enzo Minarelli, James Dashow, Peter D'Agostino, Mit Mitropoulos, Shawn Brixey, Bruno Di Bello, Antoni Muntadas, Orlan, Kit Galloway, David Rokeby, Miguel Chevalier, Norman White, Richard Kriesche, Olivier Auber, Caterina Davinio and Casey Reas.

The questions raised in various projects promoted by Artmedia, in a continuous dialogue between artists and theorists, led to discussions on topics including *Aesthetics of Communication and the anthropology of the future* (1985), *Global aesthetic communication* (1986), *Electronic performativity and the art system* (1990), *Neo-technological arts between aesthetics and communication* (1992), *Aesthetic research and technology* (1995), *Developments in aesthetics: change or mutation?* (1999), *From the Aesthetics of Communication to Net art* (2002), and *Ethics, aesthetics and techno-communication. The future of meaning* (2008).

All Artmedia symposiums have been followed by many publications. For the two held in Paris, a complete video recording is also available, and can be viewed at the Institut National de l'Audiovisuel.

An assessment of 25 years of Artmedia activity was made into a seminar on *The aesthetic object of the future*, held at the University of Salerno in 2009. The Artmedia project produced a large number of publications and documents that are being catalogued, with a view to their proper placement and use.

Key Areas of Investigation

- Electronic music

- Photochemical versus digital photography

- Aesthetics of radio

- Electroacoustic poetry

- Electronic writing and poetry

- Video art

- Generative art and software art

- Computer art

- Aesthetics of networks

- Net art

- Aesthetics of virtual

- Telerobotics and remote interactivity

- Aesthetics of (technological) flux versus aesthetics of form

Proceedings and Catalogs

Artmedia I (1985)

- Mario Costa (ed.) (1985), *Artmedia*, Salerno: Opera Universitaria di Salerno (Catalog, pp. 206).

Artmedia II (1986)

- Mario Costa (ed.) (1986), *Artmedia, II Convegno Internazionale di Estetica della comunicazione*, Salerno: Università di Salerno (Catalog, pp. 80).

Artmedia III (1990)

- Mario Costa (ed.) (1990), *Artmedia. Terzo Convegno Internazionale di Estetica dei Media e della Comunicazione. Catalogo*, Salerno: Università degli Studi di Salerno (Catalog, pp. 80).

- Mario Costa (ed.) (1990), *Artmedia. Terzo Convegno Internazionale di Estetica dei Media e della Comunicazione. Atti*, Salerno: Università degli Studi di Salerno (Proceedings, pp. 96).

Artmedia IV (1992)

- Mario Costa (ed.) (1992), *Nuovi media e sperimentazione d'artista*, Naples: Edizioni Scientifiche Italiane (including Artmedia IV Proceedings, pp. 1–156).

Artmedia V (1995)

- Università degli Studi di Salerno, Comune di Salerno (1995), *Quinto Convegno Internazionale di Estetica dei Media e della Comunicazione*, Salerno (maquette).

Artmedia VI (1997)

- Università degli Studi di Salerno, Fondazione Filiberto Menna (1997), *Artmedia VI*, Salerno (maquette).

Artmedia VII (1999)

- Mario Costa (ed.) (1999), *Artmedia VII, Settimo Convegno Internazionale di Estetica dei Media e della Comunicazione*, Salerno: Università degli Studi di Salerno (Catalog, pp. 60).

Artmedia VIII (2002)

- *Dossier Artmedia VIII*, in "Ligeia", Paris, 2002, pp. 21–245 (CNRF journal, including Artmedia VIII Proceedings).

- Mario Costa (ed.) (2004), *New Technologies: Roy Ascott, Maurizio Bolognini, Fred Forest, Richard Kriesche, Mit Mitropoulos*, Salerno: Artmedia, Museo del Sannio (Catalog, pp. 64).

Artmedia IX (2005)

- Mario Costa (ed.) (2005), *Phenomenology of New Tech Arts*, Salerno: Università di Salerno (Catalog, pp. 56).

Artmedia X (2008)

- Mario Costa, Fred Forest (eds) (2011), *Ethique, esthétique, communication technologique dans l'art contemporain ou le destin du sens*, Paris: Institut National Audiovisuel, Editions L'Harmattan (including Artmedia X Proceedings).

New Media Art

New media art is a genre that encompasses artworks created with new media technologies, including digital art, computer graphics, computer animation, virtual art, Internet art, interactive art, video games, computer robotics, 3D printing, cyborg art and art as biotechnology. The term differentiates itself by its resulting cultural objects and social events, which can be seen in opposition to those deriving from old visual arts (i.e. traditional painting, sculpture, etc.). This concern with medium is a key feature of much contemporary art and indeed many art schools and major universities now offer majors in "New Genres" or "New Media" and a growing number of graduate programs have emerged internationally. New Media Art often involves interaction between artist and observer or between observers and the artwork, which responds to them. Yet, as several theorists and curators have noted, such forms of interaction, social exchange, participation, and transformation do not distinguish new media art but rather serve as a common ground that has parallels in other strands of contemporary art practice. Such insights emphasize the forms of cultural practice that arise concurrently with emerging technological platforms, and question the focus on technological media, per se.

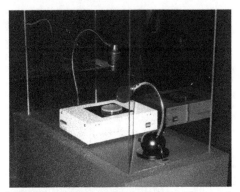

Newskool ASCII Screenshot with the words "Closed Society II"

Eduardo Kac's installation "Genesis" Ars Electronica 1999

10.000 moving cities, Marc Lee, 2013, National Museum of Modern and Contemporary Art Seoul, Korea

New Media concerns are often derived from the telecommunications, mass media and digital electronic modes of delivering the artworks involve, with practices ranging from conceptual to virtual art, performance to installation.

History

The origins of new media art can be traced to the moving photographic inventions of the late 19th century such as the zoetrope (1834), the praxinoscope (1877) and Eadweard Muybridge's zoo-praxiscope (1879). From the 1920s through the 1950s, various forms of kinetic and light art, from Thomas Wilfred's 'Lumia' (1919) and 'Clavilux' light organs to Jean Tinguely's self-destructing sculpture 'Homage to New York' (1960) can be seen as progenitors of new media art.

In 1958 Wolf Vostell becomes the first artist who incorporates a television set into one of his works. The *Black Room Cycle*. This installation is part of the collection of the Berlinische Galerie.

During the 1960s the development of then new technologies of video produced the new media art experiments of Nam June Paik, and Wolf Vostell with the installation *6 TV Dé-coll/age* in 1963 at the Smolin Gallery in New York. A. Michael Noll, and multimedia performances of E.A.T., Fluxus and Happening. In 1983, Roy Ascott introduced the concept of "distributed authorship" in his worldwide telematic project La Plissure du Texte for Frank Popper's "Electra" at the Musée d'Art Moderne de la Ville de Paris . The development of computer graphics at the end of the 1980s and real time technologies then in the 1990s combined with the spreading of the Web and the Internet favored the emergence of new and various forms of interactivity art by Lynn Hershman Leeson, David Rokeby, Ken Rinaldo, Perry Hoberman; telematic art by Roy Ascott; Internet art by Vuk Ćosić, Jodi; virtual and immersive art by Jeffrey Shaw, Maurice Benayoun and large scale urban installation by Rafael Lozano-Hemmer.

World Skin (1997), Maurice Benayoun's Virtual Reality Interactive Installation

Simultaneously advances in biotechnology have also allowed artists like Eduardo Kac to begin exploring DNA and genetics as a new art medium.

New Media Art influences on new media art have been the theories developed around hypertext, databases, and networks. Important thinkers in this regard have been Vannevar Bush and Theodor Nelson, whereas comparable ideas can be found in the literary works of Jorge Luis Borges, Italo Calvino, and Julio Cortázar. These elements have been especially revolutionary for the field of narrative and anti-narrative studies, leading explorations into areas such as non-linear and interactive narratives.

Themes

In the book *New Media Art*, Mark Tribe and Reena Jana named several themes that contemporary new media art addresses, including computer art, collaboration, identity, appropriation, open sourcing, telepresence, surveillance, corporate parody, as well as intervention and hacktivism. In the book *Postdigitale*, Maurizio Bolognini suggested that new media artists have one common denominator, which is a self-referential relationship with the new technologies, the result of finding oneself inside an epoch-making transformation determined by technological development. Nevertheless, new media art does not appear as a set of homogeneous practices, but as a complex field converging around three main elements: 1) the art system, 2) scientific and industrial research, and 3) political-cultural media activism. There are significant differences between scientist-artists, activist-artists and technological artists closer to the art system, who not only have different training and technocultures, but have different artistic production. This should be taken into account in examining the several themes addressed by new media art.

Non-linearity can be seen as an important topic to new media art by artists developing interactive, generative, collaborative, immersive artworks like Jeffrey Shaw or Maurice Benayoun who explored the term as an approach to looking at varying forms of digital projects where the content relays on the user's experience. This is a key concept since people acquired the notion that they were conditioned to view everything in a linear and clear-cut fashion. Now, art is stepping out of that form and allowing for people to build their own experiences with the piece. Non-linearity describes a project that escape from the conventional linear narrative coming from novels, theater plays and movies. Non-linear art usually requires audience participation or at least, the fact that the "visitor" is taken into consideration by the representation, altering the displayed content. The participatory aspect of new media art, which for some artists has become integral, emerged from Allan Kaprow's *Happenings* and became with Internet, a significant component of contemporary art. Art is not produced as a completed object submitted to the audience appreciation, it is a process in permanent mutation.

The inter-connectivity and interactivity of the internet, as well as the fight between corporate interests, governmental interests, and public interests that gave birth to the web today, fascinate and inspire a lot of current new media art.

Many new media art projects also work with themes like politics and social consciousness, allowing for social activism through the interactive nature of the media. New media art includes "explorations of code and user interface; interrogations of archives, databases, and networks; production via automated scraping, filtering, cloning, and recombinatory techniques; applications of user-generated content (UGC) layers; crowdsourcing ideas on social- media platforms; narrowcasting digital selves on "free" websites that claim copyright; and provocative performances that implicate audiences as participants."

One of the key themes in new media art is to create visual views of databases. Pioneers in this area include Lisa Strausfeld and Martin Wattenberg. Database aesthetics holds at least two attractions to new media artists: formally, as a new variation on non-linear narratives; and politically as a means to subvert what is fast becoming a form of control and authority.

The emergence of 3D printing has introduced a new bridge to new media art, joining the virtual and the physical worlds. The rise of this technology has allowed artists to blend the computational base of new media art with the traditional physical form of sculpture. A pioneer in this field was artist Jonty Hurwitz who created the first known anamorphosis sculpture using this technique.

Themes

G.H. Hovagimyan "A Soapopera for iMacs"

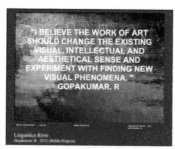

Gopakumar R. P. Linguistics River, Internet art

Michael Demers, 2009. *Color Field Paintings (Browser).*

Maurizio Bolognini's programmed machines (*Computer sigillati* series, 1992): hundreds of computers have been producing endless flows of random images.<ref>*S. Solimano (ed.) (2005). Maurizio Bolognini. Programmed Machines 1990-2005. Genoa: Villa Croce Museum of Contemporary Art, Neos. ISBN 88-87262-47-0.*

Genco Gulan "Hello, 2015. Sculpture with a Robotic Arm."

Presentation and Preservation

As the technologies used to deliver works of new media art such as film, tapes, web browsers, software and operating systems become obsolete, New Media art faces serious issues around the challenge to preserve artwork beyond the time of its contemporary production. Currently, research projects into New media art preservation are underway to improve the preservation and documentation of the fragile media arts heritage (DOCAM - Documentation and Conservation of the Media Arts Heritage).

Methods of preservation exist, including the translation of a work from an obsolete medium into a related new medium, the digital archiving of media, and the use of emulators to preserve work dependent on obsolete software or operating system environ-ments.

Education

In New Media programs, students are able to get acquainted with the newest forms of creation and communication. New Media students learn to identify what is or isn't "new" about certain technologies. Science and the market will always present new tools and platforms for artists and designers. Students learn how to sort through new emerging technological platforms and place them in a larger context of sensation, communication, production, and consumption.

When obtaining a bachelor's degree in New Media, students will primarily work through practice of building experiences that utilize new and old technologies and narrative. Through the construction of projects in various media, they acquire technical skills, practice vocabularies of critique and analysis, and gain familiarity with historical and contemporary precedents. New media studies lets students create and manipulate new technologies. The nature of New Media Art provides an opportunity for students to expand the art field in new directions, however they see fit.

In the United States, many Bachelor's and Master's level programs exist with concentrations on Media Art, New Media, Media Design, Digital Media and Interactive Arts.

Leading Art Theorists and Historians

Leading art theorists and historians in this field include Roy Ascott, Maurice Benayoun, Christine Buci-Glucksmann, Jack Burnham, Mario Costa, Edmond Couchot, Fred Forest, Oliver Grau, Margot Lovejoy, Dominique Moulon, Robert C. Morgan, Joseph Nechvatal, Christiane Paul, Catherine Perret, Frank Popper, and Edward A. Shanken.

Interactive Media

Interactive media normally refers to products and services on digital computer-based systems which respond to the user's actions by presenting content such as text, moving image, animation, video, audio, and video games.

Definition

Interactive media is a method of communication in which the output from the media comes from the input of the users. Interactive media works with the user's participation. The media still has the same purpose but the user's input adds interaction and brings interesting features to the system for better enjoyment.

Development

The analogue videodisc developed by NV Philips was the pioneering technology for interactive media. Additionally, there are several elements that encouraged the development of interactive media including the following:

- The laser disc technology was first invented in 1958. It enabled the user to access high-quality analogue images on the computer screen. This increased the ability of interactive video systems.

- The concept of the graphical user interface (GUI), which was developed in the 1970s, popularized by Apple Computer, Inc. was essentially about visual metaphors, intuitive feel and sharing information on the virtual desktop. Additional power was the only thing needed to move into multimedia.

- The sharp fall in hardware costs and the unprecedented rise in the computer speed and memory transformed the personal computer into an affordable machine capable of combining audio and color video in advanced ways.

- Another element is the release of Windows 3.0 in 1990 by Microsoft into the mainstream IBM clone world. It accelerated the acceptance of GUI as the standard mechanism for communicating with small computer systems.

- The development by NV Philips of optical digital technologies built around the compact disk (CD) in 1979 is also another leading element in the interactive media development as it raised the issue of developing interactive media.

All of the prior elements contributed in the development of the main hardware and software systems used in interactive media.

Terminology

Though the word *media* is plural, the term is often used as a singular noun.

Interactive media is related to the concepts interaction design, new media, interactivity, human computer interaction, cyberculture, digital culture, interactive design, and includes augmented reality.

An essential feature of interactivity is that it is mutual: user and machine each take an active role. Most interactive computing systems are for some human purpose and interact with humans in human contexts. Manovich complains that 'In relation to computer-based media, the concept of interactivity is a tautology. …. Therefore, to call computer media "interactive" is meaningless – it simply means stating the most basic fact about computers.'. Nevertheless, the te- rm is useful to denote an identifiable body of practices and technologies.

Interactive media are an instance of a computational method influenced by the sciences of cybernetics, autopoiesis and system theories, and challenging notions of reason and cognition, perception and memory, emotions and affection.

Any form of interface between the end user/audience and the medium may be considered interactive. Interactive media is not limited to electronic media or digital media. Board games, pop-up books, gamebooks, flip books and constellation wheels are all examples of printed interactive media. Books with a simple table of contents or index may be considered interactive due to the non-linear control mechanism in the medium, but are usually considered non-interactive since the majority of the user experience is non-interactive reading.

Advantages

Effects on Learning

Interactive media is helpful in the following four development dimensions in which young children learn: social and emotional, language development, cognitive and general knowledge, and approaches toward learning. Using computers and educational computer software in a learning environment helps children increase communication skills and their attitudes about learning. Children who use educational computer software are often found using more complex speech patterns and higher levels of verbal communication. A study found that basic interactive books that simply read a story aloud and highlighted words and phrases as they were spoken were beneficial for children with lower reading abilities. Children have different styles of learning, and interactive media helps children with visual, verbal, auditory, and tactile learning styles.

Intuitive Understanding

Interactive media makes technology more intuitive to use. Interactive products such as smartphones, iPad's/iPod's, interactive whiteboards and websites are all easy to use. The easy usage of these products encourages consumers to experiment with their products rather than reading instruction manuals.

Relationships

Interactive media promotes dialogic communication. This form of communication allows senders and receivers to build long term trust and cooperation. This plays a critical role in building relationships. Organizations also use interactive media to go further than basic marketing and develop more positive behavioral relationships.

Types

Distributed Interactive Media

The media which allows several geographically remote users to interact synchronously with the media application/system is known as Distributed Interactive Media. Some common examples of this type of Media include Online Gaming, Distributed Virtual Environment, Whiteboards which are used for interactive conferences and many more.

Examples

A couple of basic examples of interactive media are video games and websites. Websites, especially social networking websites provide the interactive use of text and graphics to its users, who interact with each other in various ways such as chatting, playing online games, sharing posts that may include their thoughts and/or pictures and so forth. Video games are also one of the common examples of Interactive Media as the players make use of the joystick/controller to interactively respond to the actions and changes taking place on the game screen generated by the game application, which in turn reacts to the response of the players through the joystick/controller.

Technologies for Implementation

Interactive media can be implemented in a wide variety of platforms and applications encompassing virtually all areas of technology. Some examples include mobile platforms such as touch screen smartphones and tablets, was well as other interactive mediums that are created exclusively to solve a unique problem or set of problems. Interactive media is not limited to a certain field of IT, it instead encompasses any technology that supplies for movie parts or feedback based on the users actions. This can include javascript and AJAX utilization in web pages, but can further be extended to any programming languages that share the same or similar functionality. One of the most recent innovations to supply for interactivity to solve a problem the plagues individuals on a daily bases is Delta Airlines "Photon Shower." This device was developed from Delta's collaboration with Professor Russell Foster of Cambridge University. The device is designed to reduce the effect of jet lag on customers that often take long flights across time zones. The systems interactivity is evident because of the way in which it solves this commonplace problem.. By observing what time zones a person has crossed and matching those to the basic known sleep cycles of the individual, the machine is able to predict when a persons body is expecting light, and when it is expecting darkness. It then bombards the individual with the appropriate light source variations for the time, as well as an instructional card to inform them of what times their body expects light and what times it expects darkness.Growth of interactive media continues to advance today, with the advent of more and more powerful machines the limit to what can be input and manipulated on a display in real time is become virtually non-existent.

Computer Graphics

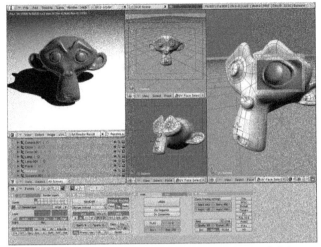

A Blender 2.45 screenshot, displaying the 3D test model Suzanne.

Computer graphics are pictures and movies created using computers – usually referring to image data created by a computer specifically with help from specialized graphical hardware and software. It is a vast and recent area in computer science. The phrase was coined by computer graphics researchers Verne Hudson and William Fetter of Boeing in 1960. It is often abbreviated as CG, though sometimes erroneously referred to as CGI.

Important topics in computer graphics include user interface design, sprite graphics, vector graphics, 3D modeling, shaders, GPU design, and computer vision, among others. The overall methodology depends heavily on the underlying sciences of geometry, optics, and physics. Computer graphics is responsible for displaying art and image data effectively and meaningfully to the user, and processing image data received from the physical world. The interaction and understanding of computers and interpretation of data has been made easier because of computer graphics. Computer graphic development has had a significant impact on many types of media and has revolutionized animation, movies, advertising, video games, and graphic design generally.

Overview

The term computer graphics has been used a broad sense to describe "almost everything on computers that is not text or sound". Typically, the term *computer graphics* refers to several different things:

- the representation and manipulation of image data by a computer

- the various technologies used to create and manipulate images

- the sub-field of computer science which studies methods for digitally synthesizing and manipulating visual content.

Computer graphics is widespread today. Computer imagery is found on television, in newspapers, for example in weather reports, or for example in all kinds of medical investigation and surgical procedures. A well-constructed graph can present complex statistics in a form that is easier to understand and interpret. In the media "such graphs are used to illustrate papers, reports, thesis", and other presentation material.

Many powerful tools have been developed to visualize data. Computer generated imagery can be categorized into several different types: two dimensional (2D), three dimensional (3D), and animated graphics. As technology has improved, 3D computer graphics have become more common, but 2D computer graphics are still widely used. Computer graphics has emerged as a sub-field of computer science which studies methods for digitally synthesizing and manipulating visual content. Over the past decade, other specialized fields have been developed like information visualization, and scientific visualization more concerned with "the visualization of three dimensional phenomena (architectural, meteorological, medical, biological, etc.), where the emphasis is on realistic renderings of volumes, surfaces, illumination sources, and so forth, perhaps with a dynamic (time) component".

History

Introduction

The precursor sciences to the development of modern computer graphics were the advances in electrical engineering, electronics, and television that took place during the first half of the twentieth century. Screens could display art since the Lumiere brothers' use of mattes to create special effects for the earliest films dating from 1895, but such displays were limited and not interactive. The first cathode ray tube, the Braun tube, was invented in 1897 - it in turn would permit the oscilloscope and the military control panel - the more direct precursors of the field, as they provided the first two-dimensional electronic displays that responded to programmatic or user input. Nevertheless, computer graphics remained relatively unknown as a discipline until the 1950s and the post-World War II period - during which time, the discipline emerged from a combination of both pure university and laboratory academic research into more advanced computers and the United States military's further development of technologies like radar, advanced aviation, and rocketry developed during the war. New kinds of displays were needed to process the wealth of information resulting from such projects, leading to the development of computer graphics as a discipline.

1950s

Early projects like the Whirlwind and SAGE Projects introduced the CRT as a viable display and interaction interface and introduced the light pen as an input device. Douglas T. Ross of the Whirlwind SAGE system performed a personal experiment in 1954 in which a small program he wrote captured the movement of his finger and displayed its vector (his traced name) on a display scope. One of the first interactive video games to feature recognizable, interactive graphics – *Tennis for Two* – was created for an oscilloscope by William Higinbotham to entertain visitors in 1958 at Brookhaven National Laboratory and simulated a tennis match. In 1959, Douglas T. Ross innovated again while working at MIT on transforming mathematic statements into computer generated machine tool vectors, and took the opportunity to create a display scope image of a Disney cartoon character.

Electronics pioneer Hewlett-Packard went public in 1957 after incorporating the decade prior, and established strong ties with Stanford University through its founders, who were alumni. This began the decades-long transformation of the southern San Francisco Bay Area into the world's leading computer technology hub - now known as Silicon Valley. The field of computer graphics developed with the emergence of computer graphics hardware.

SAGE Sector Control Room.

Further advances in computing led to greater advancements in interactive computer graphics. In 1959, the TX-2 computer was developed at MIT's Lincoln Laboratory. The TX-2 integrated a number of new man-machine interfaces. A light pen could be used to draw sketches on the computer using Ivan Sutherland's revolutionary Sketchpad software. Using a light pen, Sketchpad allowed one to draw simple shapes on the computer screen, save them and even recall them later. The light pen itself had a small photoelectric cell in its tip. This cell emitted an electronic pulse whenever it was placed in front of a computer screen and the screen's electron gun fired directly at it. By simply timing the electronic pulse with the current location of the electron gun, it was easy to pinpoint exactly where the pen was on the screen at any given moment. Once that was determined, the computer could then draw a cursor at that location. Sutherland seemed to find the perfect solution for many of the graphics problems he faced. Even today, many standards of computer graphics interfaces got their start with this early Sketchpad program. One example of this is in drawing constraints. If one wants to draw a square for example, they do not have to worry about drawing four lines perfectly to form the edges of the box. One can simply specify that they want to draw a box, and then specify the location and size of the box. The software will then construct a perfect box, with the right dimensions and at the right location. Another example is that Sutherland's software modeled objects - not just a picture of objects. In other words, with a model of a car, one could change the size of the tires without affecting the rest of the car. It could stretch the body of car without deforming the tires.

1960s

The phrase "computer graphics" itself was coined in 1960 by William Fetter, a graphic designer for Boeing. This old quote in many secondary sources comes complete with the following sentence: (*Fetter has said that the terms were actually given to him by Verne Hudson of the Wichita Division of Boeing.*) In 1961 another student at MIT, Steve Russell, created the second video game, *Spacewar*. Written for the DEC PDP-1, Spacewar was an instant success and copies started flowing to other PDP-1 owners and eventually DEC got a copy. The engineers at DEC used it as a diagnostic program on every new PDP-1 before shipping it. The sales force picked up on this quickly enough and when installing new units, would run the "world's first video game" for their new customers. (Higginbotham's *Tennis For Two* had beaten *Spacewar* by almost three years; but it was almost unknown outside of a research or academic setting.)

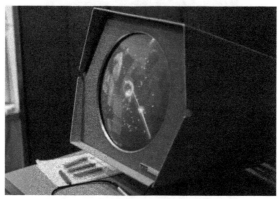

Spacewar running on the Computer History Museum's PDP-1

E. E. Zajac, a scientist at Bell Telephone Laboratory (BTL), created a film called "Simulation of a two-giro gravity attitude control system" in 1963. In this computer-generated film, Zajac showed how the attitude of a satellite could be altered as it orbits the Earth. He created the animation on an IBM 7090 mainframe computer. Also at BTL, Ken Knowlton, Frank Sinden and Michael Noll started working in the computer graphics field. Sinden created a film called *Force, Mass and Motion* illustrating Newton's laws of motion in operation. Around the same time, other scientists were creating computer graphics to illustrate their research. At Lawrence Radiation Laboratory, Nelson Max created the films *Flow of a Viscous Fluid* and *Propagation of Shock Waves in a Solid Form*. Boeing Aircraft created a film called *Vibration of an Aircraft*.

Also sometime in the early 1960s, automobiles would also provide a boost through the early work of Pierre Bézier at Renault, who used Paul de Casteljau's curves - now called Bézier curves after Bézier's work in the field - to develop 3d modeling techniques for Renault car bodies. These curves would form the foundation for much curve-modeling work in the field, as curves - unlike polygons - are mathematically complex entities to draw and model well.

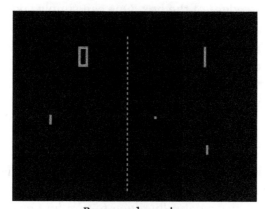

Pong arcade version

It was not long before major corporations started taking an interest in computer graphics. TRW, Lockheed-Georgia, General Electric and Sperry Rand are among the many companies that were getting started in computer graphics by the mid-1960s. IBM was quick to respond to this interest by releasing the IBM 2250 graphics terminal, the first commercially available graphics computer. Ralph Baer, a supervising engineer at Sanders Associates, came up with a home video game in 1966 that was later licensed to Magnavox and called the Odyssey. While very simplistic, and requiring fairly inexpensive electronic parts, it allowed the player to move points of light around on a screen. It was the first consumer computer graphics product. David C. Evans was director of engineering at Bendix Corporation's computer division from 1953 to 1962, after which he worked for the next five years as a visiting professor at Berkeley. There he continued his interest in computers and how they interfaced with people. In 1966, the University of Utah recruited Evans to form a computer science program, and computer graphics quickly became his primary interest. This new department would become the world's primary research center for computer graphics.

Also in 1966, Ivan Sutherland continued to innovate at MIT when he invented the first computer controlled head-mounted display (HMD). Called the Sword of Damocles because of the hardware required for support, it displayed two separate wireframe images, one for each eye. This allowed the viewer to see the computer scene in stereoscopic 3D. After receiving his Ph.D. from MIT, Sutherland became Director of Information Processing at ARPA (Advanced Research Projects Agency), and later became a professor at Harvard. In 1967 Sutherland was recruited by Evans to join the computer science program at the University of Utah - a development which would turn that department into one of the most important research centers in graphics for nearly a decade thereafter, eventually producing some of the most important pioneers in the field. There Sutherland perfected his HMD; twenty years later, NASA would re-discover his techniques in their virtual reality research. At Utah, Sutherland and Evans were highly sought after consultants by large companies, but they were frustrated at the lack of graphics hardware available at the time so they started formulating a plan to start their own company.

In 1968, Arthur Appel described the first algorithm for what would eventually become known as ray casting - a basis point for almost all of modern 3D graphics, as well as the later pursuit of photorealism in graphics.

In 1969, the ACM initiated A Special Interest Group on Graphics (SIGGRAPH) which organizes conferences, graphics standards, and publications within the field of computer graphics. By 1973, the first annual SIGGRAPH conference was held, which has become one of the focuses of the organization. SIGGRAPH has grown in size and importance as the field of computer graphics has expanded over time.

1970s

Many of the most important early breakthroughs in the transformation of graphics from utilitarian to realistic occurred at the University of Utah in the 1970s, which had hired Ivan Sutherland away from MIT. Sutherland's graphics class would contribute a number of significant pioneers to the field, including a student by the name of Edwin Catmull - a later founder of Pixar. Because of David C. Evans' and Sutherland's presence, UU was gaining quite a reputation as the place to be for computer graphics research so Catmull went there to learn 3D animation. Catmull had just come from The Boeing Company and had been working on his degree in physics. Growing up on Disney, Catmull loved animation yet quickly discovered that he did not have the talent for drawing. Now Catmull (along with many others) saw computers as the natural progression of animation and they wanted to be part of the revolution. The first animation that Catmull saw was his own. He created an animation of his hand opening and closing. It became one of his goals to produce a feature-length motion picture using computer graphics. In the same class, Fred Parke created an animation of his wife's face.

The Utah teapot by Martin Newell and its static renders became emblematic of CGI development during the 1970s.

As the UU computer graphics laboratory was attracting people from all over, John Warnock was one of those early pioneers; he would later found Adobe Systems and create a revolution in the publishing world with his PostScript page description language, and Adobe would go on later to create the industry standard photo editing software in Adobe Photoshop and the movie industry's special effects standard in Adobe After Effects. Tom Stockham led the image processing group at UU which worked closely with the computer graphics lab. Jim Clark was also there; he would later found Silicon Graphics. The first major advance in 3D computer graphics was created at UU by these early pioneers, the hidden-surface algorithm. In order to draw a representation of a 3D object on the screen, the computer must determine which surfaces are "behind" the object from the viewer's perspective, and thus should be "hidden" when the computer creates (or renders) the image. The 3D Core Graphics System (or Core) was the first graphical standard to be developed. A group of 25 experts of the ACM Special Interest Group SIGGRAPH developed this "conceptual framework". The specifications were published in 1977, and it became a foundation for many future developments in the field.

Also in the 1970s, Henri Gouraud, Jim Blinn and Bui Tuong Phong contributed to the foundations of shading in CGI via the development of the Gouraud shading and Blinn-Phong shading models, allowing graphics to move beyond a "flat" look to a look more accurately portraying depth. Jim Blinn also innovated further in 1978 by introducing bump mapping, a technique for simulating uneven surfaces, and the predecessor to many more advanced kinds of mapping used today.

The modern videogame arcade as is known today was birthed in the 1970s, with the first arcade games using real-time 2D sprite graphics. *Pong* in 1972 was one of the first hit arcade cabinet games. *Speed Race* in 1974 featured sprites moving along a vertically scrolling road. *Gun Fight* in 1975 featured human-looking sprite character graphics, while *Space Invaders* in 1978 featured a large number of sprites on screen; both used an Intel 8080 microprocessor and Fujitsu MB14241 video shifter to accelerate the drawing of sprite graphics.

1980s

The 1980s began to see the modernization and commercialization of computer graphics. As the home computer proliferated, a subject which had previously been an academics-only discipline was adopted by a much larger audience, and the number of computer graphics developers increased significantly.

Dire Straits' 1985 music video for their hit song Money For Nothing - the "I Want My MTV" song – became known as an early example of fully three-dimensional, animated computer-generated imagery.

In the early 1980s, the availability of bit-slice and 16-bit microprocessors started to revolutionise high-resolution computer graphics terminals which now increasingly became intelligent, semi-standalone and standalone workstations. Graphics and application processing were increasingly migrated to the intelligence in the workstation, rather than continuing to rely on central mainframe and mini-computers. Typical of the early move to high resolution computer graphics intelligent workstations for the computer-aided engineering market were the Orca 1000, 2000 and 3000 workstations, developed by Orcatech of Ottawa, a spin-off from Bell-Northern Research, and led by David Pearson, an early workstation pioneer. The Orca 3000 was based on Motorola 68000 and AMD bit-slice processors and had Unix as its operating system. It was targeted squarely at the sophisticated end of the design engineering sector. Artists and graphic designers began to see the personal computer, particularly the Commodore Amiga and Macintosh, as a serious design tool, one that could save time and draw more accurately than other methods. The Macintosh remains a highly popular tool for computer graphics among graphic design studios and businesses. Modern computers, dating from the 1980s, often use graphical user interfaces (GUI) to present data and information with symbols, icons and pictures, rather than text. Graphics are one of the five key elements of multimedia technology.

In the field of realistic rendering, Japan's Osaka University developed the LINKS-1 Computer Graphics System, a supercomputer that used up to 257 Zilog Z8001 microprocessors, in 1982, for the purpose of rendering realistic 3D computer graphics. According to the Information Processing Society of Japan: "The core of 3D image rendering is calculating the luminance of each pixel making up a rendered surface from the given viewpoint, light source, and object position. The LINKS-1 system was developed to realize an image rendering methodology in which each pixel could be parallel processed independently using ray tracing. By developing a new software methodology specifically for high-speed image rendering, LINKS-1 was able to rapidly render highly realistic images. It was used to create the world's first 3D planetarium-like video of the entire heavens that was made completely with computer graphics. The video was presented at the Fujitsu pavilion at the 1985 International Exposition in Tsukuba." The LINKS-1 was the world's most powerful computer, as of 1984. Also in the field of realistic rendering, the general rendering equation of David

Immel and James Kajiya was developed in 1986 - an important step towards implementing global illumination, which is necessary to pursue photorealism in computer graphics.

The continuing popularity of Star Wars and other science fiction franchises were relevant in cinematic CGI at this time, as Lucasfilm and Industrial Light & Magic became known as the "go-to" house by many other studios for topnotch computer graphics in film. Important advances in chroma keying ("bluescreening", etc.) were made for the later films of the original trilogy. Two other pieces of video would also outlast the era as historically relevant: Dire Straits' iconic, near-fully-CGI video for their song "Money For Nothing" in 1985, which popularized CGI among music fans of that era, and a scene from Young Sherlock Holmes the same year featuring the first fully CGI character in a feature movie (an animated stained-glass knight). In 1988, the first shaders - small programs designed specifically to do shading as a separate algorithm - were developed by Pixar, which had already spun off from Industrial Light & Magic as a separate entity - though the public would not see the results of such technological progress until the next decade. In the late 1980s, SGI computers were used to create some of the first fully computer-generated short films at Pixar, and Silicon Graphics machines were considered a high-water mark for the field during the decade.

The 1980s is also called the golden era of videogames; millions-selling systems from Atari, Nintendo and Sega, among other companies, exposed computer graphics for the first time to a new, young, and impressionable audience - as did MS-DOS-based personal computers, Apple IIs and Macs, and Amigas, which also allowed users to program their own games if skilled enough. Demoscenes and shareware games proliferated; John Carmack, a later 3D innovator, would start out in this period developing sprite-based games. In the arcades, advances were made in commercial, real-time 3D graphics. In 1988, the first dedicated real-time 3D graphics boards were introduced in arcades, with the Namco System 21 and Taito Air System. This innovation would be the precursor of the later home graphics processing unit or GPU, a technology where a separate and very powerful chip is used in parallel processing with a CPU to optimize graphics.

1990s

Quarxs, series poster, Maurice Benayoun, François Schuiten, 1992

The 1990s' overwhelming note was the emergence of 3D modeling on a mass scale, and an impressive rise in the quality of CGI generally. Home computers became able to take on rendering tasks that previously had been limited to workstations costing thousands of dollars; as 3D modelers became available for home systems, the popularity of Silicon Graphics workstations declined and powerful Microsoft Windows and Apple Macintosh machines running Autodesk products like 3D Studio or other home rendering software ascended in importance. By the end of the decade, the GPU would begin its rise to the prominence it still enjoys today.

The field began to see the first rendered graphics that could truly pass as photorealistic to the untrained eye (though they could not yet do so with a trained CGI artist) and 3D graphics became far more popular in gaming, multimedia and animation. At the end of the 1980s and the beginning of the nineties were created, in France, the very first computer graphics TV series: *La Vie des bêtes* by studio Mac Guff Ligne (1988), *Les Fables Géométriques* (1989-1991) by studio Fantôme, and *Quarxs*, the first HDTV computer graphics series by Maurice Benayoun and François Schuiten (studio Z-A production, 1990–1993).

In film, Pixar began its serious commercial rise in this era under Edwin Catmull, with its first major film release, in 1995 - Toy Story - a critical and commercial success of nine-figure magnitude. The studio to invent the programmable shader would go on to have many animated hits, and its work on prerendered video animation is still considered an industry leader and research trailbreaker.

In videogames, in 1992, *Virtua Racing*, running on the Sega Model 1 arcade system board, laid the foundations for fully 3D racing games and popularized real-time 3D polygonal graphics among a wider audience in the video game industry. The Sega Model 2 in 1993 and Sega Model 3 in 1996 subsequently pushed the boundaries of commercial, real-time 3D graphics. Back on the PC, *Wolfenstein 3D*, *Doom* and *Quake*, three of the first massively popular 3D first-person shooter games, were released by id Software to critical and popular acclaim during this decade using a rendering engine innovated primarily by John Carmack. The Sony Playstation and Nintendo 64, among other consoles, sold in the millions and popularized 3D graphics for home gamers. Certain late-90's first-generation 3D titles became seen as influential in popularizing 3D graphics among console users, such as platform games *Super Mario 64* and *The Legend Of Zelda: Ocarina Of Time*, and early 3D fighting games like *Virtua Fighter*, *Battle Arena Toshinden*, and *Tekken*.

Technology and algorithms for rendering continued to improve greatly. In 1996, Krishnamurty and Levoy invented normal mapping - an improvement on Jim Blinn's bump mapping. 1999 saw Nvidia release the seminal GeForce 256, the first home video card billed as a graphics processing unit or GPU, which in its own words contained "integrated transform, lighting, triangle setup/ clipping, and rendering engines". By the end of the decade, computers adopted common frameworks for graphics processing such as DirectX and OpenGL. Since then, computer graphics have only become more detailed and realistic, due to more powerful graphics hardware and 3D modeling software. AMD also became a leading developer of graphics boards in this decade, creating a "duopoly" in the field which exists this day.

2000s

CGI became ubiquitous in earnest during this era. Video games and CGI cinema had spread the reach of computer graphics to the mainstream by the late 1990s, and continued to do so at an accelerated pace in the 2000s. CGI was also adopted *en masse* for television advertisements widely in the late 1990s and 2000s, and so became familiar to a massive audience.

Still from Final Fantasy: The Spirits Within, 2001

The continued rise and increasing sophistication of the graphics processing unit was crucial to this decade, and 3D rendering capabilities became a standard feature as 3D-graphics GPUs became considered a necessity for desktop computer makers to offer. The Nvidia GeForce line of graphics cards dominated the market in the early decade with occasional significant competing presence from ATI. As the decade progressed, even low-end machines usually contained a 3D-capable GPU of some kind as Nvidia and AMD both introduced low-priced chipsets and continued to dominate the market. Shaders which had been introduced in the 1980s to perform specialized processing on the GPU would by the end of the decade become supported on most consumer hardware, speeding up graphics considerably and allowing for greatly improved texture and shading in computer graphics via the widespread adoption of normal mapping, bump mapping, and a variety of other techniques allowing the simulation of a great amount of detail.

Computer graphics used in films and video games gradually began to be realistic to the point of entering the uncanny valley. CGI movies proliferated, with traditional animated cartoon films like Ice Age and Madagascar as well as numerous Pixar offerings like Finding Nemo dominating the box office in this field. The *Final Fantasy: The Spirits Within*, released in 2001, was the first fully computer-generated feature film to use photorealistic CGI characters and be fully made with motion capture. The film was not a box-office success, however. Some commentators have suggested this may be partly because the lead CGI characters had facial features which fell into the "uncanny valley". Other animated films like *The Polar Express* drew attention at this time as well. Star Wars also resurfaced with its prequel trilogy and the effects continued to set a bar for CGI in film.

In videogames, the Sony Playstation 2 and 3, the Microsoft Xbox line of consoles, and offerings from Nintendo such as the GameCube maintained a large following, as did the Windows PC. Marquee CGI-heavy titles like the series of Grand Theft Auto, Assassin's Creed, Final Fantasy, Bioshock, Kingdom Hearts, Mirror's Edge and dozens of others continued to approach photorealism, grow the videogame industry and impress, until that industry's revenues became comparable to those of movies. Microsoft made a decision to expose DirectX more easily to the independent developer world with the XNA program, but it was not a success. DirectX itself remained a commercial success, however. OpenGL continued to mature as well, and it and DirectX improved greatly; the second-generation shader languages HLSL and GLSL began to be popular in this decade.

In scientific computing, the GPGPU technique to pass large amounts of data bidirectionally between a GPU and CPU was invented; speeding up analysis on many kinds of bioinformatics and molecular biology experiments. The technique has also been used for Bitcoin mining and has applications in computer vision.

2010s

In the early half of the 2010s, CGI is nearly ubiquitous in video, pre-rendered graphics are nearly scientifically photorealistic, and realtime graphics on a suitably high-end system may simulate photorealism to the untrained eye.

Box art from Titanfall, 2014

Texture mapping has matured into a multistage process with many layers; generally it is not uncommon to implement texture mapping, bump mapping or isosurfaces, normal mapping, lighting maps including specular highlights and reflection techniques, and shadow volumes into one rendering engine using shaders, which are maturing considerably. Shaders are now very nearly a necessity for advanced work in the field, providing considerable complexity in manipulating pixels, vertices, and textures on a per-element basis, and countless possible effects. Their shader languages HLSL and GLSL are active fields of research and development. Physically-based rendering or PBR, which implements even more maps to simulate real optic light flow, is an active research area as well. Experiments into the processing power required to provide graphics in real time at ultra-high-resolution modes like Ultra HD are beginning, though beyond reach of all but the highest-end hardware.

In cinema, most animated movies are CGI now; a great many animated CGI films are made per year, but few, if any, attempt photorealism due to continuing fears of the uncanny valley. Most are 3D cartoons.

In videogames, the Xbox One by Microsoft, Sony Playstation 4, and Nintendo Wii U currently dominate the home space and are all capable of highly advanced 3D graphics; the Windows PC is still one of the most active gaming platforms as well.

Image Types

Two-dimensional

2D computer graphics are the computer-based generation of digital images—mostly from models, such as digital image, and by techniques specific to them.

Raster graphic sprites (left) and masks (right)

2D computer graphics are mainly used in applications that were originally developed upon traditional printing and drawing technologies such as typography. In those applications, the two-dimensional image is not just a representation of a real-world object, but an independent artifact
with added semantic value; two-dimensional models are therefore preferred, because they give
more direct control of the image than 3D computer graphics, whose approach is more akin to photography than to typography.

Pixel Art

A large form of digital art being pixel art is created through the use of raster graphics software,
where images are edited on the pixel level. Graphics in most old (or relatively limited) computer and video games, graphing calculator games, and many mobile phone games are mostly
pixel art.

Sprite Graphics

A sprite is a two-dimensional image or animation that is integrated into a larger scene. Initially
including just graphical objects handled separately from the memory bitmap of a video display,
this now includes various manners of graphical overlays.

Originally, sprites were a method of integrating unrelated bitmaps so that they appeared to
be part of the normal bitmap on a screen, such as creating an animated character that can
be moved on a screen without altering the data defining the overall screen. Such sprites can
be created by either electronic circuitry or software. In circuitry, a hardware sprite is a hardware construct that employs custom DMA channels to integrate visual elements with the main
screen in that it super-imposes two discrete video sources. Software can simulate this through
specialized rendering methods.

Vector Graphics

Vector graphics formats are complementary to raster graphics. Raster graphics is the representation of images as an array of pixels and is typically used for the representation of photographic
images. Vector graphics consists in encoding information about shapes and colors that comprise

the image, which can allow for more flexibility in rendering. There are instances when working with vector tools and formats is best practice, and instances when working with raster tools and formats is best practice. There are times when both formats come together. An understanding of the advantages and limitations of each technology and the relationship between them is most likely to result in efficient and effective use of tools.

Example showing effect of vector graphics versus raster (bitmap) graphics.

Three-dimensional

3D graphics compared to 2D graphics are graphics that use a three-dimensional representation of geometric data. For the purpose of performance this is stored in the computer. This includes images that may be for later display or for real-time viewing.

Despite these differences, 3D computer graphics rely on similar algorithms as 2D computer graphics do in the frame and raster graphics (like in 2D) in the final rendered display. In computer graphics software, the distinction between 2D and 3D is occasionally blurred; 2D applications may use 3D techniques to achieve effects such as lighting, and primarily 3D may use 2D rendering techniques.

3D computer graphics are the same as 3D models. The model is contained within the graphical data file, apart from the rendering. However, there are differences that include the 3D model is the representation of any 3D object. Until visually displayed a model is not graphic. Due to printing, 3D models are not only confined to virtual space. 3D rendering is how a model can be displayed. Also can be used in non-graphical computer simulations and calculations.

Computer Animation

Computer animation is the art of creating moving images via the use of computers. It is a subfield of computer graphics and animation. Increasingly it is created by means of 3D computer graphics, though 2D computer graphics are still widely used for stylistic, low bandwidth, and faster real-time rendering needs. Sometimes the target of the animation is the computer itself, but sometimes the target is another medium, such as film. It is also referred to as CGI (Computer-generated imagery or computer-generated imaging), especially when used in films.

Example of Computer animation produced using Motion capture

Fractal landscape, an example of computer-generated imagery.

Virtual entities may contain and be controlled by assorted attributes, such as transform values (location, orientation, and scale) stored in an object's transformation matrix. Animation is the change of an attribute over time. Multiple methods of achieving animation exist; the rudimentary form is based on the creation and editing of keyframes, each storing a value at a given time, per attribute to be animated. The 2D/3D graphics software will change with each keyframe, creating an editable curve of a value mapped over time, in which results in animation. Other methods of animation include procedural and expression-based techniques: the former consolidates related elements of animated entities into sets of attributes, useful for creating particle effects and crowd simulations; the latter allows an evaluated result returned from a user-defined logical expression, coupled with mathematics, to automate animation in a predictable way (convenient for controlling bone behavior beyond what a hierarchy offers in skeletal system set up).

To create the illusion of movement, an image is displayed on the computer screen then quickly replaced by a new image that is similar to the previous image, but shifted slightly. This technique is identical to the illusion of movement in television and motion pictures.

Concepts and Principles

Images are typically created by devices such as cameras, mirrors, lenses, telescopes, microscopes, etc.

Digital images include both vector images and raster images, but raster images are more commonly used.

Pixel

In digital imaging, a pixel (or picture element) is a single point in a raster image. Pixels are placed on a regular 2-dimensional grid, and are often represented using dots or squares. Each pixel is a sample of an original image, where more samples typically provide a more accurate representation of the original. The intensity of each pixel is variable; in color systems, each pixel has typically three components such as red, green, and blue.

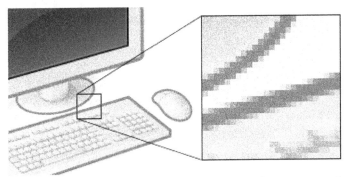

In the enlarged portion of the image individual pixels are rendered as squares and can be easily seen.

Graphics

Graphics are visual presentations on a surface, such as a computer screen. Examples are photographs, drawing, graphics designs, maps, engineering drawings, or other images. Graphics often combine text and illustration. Graphic design may consist of the deliberate selection, creation, or arrangement of typography alone, as in a brochure, flier, poster, web site, or book without any other element. Clarity or effective communication may be the objective, association with other cultural elements may be sought, or merely, the creation of a distinctive style.

Primitives

Primitives are basic units which a graphics system may combine to create more complex images or models. Examples would be sprites and character maps in 2d video games, geometric primitives in CAD, or polygons or triangles in 3d rendering. Primitives may be supported in hardware for efficient rendering, or the building blocks provided by a graphics application

Rendering

Rendering is the generation of a 2D image from a 3D model by means of computer programs. A scene file contains objects in a strictly defined language or data structure; it would contain geometry, viewpoint, texture, lighting, and shading information as a description of the virtual scene. The data contained in the scene file is then passed to a rendering program to be processed and output to a digital image or raster graphics image file. The rendering program is usually built into the computer graphics software, though others are available as plug-ins or entirely separate programs. The term "rendering" may be by analogy with an "artist's rendering" of a scene. Though the technical details of rendering methods vary, the general challenges to overcome in producing a 2D image from a 3D representation stored in a scene file are outlined as the graphics pipeline along a rendering device, such as a GPU. A GPU is a device able to assist the CPU in calculations. If a scene is to look relatively realistic and predictable under virtual lighting, the rendering software should solve the rendering equation. The rendering equation does not account for all lighting phenomena, but is a general lighting model for computer-generated imagery. 'Rendering' is also used to describe the process of calculating effects in a video editing file to produce final video output.

3D projection

> 3D projection is a method of mapping three dimensional points to a two dimensional plane. As most current methods for displaying graphical data are based on planar two dimensional media, the use of this type of projection is widespread, especially in computer graphics, engineering and drafting.

Ray Tracing

> Ray tracing is a technique for generating an image by tracing the path of light through pixels in an image plane. The technique is capable of producing a very high degree of photorealism; usually higher than that of typical scanline rendering methods, but at a greater computational cost.

Shading

Example of Shading.

> Shading refers to depicting depth in 3D models or illustrations by varying levels of darkness. It is a process used in drawing for depicting levels of darkness on paper by applying media more densely or with a darker shade for darker areas, and less densely or with a lighter shade for lighter areas. There are various techniques of shading including cross hatching where perpendicular lines of varying closeness are drawn in a grid pattern to shade an area. The closer the lines are together, the darker the area appears. Likewise, the farther apart the lines are, the lighter the area appears. The term has been recently generalized to mean that shaders are applied.

Texture Mapping

> Texture mapping is a method for adding detail, surface texture, or colour to a computer-generated graphic or 3D model. Its application to 3D graphics was pioneered by Dr Edwin Catmull in 1974. A texture map is applied (mapped) to the surface of a shape, or polygon. This process is akin to applying patterned paper to a plain white box. Multitexturing is the use of more than one texture at a time on a polygon. Procedural textures (created from adjusting parameters of an underlying algorithm that produces an output texture), and bitmap textures (created in an image editing application or imported from a digital camera) are, generally speaking, common methods of implementing texture definition on 3D models in computer graphics software, while intended placement of textures onto a

model's surface often requires a technique known as UV mapping (arbitrary, manual layout of texture coordinates) for polygon surfaces, while NURBS surfaces have their own intrinsic parameterization used as texture coordinates. Texture mapping as a discipline also encompasses techniques for creating normal maps and bump maps that correspond to a texture to simulate height and specular maps to help simulate shine and light reflections, as well as environment mapping to simulate mirror-like reflectivity, also called gloss.

Anti-aliasing

Rendering resolution-independent entities (such as 3D models) for viewing on a raster (pixel-based) device such as a liquid-crystal display or CRT television inevitably causes aliasing artifacts mostly along geometric edges and the boundaries of texture details; these artifacts are informally called "jaggies". Anti-aliasing methods rectify such problems, resulting in imagery more pleasing to the viewer, but can be somewhat computationally expensive. Various anti-aliasing algorithms (such as supersampling) are able to be employed, then customized for the most efficient rendering performance versus quality of the resultant imagery; a graphics artist should consider this trade-off if anti-aliasing methods are to be used. A pre-anti-aliased bitmap texture being displayed on a screen (or screen location) at a resolution different than the resolution of the texture itself (such as a textured model in the distance from the virtual camera) will exhibit aliasing artifacts, while any procedurally defined texture will always show aliasing artifacts as they are resolution-independent; techniques such as mipmapping and texture filtering help to solve texture-related aliasing problems.

Volume Rendering

Volume rendered CT scan of a forearm with different colour schemes for muscle, fat, bone, and blood.

Volume rendering is a technique used to display a 2D projection of a 3D discretely sampled data set. A typical 3D data set is a group of 2D slice images acquired by a CT or MRI scanner.

Usually these are acquired in a regular pattern (e.g., one slice every millimeter) and usually have a regular number of image pixels in a regular pattern. This is an example of a regular volumetric grid, with each volume element, or voxel represented by a single value that is obtained by sampling the immediate area surrounding the voxel.

3D Modeling

3D modeling is the process of developing a mathematical, wireframe representation of any three-dimensional object, called a "3D model", via specialized software. Models may be created automatically or manually; the manual modeling process of preparing geometric data for 3D computer graphics is similar to plastic arts such as sculpting. 3D models may be created using multiple approaches: use of NURBS curves to generate accurate and smooth surface patches, polygonal mesh modeling (manipulation of faceted geometry), or polygonal mesh subdivision (advanced tessellation of polygons, resulting in smooth surfaces similar to NURBS models). A 3D model can be displayed as a two-dimensional image through a process called *3D rendering*, used in a computer simulation of physical phenomena, or animated directly for other purposes. The model can also be physically created using 3D Printing devices.

Pioneers in Computer Graphics

Charles Csuri

Charles Csuri is a pioneer in computer animation and digital fine art and created the first computer art in 1964. Csuri was recognized by *Smithsonian* as the father of digital art and computer animation, and as a pioneer of computer animation by the Museum of Modern Art (MoMA) and Association for Computing Machinery-SIGGRAPH.

Donald P. Greenberg

Donald P. Greenberg is a leading innovator in computer graphics. Greenberg has authored hundreds of articles and served as a teacher and mentor to many prominent computer graphic artists, animators, and researchers such as Robert L. Cook, Marc Levoy, Brian A. Barsky, and Wayne Lytle. Many of his former students have won Academy Awards for technical achievements and several have won the SIGGRAPH Achievement Award. Greenberg was the founding director of the NSF Center for Computer Graphics and Scientific Visualization.

A. Michael Noll

Noll was one of the first researchers to use a digital computer to create artistic patterns and to formalize the use of random processes in the creation of visual arts. He began creating digital computer art in 1962, making him one of the earliest digital computer artists. In 1965, Noll along with Frieder Nake and Georg Nees were the first to publicly exhibit their computer art. During April 1965, the Howard Wise Gallery exhibited Noll's computer art along with random-dot patterns by Bela Julesz.

Other Pioneers

A modern render of the Utah teapot, an iconic model in 3D computer graphics created by Martin Newell, 1975

- Pierre Bézier
- Jim Blinn
- Jack Bresenham
- John Carmack
- Paul de Casteljau
- Ed Catmull
- Frank Crow
- James D. Foley
- William Fetter
- Henry Fuchs
- Henri Gouraud
- Nadia Magnenat Thalmann
- Benoît B. Mandelbrot
- Martin Newell
- Fred Parke
- Bui Tuong Phong
- Steve Russell
- Daniel J. Sandin
- Alvy Ray Smith
- Bob Sproull
- Ivan Sutherland
- Daniel Thalmann
- Andries van Dam
- John Warnock
- Lance Williams

Important Organizations

- SIGGRAPH
- SIGGRAPH Asia

- Bell Telephone Laboratories

- United States Armed Forces, particularly the Whirlwind computer and SAGE Project

- Boeing

- IBM

- Renault

- The computer science department of the University of Utah

- Lucasfilm and Industrial Light & Magic

- Autodesk

- Adobe Systems

- Pixar

- Silicon Graphics, Khronos Group & OpenGL

- The DirectX division at Microsoft

- Nvidia

- AMD

Study of Computer Graphics

The study of computer graphics is a sub-field of computer science which studies methods for digitally synthesizing and manipulating visual content. Although the term often refers to three-dimensional computer graphics, it also encompasses two-dimensional graphics and image processing.

As an academic discipline, computer graphics studies the manipulation of visual and geometric information using computational techniques. It focuses on the *mathematical* and *computational* foundations of image generation and processing rather than purely aesthetic issues. Computer graphics is often differentiated from the field of visualization, although the two fields have many similarities.

Interactive Art

Interactive art is a form of art that involves the spectator in a way that allows the art to achieve its purpose. Some interactive art installations achieve this by letting the observer or visitor "walk" in, on, and around them; some others ask the artist or the spectators to become part of the artwork.

Works of this kind of art frequently feature computers, interfaces and sometimes sensors to respond to motion, heat, meteorological changes or other types of input their makers programmed them to respond to. Most examples of virtual Internet art and electronic art are highly interactive. Sometimes, visitors are able to navigate through a hypertext environment; some works accept textual or visual input from outside; sometimes an audience can influence the course of a performance or can even participate in it. Some other interactive artworks are considered as immersive as the quality of interaction involve all the spectrum of surrounding stimuli. Virtual reality environnements like works by Maurice Benayoun and Jeffrey Shaw are highly interactive as the work the spectators – Maurice Benayoun call them "visitors", Char Davies "immersants" – interact with take all their fields of perception.

The Tunnel under the Atlantic (1995), Maurice Benayoun, Virtual Reality Interactive Installation : a link between Paris and Montreal

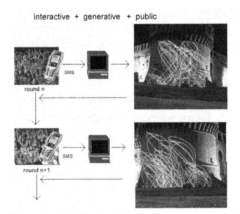

Maurizio Bolognini, *Collective Intelligence Machines* series (CIMs, from 2000): interactive installations using the mobile phone network and participation technologies taken from e-democracy.

Though some of the earliest examples of interactive art have been dated back to the 1920s, most digital art didn't make its official entry into the world of art until the late 1990s. Since this debut, countless museums and venues have been increasingly accommodating digital and interactive art into their productions. This budding genre of art is continuing to grow and evolve in a somewhat rapid manner through internet social sub-culture, as well as through large scale urban installations.

Interactivity in Art

Interactive art is a genre of art in which the viewers participate in some way by providing an input in order to determine the outcome. Unlike traditional art forms wherein the interaction of the spectator is merely a mental event, interactivity allows for various types of navigation, assembly, and/or contribution to an artwork, which goes far beyond purely psychological activity. Interactivity as a medium produces meaning.

Boundary Functions (1998) interactive floor projection by Scott Snibbe at the NTT InterCommunication Center in Tokyo.

Interactive art installations are generally computer-based and frequently rely on sensors, which gauge things such as temperature, motion, proximity, and other meteorological phenomena that the maker has programmed in order to elicit responses based on participant action. In interactive artworks, both the audience and the machine work together in dialogue in order to produce a completely unique artwork for each audience to observe. However, not all observers visualize the same picture. Because it is interactive art, each observer makes their own interpretation of the artwork and it may be completely different than another observer's views.

Interactive art can be distinguished from Generative art in that it constitutes a dialogue between the artwork and the participant; specifically, the participant has agency, or the ability, even in an unintentional manner, to act upon the artwork and is furthermore invited to do so within the context of the piece, i.e. the work affords the interaction. More often, we can consider that the work takes its visitor into account. In an increasing number of cases an installation can be defined as a responsive environment, especially those created by architects and designers. By contrast, Generative Art, which may be interactive, but not responsive per se, tends to be a monologue – the artwork may change or evolve in the presence of the viewer, but the viewer may not be invited to engage in the reaction but merely enjoy it.

History

According to the new media artist and theorist Maurice Benayoun, the first piece of interactive art should be the work done by Parrhasius during his art contest with Zeuxis described by Pliny, in the fifth century B.C. when Zeuxis tried to unveil the painted curtain. The work takes its meaning from Zeuxis' gesture and wouldn't exist without it. Zeuxis, by its gesture, became part of Parrhasius' work. This shows that the specificity of interactive art resides often less in the use of computers than in the quality of proposed "situations" and the "Other's" involvement in the process of sensemaking. Nevertheless, computers and real time computing made the task easier and opened the field of virtuality – the potential emergence of unexpected (although possibly pre-written) futures – to contemporary arts.

Some of the earliest examples of interactive art were created as early as the 1920s. An example is Marcel Duchamp's piece named *Rotary Glass Plates*. The artwork required the viewer to turn on the machine and stand at a distance of one meter in order to see an optical illusion.

The present idea of interactive art began to flourish more in the 1960s for partly political reasons. At the time, many people found it inappropriate for artists to carry the only creative power within their works. Those artists who held this view wanted to give the audience their own part of this creative process. An early example is found in the early 1960s "change-paintings" of Roy Ascott, about whom Frank Popper has written: "Ascott was among the first artists to launch an appeal for total spectator participation". Aside from the "political" view, it was also current wisdom that interaction and engagement had a positive part to play within the creative process.

In the 1970s artists began to use new technology such as video and satellites to experiment with live performances and interactions through the direct broadcast of video and audio.

Interactive art became a large phenomenon due to the advent of computer based interactivity in the 1990s. Along with this came a new kind of art-experience. Audience and machine were now able to more easily work together in dialogue in order to produce a unique artwork for each audience. In the late 1990s, museums and galleries began increasingly incorporating the art form in their shows, some even dedicating entire exhibitions to it. This continues today and is only expanding due to increased communications through digital media.

A hybrid emerging discipline drawing on the combined interests of specific artists and architects has been created in the last 10–15 years. Disciplinary boundaries have blurred, and significant number of architects and interactive designers have joined electronic artists in the creation of new, custom-designed interfaces and evolutions in techniques for obtaining user input (such as dog vision, alternative sensors, voice analysis, etc.); forms and tools for information display (such as video projection, lasers, robotic and mechatronic actuators, led lighting etc.); modes for human-human and human-machine communication (through the Internet and other telecommunications networks); and to the development of social contexts for interactive systems (such as utilitarian tools, formal experiments, games and entertainment, social critique, and political liberation).

Forms

There are many different forms of interactive art. Such forms range from interactive dance, music, and even drama. New technology, primarily computer systems and computer technology, have enabled a new class of interactive art. Examples of such interactive art are installation art, interactive architecture and interactive film.

Impact

The aesthetic impact of interactive art is more profound than expected.

Supporters of more "traditional" contemporary art saw, in the use of computers, a way to balance artistic deficiencies, some other consider that the art is not anymore in the achievement of the formal shape of the work but in the design of the rules that determine the evolution of the shape according to the quality of the dialogue.

Events and Places

There are number of globally significant festivals and exhibitions of interactive and media arts. Prix Ars Electronica is a major yearly competition and exhibition that gives awards to outstanding examples of (technology-driven) interactive art. Association of Computing Machinery's Special Interest Group in Graphics (SIGGRAPH), DEAF Dutch Electronic Arts Festival, Transmediale Germany, FILE - Electronic Language International Festival Brazil, and AV Festival England, are among the others.

CAiiA, Centre for Advanced Inquiry in the Interactive Arts, first established by Roy Ascott in 1994 at the University of Wales, Newport, and later in 2003 as the Planetary Collegium, was the first doctoral and post doc research center to be established specifically for research in the interactive art field.

Interactive architecture has now been installed on and as part of building facades, in foyers, museums and large scale public spaces, including airports, in a number of global cities. A number of leading museums, for example, the National Gallery, Tate, Victoria & Albert Museum and Science Museum in London (to cite the leading UK museums active in this field) were early adoptors in the field of interactive technologies, investing in educational resources, and more latterly, in the creative use of MP3 players for visitors. In 2004 the Victoria & Albert Museum commissioned curator and author Lucy Bullivant to write Responsive Environments (2006), the first such publication of its kind. Interactive designers are frequently commissioned for museum displays; a number specialize in wearable computing.

Venues

- National Gallery

- Tate

- onedotzero

- Victoria & Albert Museum

- Science Museum in London

- Prix Ars Electronica

- Studio Roosegaarde

- FILE - Electronic Language International Festival (Brazil)

- Beall Center for Art + Technology

- AV Festival England

- Watermans

- VIVO Media Arts Centre (Vancouver) – Includes education, exhibition, residencies.

Tools

- Wiring, the first open-source electronics prototyping platform composed of a programming language, an integrated development environment (IDE), and a single-board micro controller. It was developed starting in 2003 by Hernando Barragán and was popularized under the name of Arduino

- Arduino physical computing/electronics toolkit for interactive objects and installations

- I-CubeX sensors, actuators and interfaces for interactive media

- Max/MSP programming language for interactive media

- Processing (programming language) used for many interactive art projects

- OpenFrameworks – open source tool similar to Processing, used for many interactive projects

- Pure Data – open source programming language for interactive computer music and multimedia works

Virtual Art

Virtual art is a term for the virtualization of art, made with the technical media developed at the end of the 1980s (or a bit before, in some cases). These include human-machine interfaces such as visualization casks, stereoscopic spectacles and screens, digital painting and sculpture, generators of three-dimensional sound, data gloves, data clothes, position sensors, tactile and power feedback systems, etc. As virtual art covers such a wide array of mediums it is a catch-all term for specific focuses within it. Much contemporary art has become, in Frank Popper's terms, virtualized.

Definition

Virtual art can be considered a post-convergent art form based on the bringing together of art and technology, thus containing all previous media as subsets. Sharing this focus on art and technology are the books of Jack Burnham (*Beyond Modern Sculpture* 1968) and Gene Youngblood (*Expanded Cinema* 1970). Since virtual art can consist of virtual reality, augmented reality, or mixed reality, it can be seen in other aspects of production such as video games and movies.

In his book *From Technological to Virtual Art*, Frank Popper traces the development of immersive, interactive new media art from its historical antecedents through today's digital art, computer art, cybernetic art, multimedia and net art. Popper shows that contemporary virtual art is a further refinement of the technological art of the late twentieth century and also a departure from it. What is new about this new media art, he argues, is its humanization of technology, its emphasis on interactivity, its philosophical investigation of the real and the virtual, and its multisensory nature. He argues further that what distinguishes the artists who practice virtual art from traditional artists is their combined commitment to aesthetics and technology. Their "extra-artistic" goals – linked to their aesthetic intentions – concern not only science and society but also basic human needs and drives.

To explain and illustrate the emergence of a techno-aesthetic, Popper stresses the panoramic and multi-generational reach of virtual art. As regards to virtual art, openness is stressed both from the point of view of the artists and their creativity and from that of the follow-up users in their reciprocating thoughts and actions. This commitment to the teeming openness found in virtual art can be traced to the theories of Umberto Eco and other aestheticians.

In Virtual Worlds and Entertainment

Virtual art can be seen in worlds like Second Life, and Inworldz virtual environments in which anything is possible to the user, who is represented by an avatar. In the virtual world, the avatar's abilities ranges from ordinary walking to flying. The environment and scenery of such environments is similar to the real world, except that that it can be altered by the avatar. Worlds like Inworldz and Second Life feature an editor which allows the user to build his or her own experience just the way he or she wants it to be. The user is not bounded by physics or improbabilities that he or she faces in the real world.

Virtual art is made of many computer programs and has no boundaries, so it uses animations, movies, computer games and so on. As it becomes more and more popular and important, it results in people being able to live another virtual life. With the advancements in technology virtual art has transformed and evolved quickly from simple 8-bit representations to 3D models containing millions of polygons.

In Popular Video Games and Movies

- *Final Fantasy*
- *The Sims*
- *Heavy Rain*
- *Metal Gear Solid*
- *The Matrix*
- *Terminator*
- *Avatar*
- *The Elder Scrolls*

References

- Catricalà, Valentino (2015). Media Art. Toward a new Definition of Arts in the Age of Technology. Gli Ori. ISBN 978- 88-7336-564-8.
- Dale Hudson and Patricia R. Zimmermann. (2015). Thinking Through Digital Media Transnational Environments and Locative Places. New York: Palgrave Macmillan. P. 1. ISBN 978-1137433626
- Dix, Alan; Finlay, Janet; Abowd, Gregory D.; Beale, Russell (2004). Human-computer interaction. 3rd edn. Pearson Education. p. xvi. ISBN 9780130461094.
- Jon Peddie: The History of Visual Magic in Computers: How Beautiful Images are Made in CAD, 3D, VR and AR, Springer, 2013, p. 101, ISBN 978-1447149316
- Information Processing Society of Japan. "LINKS-1 Computer Graphics System-Computer Museum". Retrieved 15 June 2015.
- Soler-Adillon, Joan (2015-12-21). "The intangible material of interactive art: agency, behavior and emergence". Artnodes. 0 (16). doi:10.7238/a.v0i16.2744. ISSN 1695-5951.
- Robinson, Stuart. "The Disadvantages and Advantages of Interactive Media." EHow. Demand Media, 10 May

2011. Web. 23 Nov. 2014.

- DeYeso, Jennifer. "The Effect of Interactive and Traditional Media on Relationship Building." Slideshare. LinkedIn Corporation, 25 Apr. 2012. Web. 23 Nov. 2014.

- "Virtua Racing – Arcade (1992)". 15 Most Influential Games of All Time. GameSpot. 14 March 2001. Archived from the original on 2010-04-12. Retrieved 19 January 2014.

- Maurizio Bolognini, "De l'interaction à la démocratie. Vers un art génératif post-digital" / "From interactivity to democracy. Towards a post-digital generative art", in Ethique, esthétique, communication technologique, Edition L'Harmattan. Paris, 2011, pp. 229-239.

- See Mario Costa, Fred Forest (eds) (2011), Ethique, esthétique, communication technologique dans l'art contemporain ou le destin du sens, Paris: Institut National Audiovisuel, Editions L'Harmattan, and Dossier Artmedia VIII, in "Ligeia", Paris, 2002.

- Maurizio Bolognini, "From interactivity to democracy. Towards a post-digital generative art", Artmedia X Proceedings. Paris, 2010.

Advanced Technologies of Multimedia

With the fast-paced lifestyle of modern times, technology needs to accommodate changes in patterns and trends of viewership. Digitization allows for the appropriation of new media technologies for art and multimedia purposes. This chapter explores topics like non-linear media which include video on demand, hypothetical models like postliterate society, and advanced techniques like transmedia storytelling.

Non-linear Media

Non-linear media is a form of media that can be interacted with by the consumer, such as by selecting television shows to watch through a video on demand type service, by playing a video game, by clicking through a website, or by interacting through social media. Non-linear media is a move away from traditional linear media, in which content is selected by the publisher to be consumed and is then done so passively. There is no single specific form of non-linear media; rather, what might be considered non-linear changes as technology changes.

Television

The model of traditional linear television programming is for a schedule of shows to be selected by the broadcaster and then viewed at a set time. In this model, the viewer cannot fast forward through the programming or choose to watch it at a later time. Conversely, non-linear television can be considered to be any method or technology that allows viewers to select what shows they watch and when they watch them. The ability to watch a show at any time is referred to as time shifted viewing; this can be achieved by either the consumer recording shows with a device such as a PVR for later viewing, or by the publisher providing content to be selected at will at the viewers convenience.

Non-linear content is often viewed on a device other than a television, such as a personal computer or a smartphone. Video on demand (VOD) content can be transmitted over the internet via streaming services such as Netflix, Hulu, or Amazon Video, or it can be provided by a television provider as an additional option on top of their linear programming. Many producers of content now offer streaming of programs through their own websites, though sometimes the catalog that is offered will be curated in some way, such as by providing only recently released episodes. Video may also be downloaded – legally or illegally – through a peer-to-peer network such as BitTorrent, or it may be directly downloaded from a video hosting website.

As internet speeds and the number of alternate devices that are capable of viewing media on have increased, so has the number of people who consume non-linear media. The television network CBS expects that by the year 2020, 50 percent of all television content will be viewed in a non-linear fashion.

Music & Radio

Like other forms of non-linear media such as television, non-linear radio allows listeners to pick and listen to music and talk shows on a schedule that is set by the listener. Online music streaming services such as Spotify or Deezer are non-linear in that they allow listeners to create playlists from a library of music offered by a website; similarly, podcasts offer the ability to download or stream prerecorded shows similar to those that are traditionally broadcast over the radio waves; in fact, some traditional radio stations allow their shows to be downloaded on demand after the show has aired over the radio in a linear manner.

Postliterate Society

A postliterate society is a hypothetical society in which multimedia technology has advanced to the point where literacy, the ability to read or write, is no longer necessary or common. The term appears as early as 1962 in Marshall McLuhan's *The Gutenberg Galaxy*. Many science-fiction societies are postliterate, as in Ray Bradbury's *Fahrenheit 451*, Dan Simmons' novel *Ilium*, and Gary Shteyngart's *Super Sad True Love Story*.

A postliterate society is different from a pre-literate one, as the latter has not yet created writing and communicates orally (oral literature and oral history, aided by art, dance, and singing), and the former has replaced the written word with recorded sounds (CDs, audiobooks), broadcast spoken word and music (radio), pictures (JPEG) and moving images (television, film, MPG, streaming video, video games, virtual reality). A postliterate society might still include people who are aliterate, who know how to read and write but choose not to. Most if not all people would be media literate, multimedia literate, visually literate, and transliterate.

In his book *The Empire of Illusion*, Chris Hedges charts the recent, sudden rise of postliterate culture within the world culture as a whole.

Author Bruce Powe, in his 1987 book *The Solitary Outlaw*, wrote:

Literacy: the ability to read and interpret the written word. What is post-literacy? It is the condition of semi-literacy, where most people can read and write to some extent, but where the literate sensibility no longer occupies a central position in culture, society, and politics. Post-literacy occurs when the ability to comprehend the written word decays. If post-literacy is now the ground of society questions arise: what happens to the reader, the writer, and the book in post-literary environment? What happens to thinking, resistance, and dissent when the ground becomes wordless?

Transmedia Storytelling

Transmedia storytelling (also known as transmedia narrative or multiplatform storytelling, cross-media seriality) is the technique of telling a single story or story experience across multiple platforms and formats using current digital technologies, not to be confused with traditional cross-platform media franchises, sequels, or adaptations.

Henry Jenkins, author of the seminal book *Convergence Culture*, warns that this is an emerging subject and different authors have different understandings of it. He warns that the term "transmedia" *per se* means "across media" and may be applied to superficially similar, but different phenomena. In particular, the concept of "transmedia storytelling" should not to be confused with traditional cross-platform, "transmedia" media franchises, or "media mixes".

From a production standpoint, transmedia storytelling involves creating content that engages an audience using various techniques to permeate their daily lives. In order to achieve this engagement, a transmedia production will develop stories across multiple forms of media in order to deliver unique pieces of content in each channel. Importantly, these pieces of content are not only linked together (overtly or subtly), but are in narrative synchronization with each other. In his latest book, Nuno Bernardo shows TV and film producers how to use transmedia to build an entertainment brand that can conquer global audiences, readers and users in a myriad of platforms.

History

The origins of the approach to disperse the content across various commodities and media is traced to the Japanese marketing strategy of media mix, originated in early 1960s. Some, however, have traced the roots to *Pamela: Or, Virtue Rewarded* (1740) written by Samuel Richardson and even suggest that they go back further to the roots of earliest literature.

By the 1970s and 1980s, pioneering artists of telematic art made experiments of collective narrative, mixing the ancestors of today's networks, and produced both visions and critical theories of what became transmedia.

With the advent of mainstream Internet usage in the 1990s, numerous creators began to explore ways to tell stories and entertain audiences using new platforms. Many early examples took the form of what was to become known as alternate reality games (ARG), which took place in real-time with a mass audience. The term ARG was itself coined in 2001 to describe The Beast, a marketing campaign for the film *A.I.: Artificial Intelligence*. Some early works include, but are not limited to:

- Ong's Hat was most likely started sometime around 1993, and also included most of the aforementioned design principles. Ong's Hat also incorporated elements of legend tripping into its design, as chronicled in a scholarly work titled *Legend-Tripping Online: Supernatural Folklore and the Search for Ong's Hat*. ISBN 978-1628460612

- Dreadnot, an early example of an ARG-style project, was published on sfgate.com in 1996. This ARG included working voice mail phone numbers for characters, clues in the source code, character email addresses, off-site websites, and real locations in San Francisco.

- FreakyLinks (link to archived project at end of article), 2000

- *The Blair Witch Project* - feature film, 1999

- *On Line* - feature film, 2001

- The Beast - game, 2001

- Majestic - video game, 2001

The Macaulay Honors College, part of CUNY, New York, established a New Media Lab focusing on Transmedia Storytelling and content, under the direction of Robert Small.

Current State

As of 2011, both traditional and dedicated transmedia entertainment studios are beginning to embrace transmedia storytelling techniques in search of a new storytelling form that is native to networked digital content and communication channels. Developing technologies have enabled projects to now begin to include single-player experiences in addition to real-time multiplayer experiences such as alternate reality games. While the list of current and recent projects is too extensive to list here, some notable examples of transmedia storytelling include:

- Slide, a native transmedia experience for Fox8 TV in Australia.

- *Skins*, a transmedia extension of the Channel 4/Company Pictures TV show by Somethin' Else in the UK.

- *Halo*, a video game series created by Bungie and currently developed by 343 Industries that has evolved to include novels, comic books, audio plays, live action web series and an upcoming live action television series from Showtime.

- *Cathy's Book*, a transmedia novel by Sean Stewart and Jordan Weisman.

- *Year Zero*, a transmedia project by Nine Inch Nails.

- *ReGenesis*, a Canadian television series with a real-time transmedia (alternate reality game) extension that took place in sync with the episodes as they aired.

- *The Lizzie Bennet Diaries*, a web series adaptation of *Pride and Prejudice* with Twitter and Tumblr accounts.

- *Pandemic*, an independent film and event created by Lance Weiler.

- MyMusic, transmedia sitcom by Fine Brothers Productions as part of YouTube's original channels initiative, one of the more robust transmedia experiences.

- Clockwork Watch, an independent project, about a non-colonial Steampunk world, told across graphic novels, live events, online and a feature film created by Yomi Ayeni.

- ZED.TO, a crowdfunded Canadian ARG that simulates the rise and fall of a futuristic Toronto "lifestyle biotech" corporation.

- *Defiance*, a television show and video game paired to tell connective and separate stories.

- The HIVE Transmedia Project, by Daniel D.W. is a sci-fi novella series incorporating QR codes within the text to multimedia and a simulated reality story.

- *Ingress* by Niantic Labs in 2012.

- *Endgame: Proving Ground*, a web, phone, book, movie & live paid actor campaign of transreality gaming by Niantic Labs beginning in 2014.

- Simon Wilkinson has created several transmedia shows, including *Beyond the Bright Black Edge of Nowhere* (2014) and *The Cube* (2015), which both tell the story of a mass disappearance in 1950s America. After seeing the performance, audience members investigate the disappearance online through a series of websites.

- Star Wars has grown over the years and includes a large amount of novels, comic books, movies, video games and TV shows.

- The *Assassin's Creed* franchise is full of games, novels and comic book series, all expanding its universe.

In 'Digital State: How the internet is changing everything' (2013), author Simon Pont argues that transmedia storytelling is a theory that is at last starting to find its practical stride. Pont cites Ridley Scott's *Alien*-prequel *Prometheus* (2012), and specifically the three viral films produced by 20th Century Fox as part of the advance global marketing campaign, as vivid executional examples of transmedia storytelling theory.

Where Robert McKee (Story, 1998) argues that back-story is a waste of time (because if the back-story is so good then this is surely the story worth telling), Pont proposes that storytellers like J. J. Abrams and Damon Lindelof have "pretty much lined McKee's argument up against a wall and shot it". Pont goes on to argue, "Parallel and non-linear timelines, 'multi-verses', grand narratives with crazy-rich character arcs, 'back-story' has become 'more story', the opportunity to add Byzantine layers of meaning and depth. You don't create a story world by stripping away, but by layering".

In 'Ball & Flint: transmedia in 90 seconds' (2013), Pont likens transmedia story-telling to "throwing a piece of flint at an old stone wall" and "delighting in the ricochet", making story something you can now "be hit by and cut by".

Educational Uses

Transmedia storytelling mimics daily life, making it a strong constructivist pedagogical tool for educational uses. The level of engagement offered by transmedia storytelling is essential to the Me or Millennial Generation as no single media satisfy their curiosity or lifestyle. Schools have been slow to adopt the emergence of this new culture which shifts the spotlight of literacy from being one of individual expression to one of community. Whether we see it or not, Jenkins notes that we live in a transmedia, globally connected world in which we use multiple platforms to connect and communicate. Using Transmedia storytelling as a pedagogical tool, wherein students interact with platforms, such as Twitter, Facebook, Instagram, or Tumblr permits students' viewpoints, experiences, and resources to establish a shared collective intelligence that is enticing, engaging, and immersive, catching the millennial learners' attention, ensuring learners a stake in the experience. Transmedia storytelling offers the educator the ability to lead students to think critically, identify with the material and gain knowledge, offering valuable framework for the constructivist educational pedagogy that supports student centered learning. Transmedia storytelling allows for the interpretation of the story from the individual perspective, making way for personalized meaning-making.

In 'The Better Mousetrap: Brand Invention in a Media Democracy' (2012), Pont explains, "Transmedia thinking anchors itself to the world of story, the ambition principally being one of how you can 'bring story to life' in different places, in a non-linear fashion. The marketing of motion pictures is the most obvious application, where transmedia maintains that there's a 'bigger picture opportunity' to punting a big picture. Transmedia theory, applied to a movie launch, is all about promoting the story, not the 'due date of a movie starring…' In an industry built on the conventions of 'stars sell movies', where their name sits above the film's title, transmedia thinking is anti-conventional and boldly purist."

Transmedia storytelling is also used by companies like Microsoft and Kimberly-Clark to train employees and managers. Gronstedt and Ramos argues: "At the core of every training challenge is a good story waiting to be told. More and more, these stories are being told across a multitude of devices and screens, where they can reach learners more widely, and engage with them more deeply."

Web Documentary

A web documentary, interactive documentary, or multimedia documentary is a documentary production that differs from the more traditional forms—video, audio, photographic—by applying a full complement of multimedia tools. The interactive multimedia capability of the Internet provides documentarians with a unique medium to create non-linear productions that combine photography, text, audio, video, animation, and infographics.

How Web Documentaries Differ from Film Documentaries

The web documentary differs from film documentaries through the integration of a combination of multimedia assets (photos, text, audio, animation, graphic design, etc.) with web technologies. In a web documentary, the user has to interact with, or navigate through, the story.

Compared to a linear narrative where the destination of the story is pre-determined by the film-maker, a web documentary provides a user with the experience of moving through the story via clusters of information. The integration of information architecture, graphic design, imagery, titles, and sub-titles all play a role in providing visual clues to the user as to the sequence through which they should move through the web documentary. But from that point, the users have to explore the components of the story that interest them the most.

Examples of Web Documentaries

- *Casas Hechas Mujer An interactive documentary about Colombian Caribbean houses with names on their facades by Ariel E. Arteta F. "aikeart"*

- *Clouds Over Cuba* — The Cuban missile crisis and what might have been.

- *Hollow Explore the rural communities of McDowell County, West Virginia through Hollow, an interactive documentary featuring the stories of over 30 residents who live there.*

- *Mumbai Madness The daily trip of a young commuter through the hellish traffic of Mumbai*

- *Unknown Spring* — An anthology project that bears witness to the ongoing recovery of Tohoku.

- *A series of web documentary on Dhaka Markets* — 80plus1 : Journey around Dhaka: A series of web documentary on Dhaka Markets.

- *Journey to the End of Coal* — A web documentary that let the user investigate the living conditions of Chinese coal miners.

- *Out My Window* — a National Film Board of Canada collaborative documentary showing 13 interactive views from highrise apartments.

- *Green Unplugged* — a Culture Unplugged Studios short form documentary showing worldview on environment and showcased by United Nations Council For Environment.

- *Barcode* — an ARTE France and National Film Board of Canada documentary about objects and how they reveal the way we live, created with 30 directors and containing 100 videos

- *Welcome to Pine Point* — a National Film Board of Canada web documentary exploring the memories of residents from the former community of Pine Point, Northwest Territories.

- *Big Stories, Small Towns* — web documentary about life in small towns made in collaboration with the local communities. To date four towns have been featured - three from Australia and one from Cambodia.

- *Becoming Human* — "Paleoanthropology, Evolution, and Human Origins"

- Gift of a Lifetime — Audio slideshow storytelling complemented by interactive historical timeline and an interactive human body

- *Interactive Narratives* — A collection of web documentary content from various sources

- *Water's Journey: Everglades* — This web documentary includes six audio slideshows, and interactive map, an interactive historical timeline and film/animation clips

- *Hometown Baghdad* — A series chronicling the lives of three Iraqi 20-somethings in Baghdad

- *The Iron Curtain Diaries (1989-2009)* — web documentary by Matteo Scanni about the fall of the Iron Curtain

- *Farselona* — interactive scroll-doc walks the user through the "invention" of Barcelona's Gothic quarter, calling to a dual reflection on whether official history should be taken at face value and whether cities should be seen as touristic products

- *One World Journeys Expeditions* — A collection of environment and conservation themed web documentaries created between 2000 and 2002

- *Canto do Brazil* — web documentary about Brazil by a documentary photographer

- *Inside Beijing* | 融入北京 Inside Beijing is a multimedia project covering the political and cultural capital of China. It focuses mainly on two aspects connected to each other: the urban development of the metropolis and the evolution of the Chinese culture.

- *Thanatorama* — A journey into the arcane world of the funeral. Between the intimate and the universal, the sacred and the mundane, the religious rite and market rules, *Thanatorama* played on records and surveys the frontiers. At the heart of the viewer confronted with his own death. To him draw his journey, according to its beliefs, according to his curiosity.

- *Prison Valley* — *Prison Valley* is an ARTE web documentary by David Dufresne and Philippe Brault on the prison industry in the recession-hit United States. A journey into what the future might hold.

- *New York Minute* — An ARTE 6-part miniseries riding through the five boroughs and a web-based, collaborative and multilingual encyclopedia about New York's culture.

- *In Situ* — In Situ is an ARTE web documentary about urban artists in Europe, by Antoine Viviani.

- *WATERLIFE - NFB* — The interactive story of the last great supply of fresh drinking water on Earth.

- *Where is Gary* — An interactive investigation about a real con artist. The documentary maker Jean-Baptiste Dumont challenged himself to find this fascinating guy in ten weeks, with the help of the audience.

- *My Tribe Is My Life* — an interactive exploration of how young people use the internet and music subcultures to forge identities and relationships.

- *Clé 56 (original site)* — A 6 part miniseries about 2 patients of a psychiatric hospital.

- *Multimediadocumentary Is the new way to create and distribute multimedia documentary using the new mobile technologies.The projects is open to the contribution of everyone (photographers or movie maker) who have some interesting story to show.*

- *MMDoc #1 Le cittá di Olivetti by Sandro Pisani First edition of the new Multimedia documentary community network, photografy and interview of people and place inherent the project as iPad application.*

- *16 Tons* — 16 Tons is an online movie about conscience and free market, by Ümit Kıvanç. The documentary uses several versions of the song Sixteen Tons while throwing an ironic look at the history of humanity. It contains extensive sequences of animation, using photographs, paintings, drawings and etchings. The web site provides the option of watching the entire film or each chapter separately. There is comprehensive additional information and further annotation on the details of the film on the page related to each chapter.

- *Bagagem* What Esmeralina retired, the Joatan lawyer, barber and musician Jandira Afrânio have in common? They all give the intersection of Avenida de Augusto Lima and Rua da Bahia as residential reference. Residents Set Arcangelo Maletta, one of the most popular (and bohemians) buildings Belo Horizonte (MG) - Brazil, the characters in this webdocumentário declare their affection for the place and desmitificam the negative image that some city residents have the Maletta.

- *Planet Galata* — A portrait of a bridge in Istanbul.

References

- Pratten, Robert (2015). Getting Started in Transmedia Storytelling: A Practical Guide for Beginners (2nd ed.). London, UK: CreateSpace. p. 224. ISBN 978-1-5153-3916-8.

- Bernardo, Nuno (2011). The Producers Guide to Transmedia: How to Develop, Fund, Produce and Distribute Compelling Stories Across Multiple Platforms (Paperback). London, UK: beActive Books. p. 153. ISBN 978-0-9567500-0-6.

- Bernardo, Nuno (2014). Transmedia 2.0: How to Create an Entertainment Brand Using a Transmedial Approach to Storytelling (Paperback). London, UK: beActive Books. p. 162. ISBN 978-1909547018.

- Gronstedt, Anders; Ramos, Marc (January 7, 2014). Learning Through Transmedia Storytelling (Infoline). ASTD. ISBN 1562869515.

- Hartman, Dennis. "What Is Linear Marketing?". Houston Chronicle. Archived from the original on 2016-04-17. Retrieved 2016-04-17.

- "What is the difference between linear and non-linear media applications?". Borough of Manhattan Community College. Archived from the original on 2016-04-17. Retrieved 2016-04-17.

- Hasebrink, Uwe. "Linear and Non-linear Television from Viewers' Perspective". Hans-Bredow-Institut. Archived from the original on 2016-04-17. Retrieved 2016-04-17.

- Doeven, Jan (February 2013). "Trends in Broadcasting: An overview of developments" (PDF). itu.int. International Telecommunication Union. Archived from the original (PDF) on 2016-04-25. Retrieved 2016-04-25.

- "Video on demand". The Video on Demand Dictionary and Business Index. Archived from the original on 2016-04-18. Retrieved 2016-04-18.

- Ferraz, Tommy (2015-10-19). "BBC innovates in non-linear radio". Archived from the original on 2016-04-18. Retrieved 2016-04-18.

- "CBS sees 50 percent non-linear TV future". Warc. 2015-08-12. Archived from the original on 2016-04-18. Retrieved 2016-04-18.

- Lynch, Jason (2015-08-10). "Don't Panic, Says CBS: More People Are Watching TV Now Than a Decade Ago". Adweek. Prometheus Global Media. Archived from the original on 2016-04-18. Retrieved 2016-04-18.

- "Born Skippy: Radio That (Intentionally) Misses A Beat". www.newslangmedia.com. Archived from the original on 2016-04-25. Retrieved 2016-04-25.

- "After the non-linear radio - Tommy Ferraz". Tommy Ferraz. Archived from the original on 2016-04-25. Retrieved 2016-04-25.

- Teske, Paul R. J. and Horstman, Theresa. "Transmedia in the classroom: breaking the fourth wall". Paper presented at the meeting of the MindTrek, 2012.

- Scott-Stevenson, Julia (15 March 2011). "My Tribe is My Life". Special Broadcasting Service (Australia). Retrieved 7 April 2011

- Jenkins, H. "Transmedia Storytelling and Entertainment: An Annotated Syllabus", Continuum: Journal of Media & Cultural Studies, 24:6, 943-958 2010.

7

New Literacies and its Different Forms

The digital revolution has made the concept of new literacies possible. It is a relatively new field in the discipline of literacy studies and its definition remains open and is conceptualized in different ways by different academicians. Digital literacy refers to the knowledge and skill set based on digital devices like smartphones, laptops, PCs etc. This chapter elucidates the skills and competencies that are a result of digital and information literacy. The chapter also gives the reader material on how these literacies are changing the world of literary studies.

New Literacies

New literacies generally are new forms of literacy made possible by digital technology developments, although new literacies do not necessarily have to involve use of digital technologies to be recognized as such. The term "new literacies" itself is relatively new within the field of literacy studies (the first documented mention of it in an academic article title dates to 1993 in a text by David Buckingham). Its definition remains open, with new literacies being conceptualized in different ways by different groups of scholars.

For example, one group of scholars argues that literacy is now deictic, and see it as continually and rapidly changing as new technologies appear and new social practices for literacy emerge. (Leu, 2000). This group aims at developing a single, overarching theory to help explain new literacies (for example, Leu, O'Byrne, Zawilinski, McVerry, & Everett-Cacopardo, 2009). This orientation towards new literacies is largely psycholinguistic in nature. Other groups of scholars follow a more socio-cultural orientation that focuses on literacy as a social practice, which emphasizes the role of literacy with a range of socially patterned and goal-directed ways of getting things done in the world (for example, Gee & Hayes, 2012; Lankshear & Knobel, 2011; Kalantzis and Cope 2011).

Accompanying the varying conceptualizations of new literacies, there are a range of terms used by different researchers when referring to new literacies, including *21st century literacies, internet literacies, digital literacies, new media literacies, multiliteracies, information literacy, ICT literacies,* and *computer literacy.* In the *Handbook of New Literacies Research,* Coiro, Knobel, Lankshear, and Leu (2008) note that all these terms "are used to refer to phenomena we would see as falling broadly under a new literacies umbrella" (pg. 10).

Commonly recognized examples of new literacies include such practices as instant messaging, blogging, maintaining a website, participating in online social networking spaces, creating and sharing music videos, podcasting and videocasting, photoshopping images and photo sharing, emailing, shopping online, digital storytelling, participating in online discussion lists, emailing and using online chat, conducting and collating online searches, reading, writing and commenting on fan fiction, processing and evaluating online information, creating and sharing digital mashups, etc.

Definitions: At Least Two 'Camps'

The field of new literacies is characterized by two theoretically distinct approaches that overlap to some extent. One is informed by cognitive and language processing theories such as cognitive psychology, psycholinguistics, schema theory, metacognition, constructivism, and other similar theories. This orientation includes a particular focus on examining the cognitive and social pro-cesses involved in comprehending online or digital texts (Leu, 2001; Leu, Kinzer, Coiro, & Cammack, 2004; Coiro, 2003; Coiro & Dobler, 2007). Donald Leu, a prominent researcher in the field of new literacies, has outlined four defining characteristics of new literacies, according to a largely psycholinguistic orientation (Leu et al., 2007). First, new technologies (such as the internet) and the novel literacy tasks that pertain to these new technologies require new skills and strategies to effectively use them. Second, new literacies are a critical component of full participation—civic, economic, and personal in our increasingly global society. A third compo-nent to this approach is new literacies are *deictic*—that is, they change regularly as new technology emerges and older technologies fade away. With this in mind, "what may be important in reading instruction and literacy education is not to teach any single set of new literacies, but rather to teach students how to learn continuously new literacies that will appear during their lifetime." Finally, new literacies are "multiple, multimodal, and multifaceted," and as such, multiple points of view will be most beneficial in attempting to comprehensively analyze them. This orientation makes a distinction between "New Literacies" and "new literacies" theories. Lower case theories are better able to keep up with the rapidly changing nature of literacy in a deictic world since they are closer to the specific types of changes that are taking place and interest those who study them within a particular heuristic. Lower case theories also permit the field to maximize the lenses that are used and the technologies and contexts that are studied. This position argues that every scholar who studies new literacy issues is generating important insights for everyone else, even if they do not share a particular lens, technology, or context; and that this requires a second level of theorising. New Literacies (capitalized), it is argued, is a broader, more inclusive concept, and includes com-mon findings emerging across multiple, lower case theories. New Literacies theory benefits from work taking place in the multiple, lower case dimensions of new literacies by looking for what ap-pear to be the most common and consistent patterns being found in lower case theories and lines of research. This approach permits everyone to fully explore their unique, lowercase perspective of new literacies, allowing scholars to maintain close focus on many different aspects of the rapidly shifting landscape of literacy during a period of rapid change. At the same time, each also benefits from expanding their understanding of other, lowercase, new literacies perspectives. By assuming change in the model, everyone is open to a continuously changing definition of literacy, based on the most recent data that emerges consistently, across multiple perspectives, disciplines, and research traditions. Moreover, areas in which alternative findings emerge are identified, enabling each to be studied again, from multiple perspectives. From this process, common patterns emerge and are included in a broader, common, New Literacies theory. From this orientation, proponents argue, this process enables a particular theorization of New Literacies to keep up with consistent elements that will always define literacy on the Internet while it also informs each of the lower case theories of new literacies with patterns that are being regularly found by others.

The second approach to studying new literacies is overtly grounded in a focus on social practices. According to Colin Lankshear and Michele Knobel from this "social practice" perspectives, "new literacies" can refer to "new socially recognized ways of generating, communicating and negotiating meaningful content through the medium of encoded texts within contexts of participation in Discourses (or, as members of Discourses) ". From this perspective "new" refers to the presence of two dominant features of contemporary literacy practices. The first is the use of digital technologies as the means of producing, sharing, accessing and interacting with meaningful content. New literacies typically involve screens and pixels rather than paper and type, and digital code (that renders texts as image, sound, conventional text, and any combination of these within a single process) rather than material print. The second defining feature of new literacies is their highly collaborative, distributed, and participatory nature, as expressions of what Henry Jenkins calls engagement in participatory culture, and Lankshear and Knobel refer to as a distinctive *ethos*.

Research in New Literacies

Research within the field of new literacies is also diverse. A wide range of topics and issues are focused upon, and a broad range of methodologies are used.

Online Research and Comprehension

One aspect of new literacies that has attracted researchers' attention is school-age children's online research and comprehension. Specifically, researchers are interested in finding the answers to questions such as how reading online differs from traditional print-based reading. Donald Leu, Julie Coiro, Jill Castek, Laurie Henry, and others attempt to understand how students become adept at reading online to learn and how students acquire the necessary skills, strategies, and dispositions required to do so. Initial work in this area referred to online reading comprehension More recently, however, the construct "online research and comprehension" is being used since this more precisely describes the type of reading being described in their work. According to Leu and colleagues, the new literacies of online research and comprehension is a process of problem-based inquiry using information on the Internet. It includes the skills, strategies, dispositions, and social practices that take place as we read online information to learn and is based around five practices: "At least five processing practices occur during online research and comprehension: (1) reading to identify important questions, (2) reading to locate information, (3) reading to evaluate information critically, (4) reading to synthesize information, and (5) reading to communicate information. Within these five practices reside the skills, strategies, and dispositions that are distinctive to online reading comprehension as well as to others that are also important for offline reading comprehension (Leu, Reinking, et al., 2007)."

Online Fan Fiction and Adolescents

Recent research in the field of new literacies has focused on fan fiction on the internet, especially those stories published online by adolescents (Black, 2008; Thomas, 2007; Jen-kins, 2006). Online fan fiction websites, such as FanFiction.Net, are spaces where fans of all ages, but especially adolescents and younger school-age fans, are able to use these new information and communication technologies (ICTs) to write and craft fictional stories based on their favorite characters in popular media such as movies, television, and graphic novels. Adolescents are participating more and more on these kinds of sites, not only engaging with "pop culture and media, but also with a broad array of literate activities that are aligned with many school-based literacy practices"

Of course, adults are just as able to spend time in such online environments—and they do. However, it is interesting to consider that young people were born into a digitally rich world, and thus could be seen as "digital natives," and therefore interact with the online environment in a fundamentally distinct way than an older generation of people, so-called "digital immigrants." As digital natives, adolescents "use the online world to share, evaluate, create, report and program with each other differently to digital immigrants," and they engage easily and readily with new digital technologies such as instant messaging, file sharing songs and videos, and post all kinds of 'texts,' stories, photos, and videos among them. A central characteristic of digital natives is their "desire to create." Digital natives are engaged in "programming to some extent, whether it be by including a piece of HTML code that personalizes a MySpace page or creating a Flash animation. They are creating web pages, blogs, avatars and worlds; and, in stark contrast to digital immigrants, digital natives readily report and share their ideas."

Video Games

James Paul Gee described video gaming as a new literacy "in virtue of the ways game design involves a multimodal code comprising images, actions, words, sounds, and movements that players interpret according to gaming conventions". Gee notes that game players participate in their game's world as a form of social practice, especially in real-time strategy games in which players can compete with each other to build on land masses, for instance, and in which they can shape and convey their virtual identities as a certain kind of strategist. Video games continue to use new digital technologies to create the symbols players interpret to encode and decode the meanings that constitute the game. Many ways in which students learn literacies, increasingly, are happening outside of school rather than inside of school.

Other researchers have expanded the body of knowledge about video games as a new literacy, par-ticularly as they relate to classroom learning (Lacasa, Martinez, & Mendez, 2008; Sanford & Madill, 2007). In one study, researchers examined how video games, supported by discussions and dramatic performances in the classroom, can contribute to the development of narrative thought as demonstrated in written compositions in various contexts. Namely, the researchers engaged primary school children in activities designed to teach them to tell, play out, and write stories based on the most popular video game in their classroom, *Tomb Raider*. Although it was a challenging process at times, researchers discovered that the use of new digital media such as video games actually "complements the use of other written or audiovisual methods [in the classroom] and permits the development of multiple literacies in the classroom."

New Literacies and the Classroom

It has become clear to many researchers in the field that new literacies research has important implications for the classroom. Kist (2007), for example, observes how new literacies can be used in classroom settings—from the use of rap music to anime to digital storytelling, there are already instances of teachers attempting to blend new literacies with traditional literacy practices in the classroom. Kist asks: "Can new literacies indeed 'fit' into how we currently 'do' school?" Kist notes that "the new literacies instruction that does exist often comes only out of the fortitude of lonely pioneers of new literacies."

Knobel and Lankshear (2011) argue that if educators and prospective teachers engage in blogging, or participate in "affinity spaces" devoted to practices like fan fiction, video game-playing, music and video remixing, photosharing, and the like, they will better understand how new literacies can better be integrated into worthwhile classroom learning.

Leu, Coiro, Castek, Hartman, Henry and Reinking (2008) have begun to explore the use of a modified instructional model of reciprocal teaching that reflects some of the differences between offline and online reading contexts. In an instructional model known as Internet Reciprocal Teaching, each student has his/her own laptop with access to the Internet and students work in small groups to facilitate interactive group work and discussions about strategy use. In addition, Internet Reciprocal Teaching with online informational resources (as opposed to narrative texts) and strategy instruction on both the common and unique processes by which students navigate through multiple and different texts, rather than the reading of one common text. Teachers and students model their choices about which links are most relevant to a group or individual question through think-alouds. They discuss how to efficiently locate information within different kinds of websites, how to synthesize ideas across multiple texts and media, how to make judgments about the quality of the information and the author's level of expertise, and how to best represent the answers to their questions. Responsibility for monitoring and effectively using these strategies to solve online information problems is gradually released to the students using an instructional scheme with three phases: Phase 1 includes direct, whole class instruction of basic skills and strategies of Internet use; Phase 2 includes group work and the reciprocal exchange of online reading comprehension strategies by students with their peers; and Phase 3 includes online individual inquiry units, sometimes with collaborative efforts involving other students in other classes, perhaps even in other parts of the world, and periodic strategy sessions with groups. Students "are the first generation to be global publishers to access the raw material of information and to create refined knowledge products for application. They understand the social skills of working with people who they will never meet face to face. They also understand that they need to take more responsibility for managing their own learning. They do not see the boundaries of school as a solid wall. They see school as a global communications center."

Digital Literacy

Digital literacy is the knowledge, skills, and behaviors used in a broad range of digital devices such as smartphones, tablets, laptops and desktop PCs, all of which are seen as network rather than computing devices. Digital literacy initially focused on digital skills and stand-alone computers, but the focus has moved from stand-alone to network devices. Digital literacy is distinct from computer literacy and digital skills. Computer literacy preceded digital literacy, and refers to knowledge and skills in using traditional computers (such as desktop PCs and laptops) with a focus on practical skills in using software application packages. Digital skills is a more contemporary term but is limited to practical abilities in using digital devices (such as laptops and smartphones).

A digitally literate person will possess a range of digital skills, knowledge of the basic principles of computing devices, skills in using computer networks, an ability to engage in online communities and social networks while adhering to behavioral protocols, be able to find, capture and evaluate information, an understanding of the societal issues raised by digital technologies (such as big data), and possess critical thinking skills.

Digital literacy does not replace traditional forms of literacy. It builds upon the foundation of traditional forms of literacy. Digital literacy is the marrying of the two terms digital and literacy;

however, it is much more than a combination of the two terms. Digital information is a symbolic representation of data, and literacy refers to the ability to read for knowledge, write coherently, and think critically about the written word.

Digital literacy researchers explore a wide variety of topics, including how people find, use, summarize, evaluate, create, and communicate information while using digital technologies. Research also encompasses a variety of hardware platforms, such as computer hardware, cell phones and other mobile devices and software or applications, including web search or Internet applications more broadly. As a result, the area is concerned with much more than how people learn to use computers. In Scandinavian English as well as in OECD research, the term Digital Competence is preferred over literacy due to its holistic use. In 2013, European Commission published a Digital Competence Framework which also includes the notion of digital literacy, but goes further than that, for example, defining problem solving in digital environments as part of the Digital competence.

Academic and Pedagogical Concepts

From a competency perspective, literacy is the lowest level in a progression that spans literacy, fluency and mastery. From an academic perspective, digital literacy is a part of the computing subject area, alongside computer science and information technology.

Digital literacy is a new literacy, and may itself be decomposed into several sub-literacies. One such decomposition considers digital literacy as embracing computer literacy, network literacy, information literacy and social media literacy. Previous conceptualisations of digital literacy focused on the practical skills associated with using computers (now considered computer literacy). These include hardware skills, such as connecting devices, and software skills, such as using application packages. Contemporary conceptualisations of digital literacy add to these traditional skills, and embrace knowledge, skills, attitudes and behaviours, particularly with respect to networked devices (which include smartphones, tablets and personal computers). Digital literacy differs from computer literacy in a number of significant ways. While it embraces the practical skills that computer literacy incorporates, there is a much greater focus on sociological, political, cultural, economic and behavioral aspects of digital technologies.

As a pedagogical approach in curriculum design, the implementation of digital literacy affords far-reaching advantages. The internet is both a source of information and communication that has increased exponentially internationally. Subsequently, integrating technology into the classroom in a meaningful way, exposes students to a range of literacy practices called multi-literacies which broadens their outlook and widens vistas of information and knowledge which is highly constructive. This methodology embraces the constructivist theory of learning (Bruner, 1978) wherein learners draw from their existing knowledge in order to construct new learning.

Core Elements and their Educational Effects

Literacies can be grouped together in what is known as the Essential Elements of Digital Literacies which expounds the theory that having an understanding of these eight essential elements of digital literacies will enable an individual to be digitally literate. The development of these core skills correlated to the particular contexts in which an individual may develop their skills with a view to ensuring that they align with their needs. The eight elements are Cultural, Cognitive, Constructive, Communicative, Confidence, Creative, Critical and Civic. The value of each of these core elements is dependent on varying needs at different times.

- Cultural - The cultural element of Digital Literacies requires technology use in different contexts and an awareness of the values and concepts specific to the varying contexts.

- Cognitive - The cognitive component of Digital literacies aims to enable mastery of the use of technological tools, software and platforms. Gaining expertise in digital tools helps learners become more digitally literate.

- Constructive - The constructive element requires re-using and remixing existing resources depending on the need; or adapting them into new resources. Through construction, a digitally literate user creates new data and shares their creations with others digitally.

- Communicative - The communicative component requires awareness about different communication devices both digital and mobile. Being digitally literate means communicating in the digital world in several ways.

- Confidence - The confidence element of Digital Literacy means gaining competence with digital technologies and the ability to create an environment for practising skills and self-learning.

- Creative - Through the Creative element of Digital Literacy, digital learners create new data in digital environments based on personal interests. This element places emphasis on taking risks while developing searching skills and producing new things.

- Critical - The critical component requires the digital learner to develop various perspectives. While actively taking part in digital environments, the user should take different circumstances into account.

- Civic - The civic element is all about developing and acquiring the concepts of democracy and global citizenship through digital technologies. This component helps the participation of the individual in society. Part of digital literacy is the ability to form communities online.

It is recognised that the implementation of these elements in an individual's context will require constant updating and upgrading as digital information and tools change along with our understanding of them.

From a pedagogical perspective, digital literacy seeks to include knowledge and understanding of the applications and implications of digital technologies, in contrast to the skills focus of computer literacy. Digital literacy is considered a key aspect of contemporary citizenship to enable individuals to fully participate in the digital economy and the democratic process, and knowledgeably engage with debates relating to the networked society, such as those relating to personal privacy. Digital literacy may be studied at a number of levels. While fundamental concepts and skills are normally covered in the lower levels of national qualification frameworks, more advanced treatments, dealing with more sophisticated concepts and skills such as critical thinking, are higher level competencies.

- New literacies: Expounds upon the new type of literacy in regards to the technological advancements of society.

  o Layered Literacy: Describes the way that print and digital overlap, creating intertextuality

- Transliteracy: The ability to read and write across a wide variety of media formats.

- Electracy: The pedagogical skills necessary for new digital skills.

- Digital citizen: The role and rights of a person within the digital world

Digital and Media Literacy

The topic of digital and media literacy was addressed by the Knight Commission on the Information Needs of Communities in a Democracy, a blue ribbon panel of seventeen media, policy and community leaders, whose purpose was to assess the information needs of communities, and recommend measures to help Americans better meet those needs. Its report, Informing Communities: Sustaining Democracy in the Digital Age, was the first major commission on media since the Hutchins Commission in the 1940s and the Kerner and Carnegie Commissions of the 1960s. In the digital age, technological, economic and behavioral changes are dramatically altering how Americans communicate. Information is more fragmented. Communications systems no longer run along the same lines as local governance. The gap in access to digital tools and skills is wide and troubling. This new era poses major challenges to the flow of news and information people depend on to manage their complex lives. In the context of this report, digital and media literacy is seen as a constellation of life skills that are necessary for full participation in our media-saturated, information-rich society. According to Renee Hobbs, author of the white paper, Digital and Media Literacy: A Plan of Action, these include the ability to do the following:

- ACCESS. Make responsible choices and access information by locating and sharing materials and comprehending information and ideas

- ANALYZE. Analyze messages in a variety of forms by identifying the author, purpose and point of view, and evaluating the quality and credibility of the content

- CREATE. Create content in a variety of forms, making use of language, images, sound, and new digital tools and technologies

- REFLECT. Reflect on one's own conduct and communication behavior by applying social responsibility and ethical principles

- ACT. Take social action by working individually and collaboratively to share knowledge and solve problems in the family, workplace and community, and by participating as a member of a community

Digital and media literacy competencies, which constitute core competencies of citizenship in the digital age, have enormous practical value. Hobbs identifies a *10-point action plan* to enable all Americans to acquire digital and media literacy competencies.

Digital Literacy and 21st-Century Skills

Digital literacy requires certain skill sets that are interdisciplinary in nature. Warshauer and Matuchniak list information, media, and technology; learning and innovation skills; and life and career skills as the three skill sets that individuals need to master in order to be digitally literate, or the 21st century skills. In order to achieve information, media, and technology skills, one needs to achieve competency in information literacy, media literacy and ICT (information communicative technologies). Encompassed within Learning and Innovation Skills, one must also be able to be able to be exercise their creativity and innovation, critical thinking and problem solving, and communication and collaboration skills (the "Four Cs of 21st century learning"). In order to be competent in Life and Career Skills, it is also necessary to be able to exercise flexibility and adaptability, initiative and self-direction, social and cross-cultural skills, productivity and accountability, leadership and responsibility. Aviram & Eshet-Alkalai contend that there are five types of literacies that are encompassed in the umbrella term that is digital literacy.

1. Photo-visual literacy is the ability to read and deduce information from visuals.

2. Reproduction literacy is the ability to use digital technology to create a new piece of work or combine existing pieces of work together to make it your own.

3. Branching literacy is the ability to successfully navigate in the non-linear medium of digital space.

4. Information literacy is the ability to search, locate, assess and critically evaluate information found on the web and on-shelf in libraries.

5. Socio-emotional literacy refers to the social and emotional aspects of being present online, whether it may be through socializing, and collaborating, or simply consuming content.

Use in Education

Schools are continuously updating their curriculum for digital literacy to keep up with accelerating technological developments. This often includes computers in the classroom, the use of educational software to teach curriculum, and course materials being made available to students online. Some classrooms are designed to use smartboards and audience response systems. These techniques are most effective when the teacher is digitally literate as well.

Teachers often teach digital literacy skills to students who use computers for research. Such skills include verifying credible sources online and how-to cite web sites. Google and Wikipedia are used by students "for everyday life research."

Educators are often required to be certified in digital literacy to teach certain software and, more prevalently, to prevent plagiarism amongst students.

Digital Natives and Immigrants

Marc Prensky invented and popularized the terms "digital native" and "digital immigrant." A digital native, according to Prensky, is one who was born into the digital age. A digital immigrant refers to one who adopts technology later in life. These terms aid in understanding the issues of teaching digital literacy, however, simply being a digital native does not make one digitally literate.

Digital immigrants, although they adapt to the same technology as natives, possess a sort of "accent" which restricts them from communicating the way natives do. In fact, research shows that, due to the brain's malleable nature, technology has changed the way today's students read, perceive, and process information. This means that today's educators may struggle to find effective teaching methods for digital natives. Digital immigrants might resist teaching digital literacy because they themselves weren't taught that way. Prensky believes this is a problem because today's students are "a population that speaks an entirely new language" than the people who educate them.

Statistics and popular representations of the elderly and digital technologies portray them as digital immigrants. For example, in 2010 in Canada, 29% of those 75+ and 60% of those 65-74 had browsed the Internet in the past month whereas this activity almost reached 100% among those 15–24 years old. Eugene Loos identifies the most common assumptions about digital technologies and the elderly, all of which contribute to portray them as digital immigrants and to perpetuate digital ageism: senior citizens may be regarded as a homogenous group; this group does not want to or is not able to make use of digital information sources; however, it is not perceived as a problem, because as time passes, these generations will be succeeded by new generations that have no problem at all with digital technologies. The heterogeneity of cohorts, interest in technologies changing according to life events, and the importance of regular use to develop skills and literacy are examples of other elements to take into account.

Digital Visitors and Residents

In contrast to Marc Prensky, Dave White from the Department for Continuing Education at the University of Oxford has been publicising his concept of digital visitors and residents. Briefly, the concept is that visitors leave no online social trace where as residents live a portion of their lives online. These are not two separate categories of people but rather a description of a continuum of behaviours. It is probable that many individuals demonstrate both visitor and residential behaviours in different contexts. Dave White has developed a mapping tool which explores this concept.

Digital Writing

Digital writing is a new type of composition being taught increasingly within universities. Digital writing is a pedagogy focused on technology's impact on writing environments; it is not simply using a computer to write. Rather than the traditional print perspective, digital writing enables students to explore modern technologies and learn how different writing spaces affect the meaning, audience, and readability of text. Educators in favor of digital writing argue that it is necessary because "technology fundamentally changes how writing is produced, delivered, and received." The goal of teaching digital writing is that students will increase their ability to produce a relevant, high-quality product, instead of just a standard academic paper.

One aspect of digital writing is the use of hypertext. As opposed to printed text, hypertext invites readers to explore information in a non-linear fashion. Hypertext consists of traditional text and hyperlinks that send readers to other texts. These links may refer to related terms or concepts, or they may enable readers to choose the order in which they read. The process of digital writing requires the composer to make unique "decisions regarding linking and omission." These decisions "give rise to questions about the author's responsibilities to the [text] and to objectivity."

Use in Society

Digital literacy helps people communicate and keep up with societal trends. Literacy in social network services and Web 2.0 sites helps people stay in contact with others, pass timely information and even sell goods and services. This is mostly popular among younger generations, though sites like LinkedIn have made it valuable to older professionals.

Digital literacy can also prevent people from believing hoaxes that are spread online or are the result of photo manipulation. E-mail frauds and phishing often take advantage of the digitally illiterate, costing victims money and making them vulnerable to identity theft.

Research has demonstrated that the differences in the level of digital literacy depend mainly on age and education level, while the influence of gender is decreasing (Hargittai, 2002; van Dijk, 2005; van Dijk and van Deursen, 2009). Among young people, in particular, digital literacy is high in its operational dimension (e.g. rapidly move through hypertext, familiarity with different kinds of online resources) while the skills to critically evaluate content found online show a deficit (Gui and Argentin, 2011).

Building on digital literacy is the concept of digital creativity which is the expression of creative skills in the digital medium. This can include programming, web sites and the generation and manipulation of digital images.

Social Networking

With the emergence of social networking, one who is digitally literate now has a major voice online. The level of digital literacy needed to voice an opinion online today compared to the Internet before social networks is minute. Websites like Facebook and Twitter, as well as personal websites and blogs have enabled a new type of journalism that is subjective, personal, and "represents a global conversation that is connected through its community of readers." These online communities foster group interactivity among the digitally literate. Social networks also help users establish a digital identity, or a "symbolic digital representation of identity attributes." Without digital literacy or the assistance of someone who is digitally literate, one cannot possess a personal digital identity. This is closely allied to Web Literacy.

Digital Divide

Digital literacy and digital access have become increasingly important competitive differentiators. Bridging the economic and developmental divides is in large measure a matter of increasing digital literacy and access for peoples who have been left out of the information and communications technology (ICT) revolutions.

Scholar Howard Besser contends that the digital divide is more than just a gap between those who have access to technology and those who don't. This issue encompasses aspects such as information literacy, appropriateness of content, and access to content. Beyond access, a digital divide exists between those who apply critical thinking to technology or not, those who speak English or not, and those who create digital content or merely consume it.

Research published in 2012 found that the digital divide, as defined by access to information technology, does not exist amongst youth in the United States. Young people of all races and ethnicities report being connected to the internet at rates of 94-98%. There remains, however, a Civic Opportunity Gap, where youth from poorer families and those attending lower socioeconomic status schools are less likely to encounter opportunities to apply their digital literacies toward civic ends.

Community Informatics overlaps to a considerable degree with digital literacy by being concerned with ensuring the opportunity not only for ICT access at the community level but also, according to Michael Gurstein, that the means for the "effective use" of ICTs for community betterment and empowerment are available. Digital literacy is of course, one of the significant elements in this process.

The United Nations Global Alliance for ICT and Development (GAID) seeks to address this set of issues at an international and global level. Many organizations (e.g. *Per* Scholas for underserved communities in the United States and InterConnection for underserved communities around the world as well as the U.S.) focus on addressing this concern at national, local and community levels.

Digital Citizenship

Digital citizenship has nine components:

- Digital access: full electronic participation in society.

- Digital commerce: electronic buying and selling of goods.

- Digital communication: electronic exchange of information.

- Digital literacy: process of teaching and learning about technology and the use of technology.

- Digital etiquette: electronic standards of conduct or procedure.

- Digital law: electronic responsibility for actions and deeds.

- Digital rights and responsibilities: those freedoms extended to everyone in a digital world.

- Digital health and wellness: physical and psychological well-being in a digital technology world.

- Digital security (self-protection): electronic precautions to guarantee safety.

Global Impact

Government officials around the world have emphasized the importance of digital literacy for their economy. According to HotChalk, an Online resource for educators: "Nations with centralized education systems, such as China, are leading the charge and implementing digital literacy training programs faster than anyone else. For those countries, the news is good."

Many developing nations are also focusing on digital literacy education to compete globally.

Economically, socially and regionally marginalised people have benefited from the ECDL Foundation's ECDL / ICDL programme through funding and support from Corporate Social Responsibility initiatives, international development agency funding and non-governmental organisations(NGO's).

The Philippines' Education Secretary Jesli Lapus has emphasized the importance of digital literacy in Filipino education. He claims a resistance to change is the main obstacle to improving the nation's education in the globalized world. In 2008, Lapus was inducted into Certiport's "Champions of Digital Literacy" Hall of Fame for his work to emphasize digital literacy.

Use in the Workforce

Those who are digitally literate are more likely to be economically secure. Many jobs require a working knowledge of computers and the Internet to perform basic functions. As wireless technology improves, more jobs require proficiency with cell phones and PDAs (sometimes combined into smart phones).

White collar jobs are increasingly performed primarily on computers and portable devices. Many of these jobs require proof of digital literacy to be hired or promoted. Sometimes companies will administer their own tests to employees, or official certification will be required.

As technology has become cheaper and more readily available, more blue-collar jobs have required digital literacy as well. Manufacturers and retailers, for example, are expected to collect and analyze data about productivity and market trends to stay competitive. Construction workers often use computers to increase employee safety.

Job recruiters often use employment Web sites to find potential employees, thus magnifying the importance of digital literacy in securing a job.

The 2014 Workforce Innovation and Opportunity Act (WIOA)...defines digital literacy skills as a workforce preparation activity.

Information Literacy

The United States National Forum on Information Literacy defines information literacy as "... the ability to know when there is a need for information, to be able to identify, locate, evaluate, and effectively use that information for the issue or problem at hand." The American Library Association defines "information literacy" as a set of abilities requiring individuals to "recognize when information is needed and have the ability to locate, evaluate, and use effectively the needed information. Other definitions incorporate aspects of "skepticism, judgement, free thinking, questioning, and understanding..." or incorporate competencies that an informed citizen of an information society ought to possess to participate intelligently and actively in that society.

A number of efforts have been made to better define the concept and its relationship to other skills and forms of literacy. Although other educational goals, including traditional literacy, computer literacy, library skills, and critical thinking skills, are related to information literacy and important foundations for its development, information literacy itself is emerging as a distinct skill set and a necessary key to one's social and economic well-being in an increasingly complex information society. According to McTavish (2009), in order to increase and maximize people's contributions to a healthy, democratic and pluralistic society and maintain a prosperous and sustainable economy, governments and industries around the world are challenging education systems to focus people's attention on literacy. In Canada, because of a great focus on a supposed literacy crisis, it has caused some alarm in some educational sectors. Brink (2006) researched government organization, such as Human Resources and Skill Development Canada, claims that almost half of working-age Canadians do not have the literacy skills they need to meet the ever-increasing demands of modern life.

History of the Concept

The phrase *information literacy* first appeared in print in a 1974 report by Paul G. Zurkowski written on behalf of the National Commission on Libraries and Information Science. Zurkowski used the phrase to describe the "techniques and skills" learned by the information literate "for utilizing the wide range of information tools as well as primary sources in molding information solutions to their problems" and drew a relatively firm line between the "literates" and "information illiterates".

The Presidential Committee on Information Literacy released a report on January 10, 1989, outlining the importance of information literacy, opportunities to develop information literacy, and an Information Age School. The report's final name is the Presidential Committee on Information Literacy: Final Report.

The recommendations of the Presidential Committee led to the creation later that year of the National Forum on Information Literacy, a coalition of more than 90 national and international organizations.

In 1998, the American Association of School Librarians and the Association for Educational Communications and Technology published *Information Power: Building Partnerships for Learning*, which further established specific goals for information literacy education, defining some nine standards in the categories of "information literacy", "independent learning", and "social responsibility".

Also in 1998, the Presidential Committee on Information Literacy produced an update on its Final Report. This update outlined the six main recommendations of the original report and examined areas where it made progress and areas that still needed work. The updated report supports further information literacy advocacy and reiterates its importance.

In 1999, the Society of College, National and University Libraries (SCONUL) in the UK, published "The Seven Pillars of Information Literacy" model to "facilitate further development of ideas amongst practitioners in the field ... stimulate debate about the ideas and about how those ideas might be used by library and other staff in higher education concerned with the development of students' skills." A number of other countries have developed information literacy standards since then.

In 2003, the National Forum on Information Literacy, together with UNESCO and the National Commission on Libraries and Information Science, sponsored an international conference in Prague with representatives from some twenty-three countries to discuss the importance of information literacy within a global context. The resulting Prague Declaration described information literacy as a "key to social, cultural, and economic development of nations and communities, institutions and individuals in the 21st century" and declared its acquisition as "part of the basic human right of life long learning".

The Alexandria Proclamation linked Information literacy with lifelong learning. More than that, it sets Information Literacy as a basic Human right that it *"promotes social inclusion of all nations"*.

On May 28, 2009, U.S. California Governor Arnold Schwarzenegger signed Executive Order S-06-09, establishing a California ICT Digital Literacy Leadership Council, which in turn, was directed to establish an ICT Digital Literacy Advisory Committee. "The Leadership Council, in consultation with the Advisory Committee, shall develop an ICT Digital Literacy Policy, to ensure that California residents are digitally literate." The Executive Order states further: "ICT Digital Literacy is defined as using digital technology, communications tools and/or networks to access, manage, integrate, evaluate, create, and communicate information in order to function in a knowledge-based economy and society..." The Governor directs "...The Leadership Council, in consultation with the Advisory Committee... [to] develop a California Action Plan for ICT Digital Literacy (Action Plan)." He also directs "The California Workforce Investment Board (WIB)... [to] develop a technology literacy component for its five-year Strategic State Plan." His Executive Order ends with the following: "I FURTHER REQUEST that the Legislature and Superintendent of Public Instruction consider adopting similar goals, and that they join the Leadership Council in issuing a "Call to Action" to schools, higher education institutions, employers, workforce training agencies, local governments, community organizations, and civic leaders to advance California as a global leader in ICT Digital Literacy".

Information literacy rose to national consciousness in the U.S. with President Barack Obama's Proclamation designating October 2009 as National Information Literacy Awareness Month. President Obama's Proclamation stated that

"Rather than merely possessing data, we must also learn the skills necessary to acquire, collate, and evaluate information for any situation... Though we may know how to find the information we need, we must also know how to evaluate it. Over the past decade, we have seen a crisis of authenticity emerge. We now live in a world where anyone can publish an opinion or perspective, whether true or not, and have that opinion amplified within the information marketplace. At the same time, Americans have unprecedented access to the diverse and independent sources of information, as well as institutions such as libraries and universities, that can help separate truth from fiction and signal from noise."

Obama's proclamation ended with:

"Now, therefore, I, Barack Obama, President of the United States of America, by virtue of the authority vested in me by the Constitution and the laws of the United States, do hereby proclaim October 2009 as National Information Literacy Awareness Month. I call upon the people of the United States to recognize the important role information plays in our daily lives, and appreciate the need for a greater understanding of its impact."

Presidential Committee on Information Literacy

The Presidential Committee on Information Literacy was formed in 1987 by the American Library Association's president at the time Margaret Chisholm. The committee was formed with three specific purposes

1. to define Information Literacy within the higher literacies and its importance to student performance, lifelong learning, and active citizenship

2. to design one or more models for information literacy development appropriate to formal and informal learning environments throughout people's lifetimes

3. to determine implications for the continuing education and development for teachers

The American Library Association's Presidential Committee on Information Literacy defined information literacy as the ability "to recognize when information is needed and have the ability to locate, evaluate, and use effectively the needed information" and highlighted information literacy as a skill essential for lifelong learning and the production of an informed and prosperous citizenry.

The committee outlined six principal recommendations: to "reconsider the ways we have organized information institutionally, structured information access, and defined information's role in our lives at home in the community, and in the work place"; to promote "public awareness of the problems created by information illiteracy"; to develop a national research agenda related to information and its use; to ensure the existence of "a climate conducive to students' becoming information literate"; to include information literacy concerns in teacher education; and to promote public awareness of the relationship between information literacy and the more general goals of "literacy, productivity, and democracy."

In March 1998 the Presidential Committee on Information Literacy re-evaluated its Final Report and published an update. The update looks at what the Final Report set out to accomplish, its six main goals, and how far it had come to that point in meeting those objectives. Before identifying what still needs to be done, the updated report recognizes what the previous report and the National Forum were able to accomplish. In realizing it still had not met all objectives, it set out further recommendations to ensure all were met. The updated report ends with an invitation, asking the National Forum and regular citizens to recognize that "the result of these combined efforts will be a citizenry which is made up of effective lifelong learners who can always find the information needed for the issue or decision at hand. This new generation of information literate citizens will truly be America's most valuable resource", and to continue working toward an information literate world.

One of the most important things to come out of the Presidential Committee on Information Literacy was the creation of the National Forum on Information Literacy.

National Forum on Information Literacy

Background

In 1983, the seminal report "A Nation at Risk: The Imperative for Educational Reform" declared that a "rising tide of mediocrity" was eroding the very foundations of the American educational system. It was, in fact, the genesis of the current educational reform movement within the United States. Ironically, the report did not include in its set of reform recommendations the academic and/or the public library as one of the key architects in the redesign of our K-16 educational system. This report and several others that followed, in conjunction with the rapid emergence of the information society, led the American Library Association (ALA) to convene a blue ribbon panel of national educators and librarians in 1987. The ALA Presidential Committee on Information Literacy was charged with the following tasks:

(1) to define information literacy within the higher literacies and its importance to student performance, lifelong learning, and active citizenship;

(2) to design one or more models for information literacy development appropriate to formal and informal learning environments throughout people's lifetimes; and

(3) to determine implications for the continuing education and development of teachers.

In the release of its Final Report in 1989, the American Library Association Presidential Committee on Information Literacy summarized in its opening paragraphs the ultimate mission of the National Forum on Information Literacy:

"How our country deals with the realities of the Information Age will have enormous impact on our democratic way of life and on our nation's ability to compete internationally. Within America's information society, there also exists the potential of addressing many long-standing social and economic inequities. To reap such benefits, people—as individuals and as a nation—must be information literate. To be information literate, a person must be able to recognize when information is needed and have the ability to locate, evaluate, and use effectively the needed information. Producing such a citizenry will require that schools and colleges appreciate and integrate the concept of information literacy into their learning programs and that they play a leadership role in equipping individuals and institutions to take advantage of the opportunities inherent within the information society.

Ultimately, information literate people are those who have learned how to learn. They know how to learn because they know how knowledge is organized, how to find information, and how to use information in such a way that others can learn from them. They are people prepared for lifelong learning because they can always find the information needed for any task or decision at hand."

Acknowledging that the major obstacle to people becoming information literate citizens, who are prepared for lifelong learning, "is a lack of public awareness of the problems created by information illiteracy," the report recommended the formation of a coalition of national organizations to promote information literacy."

Thus, in 1989, the A.L.A. Presidential Committee established the National Forum on Information Literacy, a volunteer network of organizations committed to raising public awareness on the importance of information literacy to individuals, communities, the economy, and to engage citizenship participation.

The Forum Today

Since 1989, the National Forum on Information Literacy has evolved steadily under the leadership of its first chair, Dr. Patricia Senn Breivik. Today, the Forum represents over 90 national and international organizations, all dedicated to mainstreaming the philosophy of information literacy across national and international landscapes, and throughout every educational, domestic, and workplace venue.

Although the initial intent of the Forum was to raise public awareness and support on a national level, over the last several years, the National Forum on Information Literacy has made significant strides internationally in promoting the importance of integrating information literacy concepts and skills throughout all educational, governmental, and workforce development programs. For example, the National Forum co-sponsored with UNESCO and IFLA several "experts meetings", resulting in the Prague Declaration (2003) and the Alexandria Proclamation (2005) each underscoring the importance of information literacy as a basic fundamental human right and lifelong learning skill.

In the United States, however, information literacy skill development has been the exception and not the rule, particularly as it relates to the integration of information literacy practices within our educational and workforce development infrastructures. In a 2000 peer-reviewed publication, Nell K. Duke, found that students in first grade classrooms were exposed to an average of 3.6 minutes of informational text in a school day. In October 2006, the first national Summit on Information Literacy brought together over 100 representatives from education, business, and government to address America's information literacy deficits as a nation currently competing in a global marketplace. This successful collaboration was sponsored by the National Forum on Information Literacy, Committee for Economic Development, Educational Testing Service, the Institute for a Competitive Workforce, and National Education Association (NEA). The Summit was held at NEA headquarters in Washington, D.C.

A major outcome of the Summit was the establishment of a national ICT literacy policy council to provide leadership in creating national standards for ICT literacy in the United States.

As stated on the Forum's Main Web page, it recognizes that achieving information literacy has been much easier for those with money and other advantages. For those who are poor, non-White, older, disabled, living in rural areas or otherwise disadvantaged, it has been much harder to overcome the digital divide. A number of the Forum's members address the specific challenges for those disadvantaged. For example, The Children's Partnership advocates for the nearly 70 million children and youth in the country, many of whom are disadvantaged. The Children's Partnership currently runs three programs, two of which specifically address the needs of those with low-incomes: Online content for Low-Income and Underserved Americans Initiative, and the California Initiative Program. Another example is the National Hispanic Council on Aging, which is:

Dedicated to improving the quality of life for Latino elderly, families, and communities through advocacy, capacity and institution building, development of educational materials, technical assistance, demonstration projects, policy analysis and research (National Hispanic Council on Aging, and, Mission Statement section).

The National Forum on Information Literacy will continue to work closely with educational, business, and non-profit organizations in the U.S. to promote information literacy skill development at every opportunity, particularly in light of the ever growing social, economic, and political urgency of globalization, prompting citizens to re-energize our promotional and collaborative efforts.

Global Information Literacy

The International Federation of Library Associations and Institutions (IFLA)

IFLA has established an Information Literacy Section. The Section has, in turn, developed and mounted an Information Literacy Resources Directory, called InfoLit Global. Librarians, educators and information professionals may self-register and upload information-literacy-related materials (IFLA, Information Literacy Section, n.d.) According to the IFLA website, "The primary purpose of the Information Literacy Section is to foster international cooperation in the development of information literacy education in all types of libraries and information institutions."

The International Alliance for Information Literacy (IAIL)

This alliance was created from the recommendation of the Prague Conference of Information Literacy Experts in 2003. One of its goals is to allow for the sharing of information literacy research and knowledge between nations. The IAIL also sees "life-long learning" as a basic human right, and their ultimate goal is to use information literacy as a way to allow everyone to participate in the "Information Society" as a way of fulfilling this right. The following organizations are founding members of IAIL:

- Australian and New Zealand Institute for Information Literacy (ANZIIL); based in Australia and New Zealand. Official website

- European Network on Information Literacy (EnIL); based in the European Union. Official website

- National Forum on Information Literacy (NFIL); based in the United States. Official website

- NORDINFOlit; based in Scandinavia

- SCONUL (Society of College, National and University Libraries) Advisory Committee on Information Literacy; based in the United Kingdom. Official website

United Nations Educational, Scientific, and Cultural Organization (UNESCO) Media and Information Literacy

According to the UNESCO website, this is their "action to provide people with the skills and abilities for critical reception, assessment and use of information and media in their professional and personal lives." Their goal is to create information literate societies by creating and maintaining educational policies for information literacy. They work with teachers around the world, training them in the importance of information literacy and providing resources for them to use in their classrooms.

UNESCO publishes studies on information literacy in many countries, looking at how information literacy is currently taught, how it differs in different demographics, and how to raise awareness. They also publish pedagogical tools and curricula for school boards and teachers to refer to and use.

Specific Aspects (Shapiro and Hughes, 1996)

In "Information Literacy as a Liberal Art", Jeremy J. Shapiro and Shelley K. Hughes advocated a more holistic approach to information literacy education, one that encouraged not merely the addition of information technology courses as an adjunct to existing curricula, but rather a radically new conceptualization of "our entire educational curriculum in terms of information".

Drawing upon Enlightenment ideals like those articulated by Enlightenment philosopher Condorcet, Shapiro and Hughes argued that information literacy education is "essential to the future of democracy, if citizens are to be intelligent shapers of the information society rather than its pawns, and to humanistic culture, if information is to be part of a meaningful existence rather than a routine of production and consumption".

To this end, Shapiro and Hughes outlined a "prototype curriculum" that encompassed the concepts of computer literacy, library skills, and "a broader, critical conception of a more humanistic sort", suggesting seven important components of a holistic approach to information literacy:

- Tool literacy, or the ability to understand and use the practical and conceptual tools of current information technology relevant to education and the areas of work and professional life that the individual expects to inhabit.

- Resource literacy, or the ability to understand the form, format, location and access methods of information resources, especially daily expanding networked information resources.

- Social-structural literacy, or understanding how information is socially situated and produced.

- Research literacy, or the ability to understand and use the IT-based tools relevant to the work of today's researcher and scholar.

- Publishing literacy, or the ability to format and publish research and ideas electronically, in textual and multimedia forms ... to introduce them into the electronic public realm and the electronic community of scholars.

- Emerging technology literacy, or the ability to continuously adapt to, understand, evaluate and make use of the continually emerging innovations in information technology so as not to be a prisoner of prior tools and resources, and to make intelligent decisions about the adoption of new ones.

- Critical literacy, or the ability to evaluate critically the intellectual, human and social strengths and weaknesses, potentials and limits, benefits and costs of information technologies.

Ira Shor further defines critical literacy as "[habits] of thought, reading, writing, and speaking which go beneath surface meaning, first impressions, dominant myths, official pronouncements, traditional clichés, received wisdom, and mere opinions, to understand the deep meaning, root causes, social context, ideology, and personal consequences of any action, event, object, process, organization, experience, text, subject matter, policy, mass media, or discourse".

Information Literacy Skills

Big6 Skills

Based on the Big6 by Mike Eisenberg and Bob Berkowitz.

1. The first step in the information literacy strategy is to clarify and understand the requirements of the problem or task for which information is sought. Basic questions asked at this stage:

1. What is known about the topic?

2. What information is needed?

3. Where can the information be found?

2. Locating: The second step is to identify sources of information and to find those resources. Depending upon the task, sources that will be helpful may vary. Sources may include books, encyclopedias, maps, almanacs, etc. Sources may be in electronic, print, social bookmarking tools, or other formats.

3. Selecting/analyzing: Step three involves examining the resources that were found. The information must be determined to be useful or not useful in solving the problem. The useful resources are selected and the inappropriate resources are rejected.

4. Organizing/synthesizing: It is in the fourth step this information which has been selected is organized and processed so that knowledge and solutions are developed. Examples of basic steps in this stage are:

    1. Discriminating between fact and opinion

    2. Basing comparisons on similar characteristics

    3. Noticing various interpretations of data

    4. Finding more information if needed

    5. Organizing ideas and information logically

5. Creating/presenting: In step five the information or solution is presented to the appropriate audience in an appropriate format. A paper is written. A presentation is made. Drawings, illustrations, and graphs are presented.

6. Evaluating: The final step in the information literacy strategy involves the critical evaluation of the completion of the task or the new understanding of the concept. Was the problem solved? Was new knowledge found? What could have been done differently? What was done well?

The Big6 skills have been used in a variety of settings to help those with a variety of needs. For example, the library of Dubai Women's College, in Dubai, United Arab Emirates which is an English as a second language institution, uses the Big6 model for its information literacy workshops. According to Story-Huffman (2009), using Big6 at the college "has transcended cultural and physical boundaries to provide a knowledge base to help students become information literate" (para. 8). In primary grades, Big6 has been found to work well with variety of cognitive and language levels found in the classroom.

Differentiated instruction and the Big6 appear to be made for each other. While it seems as though all children will be on the same Big6 step at the same time during a unit of instruction, there is no reason students cannot work through steps at an individual pace. In addition, the Big 6 process allows for seamless differentiation by interest.

A number of weaknesses in the Big6 approach have been highlighted by Philip Doty:

This approach is problem-based, is designed to fit into the context of Benjamin Bloom's taxonomy of cognitive objectives, and aims toward the development of critical thinking. While the Big6 approach has a great deal of power, it also has serious weaknesses. Chief among these are the fact that users often lack well-formed statements of information needs, as well as the model's reliance on problem-solving rhetoric. Often, the need for information and its use are situated in circumstances that are not as well-defined, discrete, and monolithic as problems.

Eisenberg (2004) has recognized that there are a number of challenges to effectively applying the Big6 skills, not the least of which is information overload which can overwhelm students. Part of Eisenberg's solution is for schools to help students become discriminating users of information.

Another Conception

This conception, used primarily in the library and information studies field, and rooted in the concepts of library instruction and bibliographic instruction, is the ability "to recognize when information is needed and have the ability to locate, evaluate and use effectively the needed information". In this view, information literacy is the basis for lifelong learning.

In the publication Information power: Building partnerships for learning (AASL and AECT, 1998), three categories, nine standards, and twenty-nine indicators are used to describe the information literate student. The categories and their standards are as follows:

Category 1: Information Literacy

Standards:

1. The student who is information literate accesses information efficiently and effectively.

2. The student who is information literate evaluates information critically and competently.

3. The student who is information literate uses information accurately and creatively.

Category 2: Independent Learning

Standards:

1. The student who is an independent learner is information literate and pursues information related to personal interests.

2. The student who is an independent learner is information literate and appreciates literature and other creative expressions of information.

3. The student who is an independent learner is information literate and strives for excellence in information seeking and knowledge generation.

Category 3: Social Responsibility

Standards:

1. The student who contributes positively to the learning community and to society is information literate and recognizes the importance of information to a democratic society.

2. The student who contributes positively to the learning community and to society is information literate and practices ethical behavior in regard to information and information technology.

3. The student who contributes positively to the learning community and to society is information literate and participates effectively in groups to pursue and generate information.

Since information may be presented in a number of formats, the term "information" applies to more than just the printed word. Other literacies such as visual, media, computer, network, and basic literacies are implicit in information literacy.

Many of those who are in most need of information literacy are often amongst those least able to access the information they require:

Minority and at-risk students, illiterate adults, people with English as a second language, and economically disadvantaged people are among those most likely to lack access to the information that can improve their situations. Most are not even aware of the potential help that is available to them.

As the Presidential Committee report points out, members of these disadvantaged groups are often unaware that libraries can provide them with the access, training and information they need. In Osborne (2004), many libraries around the country are finding numerous ways to reach many of these disadvantaged groups by discovering their needs in their own environments (including prisons) and offering them specific services in the libraries themselves.

Effects on Education

The rapidly evolving information landscape has demonstrated a need for education methods and practices to evolve and adapt accordingly. Information literacy is a key focus of educational institutions at all levels and in order to uphold this standard, institutions are promoting a commitment to lifelong learning and an ability to seek out and identify innovations that will be needed to keep pace with or outpace changes.

Educational methods and practices, within our increasingly information-centric society, must facilitate and enhance a student's ability to harness the power of information. Key to harnessing the power of information is the ability to evaluate information, to ascertain among other things its relevance, authenticity and modernity. The information evaluation process is crucial life skill and a basis for lifelong learning. According to Lankshear and Knobel, what is needed in our education system is a new understanding of literacy, information literacy and on literacy teaching. Educators need to learn to account for the context of our culturally and linguistically diverse and increasingly globalized societies. We also need to take account for the burgeoning variety of text forms associated with information and multimedia technologies.

Evaluation consists of several component processes including metacognition, goals, personal disposition, cognitive development, deliberation, and decision-making. This is both a difficult and complex challenge and underscores the importance of being able to think critically.

Critical thinking is an important educational outcome for students. Education institutions have experimented with several strategies to help foster critical thinking, as a means to enhance information evaluation and information literacy among students. When evaluating evidence, students should be encouraged to practice formal argumentation. Debates and formal presentations must also be encouraged to analyze and critically evaluate information.

Education professionals must underscore the importance of high information quality. Students must be trained to distinguish between fact and opinion. They must be encouraged to use cue words such as "I think" and "I feel" to help distinguish between factual information and opinions. Information related skills that are complex or difficult to comprehend must be broken down into smaller parts. Another approach would be to train students in familiar contexts. Education professionals should encourage students to examine "causes" of behaviors, actions and events. Research shows that people evaluate more effectively if causes are revealed, where available.

Some call for increased critical analysis in Information Literacy instruction. Smith (2013) identifies this as beneficial "to individuals, particularly young people during their period of formal education. It could equip them with the skills they need to understand the political system and their place within it, and, where necessary, to challenge this" (p. 16).

Education in the US

Standards

National content standards, state standards, and information literacy skills terminology may vary, but all have common components relating to information literacy.

Information literacy skills are critical to several of the National Education Goals outlined in the Goals 2000: Educate America Act, particularly in the act's aims to increase "school readiness", "student achievement and citizenship", and "adult literacy and lifelong learning". Of specific relevance are the "focus on lifelong learning, the ability to think critically, and on the use of new and existing information for problem solving", all of which are important components of information literacy.

In 1998, the American Association of School Librarians and the Association for Educational Communications and Technology published "Information Literacy Standards for Student Learning", which identified nine standards that librarians and teachers in K-12 schools could use to describe information literate students and define the relationship of information literacy to independent learning and social responsibility:

- Standard One: The student who is information literate accesses information efficiently and effectively.

- Standard Two: The student who is information literate evaluates information critically and competently.

- Standard Three: The student who is information literate uses information accurately and creatively.

- Standard Four: The student who is an independent learner is information literate and pursues information related to personal interests.

- Standard Five: The student who is an independent learner is information literate and appreciates literature and other creative expressions of information.

- Standard Six: The student who is an independent learner is information literate and strives for excellence in information seeking and knowledge generation.

- Standard Seven: The student who contributes positively to the learning community and to society is information literate and recognizes the importance of information to a democratic society.

- Standard Eight: The student who contributes positively to the learning community and to society is information literate and practices ethical behavior in regard to information and information technology.

- Standard Nine: The student who contributes positively to the learning community and to society is information literate and participates effectively in groups to pursue and generate information.

In 2007 AASL expanded and restructured the standards that school librarians should strive for in their teaching. These were published as "Standards for the 21st Century Learner" and address several literacies: information, technology, visual, textual, and digital. These aspects of literacy were organized within four key goals: that "learners use of skills, resources, & tools" to "inquire, think critically, and gain knowledge"; to "draw conclusions, make informed decisions, apply knowledge to new situations, and create new knowledge"; to "share knowledge and participate ethically and productively as members of our democratic society"; and to "pursue personal and aesthetic growth".

In 2000, the Association of College and Research Libraries (ACRL), a division of the American Library Association (ALA), released "Information Literacy Competency Standards for Higher Education", describing five standards and numerous performance indicators considered best practices for the implementation and assessment of postsecondary information literacy programs. The five standards are:

- Standard One: The information literate student determines the nature and extent of the information needed.

- Standard Two: The information literate student accesses needed information effectively and efficiently.

- Standard Three: The information literate student evaluates information and its sources critically and incorporates selected information into his or her knowledge base and value system.

- Standard Four: The information literate student, individually or as a member of a group, uses information effectively to accomplish a specific purpose.

- Standard Five: The information literate student understands many of the economic, legal, and social issues surrounding the use of information and accesses and uses information ethically and legally.

These standards are meant to span from the simple to more complicated, or in terms of Bloom's Taxonomy of Educational Objectives, from the "lower order" to the "higher order". Lower order skills would involve for instance being able to use an online catalog to find a book relevant to an information need in an academic library. Higher order skills would involve critically evaluating and synthesizing information from multiple sources into a coherent interpretation or argument.

K-12 Education Restructuring

Today instruction methods have changed drastically from the mostly one-directional teacher-student model, to a more collaborative approach where the students themselves feel empowered. Much of this challenge is now being informed by the American Association of School Librarians that published new standards for student learning in 2007.

Within the K-12 environment, effective curriculum development is vital to imparting Information Literacy skills to students. Given the already heavy load on students, efforts must be made to avoid curriculum overload. Eisenberg strongly recommends adopting a collaborative approach to curriculum development among classroom teachers, librarians, technology teachers, and other educators. Staff must be encouraged to work together to analyze student curriculum needs, develop a broad instruction plan, set information literacy goals, and design specific unit and lesson plans that integrate the information skills and classroom content. These educators can also collaborate on teaching and assessment duties

Educators are selecting various forms of resource-based learning (authentic learning, problem-based learning and work-based learning) to help students focus on the process and to help students learn from the content. Information literacy skills are necessary components of each. Within a school setting, it is very important that a students' specific needs as well as the situational context be kept in mind when selecting topics for integrated information literacy skills instruction. The primary goal should be to provide frequent opportunities for students to learn and practice information problem solving. To this extent, it is also vital to facilitate repetition of information seeking actions and behavior. The importance of repetition in information literacy lesson plans cannot be underscored, since we tend to learn through repetition. A students' proficiency will improve over time if they are afforded regular opportunities to learn and to apply the skills they have learnt.

The process approach to education is requiring new forms of student assessment. Students demonstrate their skills, assess their own learning, and evaluate the processes by which this learning has been achieved by preparing portfolios, learning and research logs, and using rubrics.

Efforts in K-12 Education

Information literacy efforts are underway on individual, local, and regional bases.

Many states have either fully adopted AASL information literacy standards or have adapted them to suit their needs. States such as Oregon (OSLIS, 2009) increasing rely on these guidelines for curriculum development and setting information literacy goals. Virginia, on the other hand, chose to undertake a comprehensive review, involving all relevant stakeholders and formulate its own guidelines and standards for information literacy. At an international level, two framework documents jointly produced by UNESCO and the IFLA (International Federation of Library Associations and Institutions) developed two framework documents that laid the foundations in helping define the educational role to be played by school libraries: the School library manifesto (1999),.

Another immensely popular approach to imparting information literacy is the Big6 set of skills. Eisenberg claims that the Big6 is the most widely used model in K-12 education. This set of skills seeks to articulate the entire information seeking life cycle. The Big6 is made up of six major stages and two sub-stages under each major stages. It defines the six steps as being: task definition, information seeking strategies, location and access, use of information, synthesis, and evaluation. Such approaches seek to cover the full range of information problem-solving actions that a person would normally undertake, when faced with an information problem or with making a decision based on available resources.

Efforts in Higher Education

Information literacy instruction in higher education can take a variety of forms: stand-alone courses or classes, online tutorials, workbooks, course-related instruction, or course-integrated instruction. One attempt in the area of physics was published in 2009.

The six regional accreditation boards have added information literacy to their standards, Librarians often are required to teach the concepts of information literacy during "one shot" classroom lectures. There are also credit courses offered by academic librarians to prepare college students to become information literate.

Distance Education

Now that information literacy has become a part of the core curriculum at many post-secondary institutions, it is incumbent upon the library community to be able to provide information literacy instruction in a variety of formats, including online learning and distance education. The Association of College and Research Libraries (ACRL) addresses this need in its Guidelines for Distance Education Services (2000):

Library resources and services in institutions of higher education must meet the needs of all their faculty, students, and academic support staff, wherever these individuals are located, whether on a main campus, off campus, in distance education or extended campus programs—or in the absence of a campus at all, in courses taken for credit or non-credit; in continuing education programs; in courses attended in person or by means of electronic transmission; or any other means of distance education.

Within the e-learning and distance education worlds, providing effective information literacy programs brings together the challenges of both distance librarianship and instruction. With the prevalence of course management systems such as WebCT and Blackboard, library staff are embedding information literacy training within academic programs and within individual classes themselves.

Information Literacy Assessment Tools

- iCritical Thinking, former variation known as iSkills, and before that ICT Literacy Assessment, from the Educational Testing Service (ETS)

- Standardized Assessment of Information Literacy Skills (Project SAILS) developed and maintained at Kent State University in Ohio

- Information Literacy Test (ILT) developed collaboratively by the James Madison Center for Assessment and Research Studies and JMU libraries

- Research Readiness Self-Assessment (RRSA) from Central Michigan University originally designed by Lana V. Ivanitskaya, Ph.D. and Anne Marie Casey, A.M.L.S. and developed in collaboration with many of their colleagues.

- More Assessments of Information Literacy

- WASSAIL, an open-source assessment platform for storing questions and answers, producing tests, and generating reports.

Information Literacy Conferences

There are several national and international conferences dedicated to information literacy.

- European Conference on Information Literacy: ECIL held its first conference during October 2013 in Istanbul, Turkey.

- Georgia International Conference on Information Literacy: Annual conference on information literacy in Savannah, Georgia, bringing together P-20 librarians and faculty across the curriculum.

- IFLA World Library and Information Congress, Information Literacy Section: There is an annual satellite conference associated with the IFLA World Library and Information Congress organised by the IFLA Information Literacy Section.

- Information Literacy Summit: The annual Information Literacy Summit is held at Moraine Valley Community College in Palos Hills, IL.

- Librarians' Information Literacy Annual Conference: Within the UK, since 2005 there has been a Librarians' Information Literacy Annual Conference, or LILAC for short, organised by an Information Literacy Group that is now a special interest group of CILIP.

- LOEX conference: LOEX was founded in 1971 after the "First Annual Conference on Library Orientation" at Eastern Michigan University. The annual LOEX conference is the preeminent information literacy gathering in the United States.

References

- Section, edited by Jesús Lau ; IFLA Information Literacy (2008). Information literacy : international perspectives (2008. ed.). München: K.G. Saur. p. 23. ISBN 3598220375.

- Endrizzi, L. (April 2006). "Information Literacy". Lettre d'information n° 17. Institut Français de l'Éducation. Retrieved February 2, 2013.

- Squire, Kurt (2011). Video Games and Learning: Teaching and Participatory Culture in the Digital Age. New York: Teachers College Press.

- Lankshear, C., & Knobel, M. (2011). New literacies: Everyday practices & classroom learning (3rd ed.). pg. 255. New York: Open University Press and McGraw Hill.

- as proposed by Doug Belshaw at his 2011 Presentation to the Association of Independent Schools of New South Wales (Australia) ICT Managers Conference

- Prensky, Marc. "Digital Natives, Digital Immigrants" (PDF). On the Horizon. MCB University Press. Retrieved 30 November 2011.

8

Hypermedia and Streaming Media

An extension of the term hypertext, hypermedia refers to nonlinear media that includes things like graphics, audio, plain text and hyperlinks. The details included are hypermedia, its tools and their applications in the current scenario. This chapter discusses the methods of hypermedia in a critical manner, providing key analysis to the subject matter.

Hypermedia

Hypermedia, an extension of the term hypertext, is a nonlinear medium of information which includes graphics, audio, video, plain text and hyperlinks. This contrasts with the broader term *multimedia*, which may include non-interactive linear presentations as well as hypermedia. It is also related to the field of electronic literature. The term was first used in a 1965 article by Ted Nelson.

The World Wide Web is a classic example of hypermedia, whereas a non-interactive cinema presentation is an example of standard multimedia due to the absence of hyperlinks.

The first hypermedia work was, arguably, the Aspen Movie Map. Bill Atkinson's HyperCard popularized hypermedia writing, while a variety of literary hypertext and hypertext works, fiction and nonfiction, demonstrated the promise of links. Most modern hypermedia is delivered via electronic pages from a variety of systems including media players, web browsers, and stand-alone applications (i. e., software that does not require network access). Audio hypermedia is emerging with voice command devices and voice browsing.

Development Tools

Hypermedia may be developed a number of ways. Any programming tool can be used to write programs that link data from internal variables and nodes for external data files. Multimedia development software such as Adobe Flash, Adobe Director, Macromedia Authorware, and MatchWare Mediator may be used to create stand-alone hypermedia applications, with emphasis on entertainment content. Some database software such as Visual FoxPro and FileMaker Developer may be used to develop stand-alone hypermedia applications, with emphasis on educational and business content management.

Hypermedia applications may be developed on embedded devices for the mobile and the digital signage industries using the Scalable Vector Graphics (SVG) specification from W3C (World Wide Web Consortium). Software applications such as Ikivo Animator and Inkscape simplify the development of hypermedia content based on SVG. Embedded devices such as iPhone natively support SVG specifications and may be used to create mobile and distributed hypermedia applications.

Hyperlinks may also be added to data files using most business software via the limited scripting and hyperlinking features built in. Documentation software such as the Microsoft Office Suite and LibreOffice allow for hypertext links to other content within the same file, other external files, and URL links to files on external file servers. For more emphasis on graphics and page layout, hyperlinks may be added using most modern desktop publishing tools. This includes presentation programs, such as Microsoft Powerpoint and LibreOffice Impress, add-ons to print layout programs such as Quark Immedia, and tools to include hyperlinks in PDF documents such as Adobe InDesign for creating and Adobe Acrobat for editing. Hyper Publish is a tool specifically designed and optimized for hypermedia and hypertext management. Any HTML editor may be used to build HTML files, accessible by any web browser. CD/DVD authoring tools such as DVD Studio Pro may be used to hyperlink the content of DVDs for DVD players or web links when the disc is played on a personal computer connected to the internet.

Learning

There have been a number of theories concerning hypermedia and learning. One important claim in the literature on hypermedia and learning is that it offers more control over the instructional environment to the reader or student. Another claim is that it makes level the playing field among students of varying abilities and enhances collaborative learning. A claim from psychology includes the notion that hypermedia more closely models the structure of the brain, in comparison with printed text.

Language Learning

Hypermedia has found a place in foreign language instruction as well. Hypermedia reading texts can be purchased or prepared so that students can click on unfamiliar words or phrases in a foreign language and then access all the information needed to understand the word or phrase. Information can be in any medium, for example, text-based translations, definitions, grammatical explanations, and cultural references. Also, audio recordings of the pronunciation as well as images, animations and video for visualization. Some of the innovations in this area were the original products from Transparent Language as well as Ottmar Foelsche's Annotext and Thom Thibeault's hypermedia editor, FLAn.

Application Programming Interfaces

Hypermedia is used as a medium and constraint in certain application programming interfaces. HATEOAS, Hypermedia as the Engine of Application State, is a constraint of the REST application architecture where a client interacts with the server entirely through hypermedia provided dynamically by application servers. This means that in theory no API documentation is needed, because the client needs no prior knowledge about how to interact with any particular application or server beyond a generic understanding of hypermedia. In other service-oriented architectures (SOA), clients and servers interact through a fixed interface shared through documentation or an interface description language (IDL).

Cultural References

Hyperland is a 1990 documentary film that focuses on Douglas Adams and explains adaptive hypertext and hypermedia.

Streaming Media

A typical webcast, streaming in an embedded media player

A live stream from a camera pointed at a fish tank, Schou FishCam

Streaming media is multimedia that is constantly received by and presented to an end-user while being delivered by a provider. The verb "to stream" refers to the process of delivering media in this manner; the term refers to the delivery method of the medium, rather than the medium itself, and is an alternative to file downloading.

A client media player can begin to play the data (such as a movie) before the entire file has been transmitted. Distinguishing delivery method from the media distributed applies specifically to telecommunications networks, as most of the delivery systems are either inherently streaming (e.g. radio, television) or inherently nonstreaming (e.g. books, video cassettes, audio CDs). For example, in the 1930s, elevator music was among the earliest popularly available streaming media; nowadays Internet television is a common form of streamed media. The term "streaming media" can apply to media other than video and audio such as live closed captioning, ticker tape, and re-al-time text, which are all considered "streaming text". The term "streaming" was first used in the early 1990s as a better description for video on demand on IP networks; at the time such video was usually referred to as "store and forward video", which was misleading nomenclature.

As of 2016, streaming is generally taken to refer to cases where a user watches digital video content and/or listens to digital audio content on a computer screen and speakers (ranging from a desktop computer to a smartphone) over the Internet. With streaming content, the user does not have to download the entire digital video or digital audio file before they start to watch/listen to it. There are challenges with streaming content on the Internet. If the user does not have enough bandwidth in their Internet connection, they may experience stops in the content and some users may not be able to stream certain content due to not having compatible computer or software systems. As of 2016, popular streaming website include YouTube, which contains video and audio files on a huge range of topics and Netflix, which streams movies and TV shows.

Live streaming refers to Internet content delivered in real-time, as events happen, much as live television broadcasts its contents over the airwaves via a television signal. Live internet streaming requires a form of source media (e.g. a video camera, an audio interface, screen capture software), an encoder to digitize the content, a media publisher, and a content delivery network to distribute and deliver the content. Live streaming does not need to be recorded at the origination point, although it frequently is.

History

In the early 1920s, George O. Squier was granted patents for a system for the transmission and distribution of signals over electrical lines which was the technical basis for what later became *Muzak*, a technology streaming continuous music to commercial customers without the use of radio. Attempts to display media on computers date back to the earliest days of computing in the mid-20th century. However, little progress was made for several decades, primarily due to the high cost and limited capabilities of computer hardware. From the late 1980s through the 1990s, consumer-grade personal computers became powerful enough to display various media. The primary technical issues related to streaming were: having enough CPU power and bus bandwidth to support the required data rates and creating low-latency interrupt paths in the operating system to prevent buffer underrun and thus enable skip-free streaming of the content. However, computer networks were still limited in the mid-1990s, and audio and video media were usually delivered over non-streaming channels, such as by downloading a digital file from a remote server and then saving it to a local drive on the end user's computer or storing it as a digital file and playing it back from CD-ROMs.

Late 1990s-early 2000s

During the late 1990s and early 2000s, users had increased access to computer networks, especially the Internet, and especially during the early 2000s, users had access to increased network bandwidth, especially in the "last mile". These technological improvement facilitated the streaming of audio and video content to computer users in their homes and workplaces. As well, there was an increasing use of standard protocols and formats, such as TCP/IP, HTTP, HTML and the Internet became increasingly commercialized, which led to an infusion of investment into the sector. The band Severe Tire Damage was the first group to perform live on the Internet. On June 24, 1993, the band was playing a gig at Xerox PARC while elsewhere in the building, scientists were discussing new technology (the Mbone) for broadcasting on the Internet using multicasting. As proof of PARC's technology, the band's performance was broadcast and could be seen live in Australia and elsewhere.

Microsoft Research developed Microsoft TV application which was compiled under MS Windows Studio Suite and tested in conjunction with Connectix QuickCam. RealNetworks was also a pioneer in the streaming media markets, when it broadcast a baseball game between the New York Yankees and the Seattle Mariners over the Internet in 1995. The first symphonic concert on the Internet took place at the Paramount Theater in Seattle, Washington on November 10, 1995. The concert was a collaboration between The Seattle Symphony and various guest musicians such as Slash (Guns 'n Roses, Velvet Revolver), Matt Cameron (Soundgarden, Pearl Jam), and Barrett Martin (Screaming Trees). When *Word Magazine* launched in 1995, they featured the first-ever streaming soundtracks on the Internet. Using local downtown musicians the first music stream was "Big Wheel" by Karthik Swaminathan and the second being "When We Were Poor" by Karthik Swaminathan with Marc Ribot and Christine Bard.

Business Developments

Microsoft developed a media player known as ActiveMovie in 1995 that allowed streaming media and included a proprietary streaming format, which was the precursor to the streaming feature later in Windows Media Player 6.4 in 1999. In June 1999 Apple also introduced a streaming media format in its QuickTime 4 application. It was later also widely adopted on websites along with RealPlayer and Windows Media streaming formats. The competing formats on websites required each user to download the respective applications for streaming and resulted in many users having to have all three applications on their computer for general compatibility. Around 2002, the interest in a single, unified, streaming format and the widespread adoption of Adobe Flash prompted the development of a video streaming format through Flash, which is the format used in Flash-based players on many popular video hosting sites today such as YouTube. Increasing consumer demand for live streaming has prompted YouTube to implement a new live streaming service to users. Presently the company also offers a (secured) link returning the available connection speed of the user.

Consumerization

These advances in computer networking, combined with powerful home computers and modern operating systems, made streaming media practical and affordable for ordinary consumers. Stand-alone Internet radio devices emerged to offer listeners a no-computer option for listening to audio streams. These audio streaming services have become increasingly popular over recent years, as streaming music hit a record of 118.1 billion streams in 2013. In general, multimedia content has a large volume, so media storage and transmission costs are still significant. To offset this somewhat, media are generally compressed for both storage and streaming. Increasing consumer demand for streaming of high definition (HD) content has led the industry to develop a number of technologies such as WirelessHD or ITU-T G.hn, which are optimized for streaming HD content without forcing the user to install new networking cables. In 1996, digital pioneer Marc Scarpa produced the first large-scale, online, live broadcast in history, the Adam Yauch-led Tibetan Freedom Concert, an event that would define the format of social change broadcasts. Scarpa continued to pioneer in the streaming media world with projects such as Woodstock '99, Townhall with President Clinton, and more recently Covered CA's campaign "Tell a Friend Get Covered" which was live streamed on YouTube.

As of 2016, a media stream can be streamed either live or on demand. Live streams are generally provided by a means called "true streaming". True streaming sends the information straight to the computer or device without saving the file to a hard disk. On-demand streaming is provided by a means called *progressive streaming* or *progressive download*. Progressive streaming saves the file to a hard disk and then is played from that location. On-demand streams are often saved to hard disks and servers for extended amounts of time; while the live streams are only available at one time only (e.g., during the football game). Streaming media is increasingly being coupled with use of social media. For example, sites such as YouTube encourage social interaction in webcasts through features such as live chat, online surveys, and more. Furthermore, streaming media is increasingly being used for social business and e-learning. Due the popularity of the streaming medias, many developers have introduced free HD movie streaming apps for the people who use smaller devices such as tablets and smartphones for everyday need.

Bandwidth and Storage

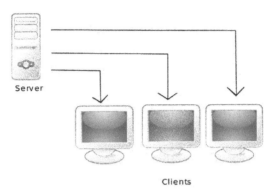

Clients

Unicast connections require multiple connections from the same streaming server even when it streams the same content

A broadband speed of 2 Mbit/s or more is recommended for streaming standard definition video without experiencing buffering or skips, especially live video, for example to a Roku, Apple TV, Google TV or a Sony TV Blu-ray Disc Player. 5 Mbit/s is recommended for High Definition content and 9 Mbit/s for Ultra-High Definition content. Streaming media storage size is calculated from the streaming bandwidth and length of the media using the following formula (for a single user and file) requires a storage size in megabytes which is equal to length (in seconds) × bit rate (in bit/s) / (8 × 1024 × 1024). For example, one hour of digital video encoded at 300 kbit/s (this was a typical broadband video in 2005 and it was usually encoded in a 320 × 240 pixels window size) will be: (3,600 s × 300,000 bit/s) / (8×1024×1024) requires around 128 MB of storage.

If the file is stored on a server for on-demand streaming and this stream is viewed by 1,000 people at the same time using a Unicast protocol, the requirement is 300 kbit/s × 1,000 = 300,000 kbit/s = 300 Mbit/s of bandwidth. This is equivalent to around 135 GB per hour. Using a multicast protocol the server sends out only a single stream that is common to all users. Therefore, such a stream would only use 300 kbit/s of serving bandwidth. for more information on these protocols. The calculation for live streaming is similar. Assuming that the seed at the encoder is 500 kbit/s and if the show lasts for 3 hours with 3,000 viewers, then the calculation is number of MBs transferred = encoder speed (in bit/s) × number of seconds × number of viewers / (8*1024*1024). The results of this calculation are as follows: number of MBs transferred = 500 x 1024 (bit/s) × 3 × 3,600 (= 3 hours) × 3,000 (number of viewers) / (8*1024*1024) = 1,977,539 MB

Protocols

The audio stream is compressed to make the file size smaller using an audio coding format such as MP3, Vorbis, AAC or Opus. The video stream is compressed using a video coding format to make the file size smaller. Video coding formats include H.264, HEVC, VP8 or VP9. Encoded audio and video streams are assembled in a container "bitstream" such as MP4, FLV, WebM, ASF or ISMA. The bitstream is delivered from a streaming server to a streaming client (e.g., the computer user with their Internet-connected laptop) using a transport protocol, such as Adobe's RTMP or RTP. In the 2010s, technologies such as Apple's HLS, Microsoft's Smooth Streaming, Adobe's HDS and non-proprietary formats such as MPEG-DASH have emerged to enable adaptive bitrate streaming over HTTP as an alternative to using proprietary transport protocols. Often, a streaming transport protocol is used to send video from an event venue to a "cloud" transcoding service and CDN, which then uses HTTP-based transport protocols to distribute the video to individual homes and users. The streaming client (the end user) may interact with the streaming server using a control protocol, such as MMS or RTSP.

Protocol Challenges

Designing a network protocol to support streaming media raises many problems. Datagram protocols, such as the User Datagram Protocol (UDP), send the media stream as a series of small packets. This is simple and efficient; however, there is no mechanism within the protocol to guarantee delivery. It is up to the receiving application to detect loss or corruption and recover data using error correction techniques. If data is lost, the stream may suffer a dropout. The Real-time Streaming Protocol (RTSP), Real-time Transport Protocol (RTP) and the Real-time Transport Control Protocol (RTCP) were specifically designed to stream media over networks. RTSP runs over a variety of transport protocols, while the latter two are built on top of UDP.

Another approach that seems to incorporate both the advantages of using a standard web protocol and the ability to be used for streaming even live content is adaptive bitrate streaming. HTTP adaptive bitrate streaming is based on HTTP progressive download, but contrary to the previous approach, here the files are very small, so that they can be compared to the streaming of packets, much like the case of using RTSP and RTP. Reliable protocols, such as the Transmission Control Protocol (TCP), guarantee correct delivery of each bit in the media stream. However, they accomplish this with a system of timeouts and retries, which makes them more complex to implement. It also means that when there is data loss on the network, the media stream stalls while the protocol handlers detect the loss and retransmit the missing data. Clients can minimize this effect by buffering data for display. While delay due to buffering is acceptable in video on demand scenarios, users of interactive applications such as video conferencing will experience a loss of fidelity if the delay caused by buffering exceeds 200 ms.

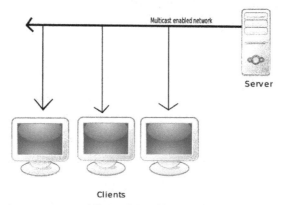

Multicasting broadcasts the same copy of the multimedia over the entire network to a group of clients

Unicast protocols send a separate copy of the media stream from the server to each recipient. Unicast is the norm for most Internet connections, but does not scale well when many users want to view the same television program concurrently. Multicast protocols were developed to reduce the server/network loads resulting from duplicate data streams that occur when many recipients receive unicast content streams independently. These protocols send a single stream from the source to a group of recipients. Depending on the network infrastructure and type, multicast transmission may or may not be feasible. One potential disadvantage of multicasting is the loss of video on demand functionality. Continuous streaming of radio or television material usually precludes the recipient's ability to control playback. However, this problem can be mitigated by elements such as caching servers, digital set-top boxes, and buffered media players.

IP Multicast provides a means to send a single media stream to a group of recipients on a computer network. A multicast protocol, usually Internet Group Management Protocol, is used to manage delivery of multicast streams to the groups of recipients on a LAN. One of the challenges in deploying IP multicast is that routers and firewalls between LANs must allow the passage of packets destined to multicast groups. If the organization that is serving the content has control over the network between server and recipients (i.e., educational, government, and corporate intranets), then routing protocols such as Protocol Independent Multicast can be used to deliver stream content to multiple Local Area Network segments. As in mass delivery of content, multicast protocols need much less energy and other resources, widespread introduction of reliable multicast (broadcast-like) protocols and their preferential use, wherever possible, is a significant ecological and economic challenge. Peer-to-peer (P2P) protocols arrange for prerecorded streams to be sent between computers. This prevents the server and its network connections from becoming a bottleneck. However, it raises technical, performance, security, quality, and business issues.

Applications and Marketing

Useful - and typical - applications of the "streaming" concept are, for example, long video lectures performed "online" on the Internet. An advantage of this presentation is that these lectures can be very long, indeed, although they can always be interrupted or repeated at arbitrary places. There are also new marketing concepts. For example, the Berlin Philharmonic Orchestra sells Internet live streams of whole concerts, instead of several CDs or similar fixed media, by their so-called "Digital Concert Hall" using YouTube for "trailing" purposes only. These "online concerts" are also spread over a lot of different places - cinemas - at various places on the globe. A similar concept is used by the Metropolitan Opera in New York. Many successful startup ventures have based their business on streaming media. Some of the most popular live streaming app services are Periscope, Stringwire, Meerkat, Hang w/ and Facebook.

Internet Radio

Internet radio (also web radio, net radio, streaming radio, e-radio, online radio, webcasting) is an audio service transmitted via the Internet. Broadcasting on the Internet is usually referred to as webcasting since it is not transmitted broadly through wireless means.

Internet radio involves streaming media, presenting listeners with a continuous stream of audio that typically cannot be paused or replayed, much like traditional broadcast media; in this respect, it is distinct from on-demand file serving. Internet radio is also distinct from podcasting, which involves downloading rather than streaming.

An Internet radio studio

Internet radio services offer news, sports, talk, and various genres of music—every format that is available on traditional broadcast radio stations. Many Internet radio services are associated with a corresponding traditional (terrestrial) radio station or radio network, although low start-up and ongoing costs have allowed a substantial proliferation of independent Internet-only radio stations.

Internet Radio Technology

Internet radio services are usually accessible from anywhere in the world with a suitable internet connection available; one could, for example, listen to an Australian station from Europe and America. This has made internet radio particularly suited to and popular among expatriate listeners. Nevertheless, some major networks like CBS Radio, Pandora Radio, and Citadel Broadcasting (except for news/talk and sports stations) in the United States, and Chrysalis in the United Kingdom, restrict listening to in-country due to music licensing and advertising issues.

Internet radio is also suited to listeners with special interests that are often not adequately served by local radio stations.

Listening

An early Kerbango Internet radio receiver

Internet radio is typically listened to on a standard home PC or similar device, through an embedded player program located on the respective station's website. In recent years, dedicated devices that resemble and offer the listener a similar experience to a traditional radio receiver have arrived on the market.

Streaming

Streaming technology is used to distribute Internet radio, typically using a lossy audio codec. Streaming audio formats include MP3, Ogg Vorbis, Windows Media Audio, RealAudio, and HE-AAC (or aacPlus). Audio data is continuously transmitted serially (streamed) over the local network or internet in TCP or UDP packets, then reassembled at the receiver and played a second or two later. The delay is called lag, and is introduced at several stages of digital audio broadcasting.

Simulation

A local tuner simulation program includes all the online radios that can also be heard in the air in the city.

Popularity

In 2003, revenue from online streaming music radio was US$49 million. By 2006, that figure rose to US$500 million. A February 21, 2007 "survey of 3,000 Americans released by consultancy Bridge Ratings & Research" found that "[a]s much as 19% of U.S. consumers 12 and older listen to Web-based radio stations." In other words, there were "some 57 million weekly listeners of Internet radio programs. More people listen to online radio than to satellite radio, high-definition radio, podcasts, or cell-phone-based radio combined." An April 2008 Arbitron survey showed that, in the US, more than one in seven persons aged 25–54 years old listen to online radio each week. In 2008, 13 percent of the American population listened to the radio online, compared to 11 percent in 2007. Internet radio functionality is also built into many dedicated Internet radio devices, which give an FM like receiver user experience.

In the fourth quarter (Q4) of 2012, Pandora and other subscription-based and free Internet radio services accounted for nearly one quarter (23 percent) of the average weekly music listening time among consumers between the ages of 13 and 35, an increase from a share of 17 percent the previous year.

As Internet-radio listening rose among the 13-to-35 age group, listening to AM/FM radio, which now accounts for 24 percent of music-listening time, declined 2 percentage points. In the 36-and-older age group, by contrast, Internet radio accounted for just 13 percent of music listening, while AM/FM radio dominated listening methods with a 41 percent share.

Currently, 47% of all Americans ages 12 and older -- an estimated 124 million people -- said they have listened to online radio in the last month, while 36% (94 million people) have listened in the last week. These figures are up from 45% and 33%, respectively, in 2013. The average amount of time spent listening increased from 11 hours, 56 minutes per week in 2013 to 13 hours 19 minutes in 2014. As might be expected, usage numbers are much higher for teens and younger adults, with 75% of Americans ages 12-24 listening to online radio in the last month, compared to 50% of Americans ages 25-54 and 21% of Americans 55+. The weekly figures for the same age groups were 64%, 37% and 13%, respectively.

History

Internet radio was pioneered by Carl Malamud. In 1993, Malamud launched "Internet Talk Radio" which was the "first computer-radio talk show, each week interviewing a computer expert.". The first Internet concert was broadcast on June 24, 1993 by the band Severe Tire Damage

In November 1994, a Rolling Stones concert was the "first major cyberspace multicast concert." Mick Jagger opened the concert by saying, "I want to say a special welcome to everyone that's, uh, climbed into the Internet tonight and, uh, has got into the M-bone. And I hope it doesn't all collapse."

On November 7, 1994, WXYC (89.3 FM Chapel Hill, NC USA) became the first traditional radio station to announce broadcasting on the Internet. WXYC used an FM radio connected to a system at SunSite, later known as Ibiblio, running Cornell's CU-SeeMe software. WXYC had begun test broadcasts and bandwidth testing as early as August 1994. WREK (91.1 FM, Atlanta, GA USA) started streaming on the same day using their own custom software called CyberRadio1. However, unlike WXYC, this was WREK's beta launch and the stream was not advertised until a later date.

Time magazine said that RealAudio took "advantage of the latest advances in digital compression" and delivered "AM radio-quality sound in so-called real time." Eventually, companies such as Nullsoft and Microsoft released streaming audio players as free downloads. As the software audio players became available, "many Web-based radio stations began springing up."

In 1995, Scott Bourne founded NetRadio.com as the world's first Internet-only radio network. NetRadio.com was a pioneer in Internet radio. It was the first Internet-only network to be licensed by ASCAP. NetRadio eventually went on to an IPO in October 1999. Most of the current Internet radio providers followed the path that NetRadio.com carved out in digital media.

In March 1996, Virgin Radio - London, became the first European radio station to broadcast its full program live on the internet. It broadcast its FM signal, live from the source, simultaneously on the Internet 24 hours a day.

Internet radio attracted significant media and investor attention in the late 1990s. In 1998, the initial public stock offering for Broadcast.com set a record at the time for the largest jump in price in stock offerings in the United States. The offering price was US$18 and the company's shares opened at US$68 on the first day of trading. The company was losing money at the time and indicated in a prospectus filed with the Securities Exchange Commission that they expected the losses to continue indefinitely. Yahoo! purchased Broadcast.com on July 20, 1999 for US$5.7 billion.

With the advent of streaming RealAudio over HTTP, streaming became more accessible to a number of radio shows. One such show, TechEdge Radio in 1997 was broadcast in 3 formats - live on the radio, live from a RealAudio server and streamed from the web over HTTP.

In 1998, the longest running internet radio show, "The Vinyl Lounge", commenced netcasting from Sydney, Australia, from Australia's first Internet Radio Station, NetFM (www.netfm.net). In 1999, Australian Telco "Telstra" launched The Basement Internet Radio Station but it was later shut down in 2003 as it was not a viable business for the Telco.

From 2000 onwards, most Internet Radio Stations increased their stream quality as bandwidth became more economical. Today, most stations stream between 64 kbit/s and 128 kbit/s providing near CD quality audio.

US Royalty Controversy

In October 1998, the US Congress passed the Digital Millennium Copyright Act (DMCA). One result of the DMCA is that performance royalties are to be paid for satellite radio and Internet radio broadcasts in addition to publishing royalties. In contrast, traditional radio broadcasters pay only publishing royalties and no performance royalties.

A rancorous dispute ensued over how performance royalties should be assessed for Internet broadcasters. Some observers said that royalty rates that were being proposed were overly burdensome and intended to disadvantage independent Internet-only stations—that "while Internet giants like AOL may be able to afford the new rates, many smaller Internet radio stations will have to shut down." The Digital Media Association (DiMA) said that even large companies, like Yahoo! Music, might fail due to the proposed rates. Some observers said that some U.S.-based Internet broadcasts might be moved to foreign jurisdictions where US royalties do not apply.

Many of these critics organized SaveNetRadio.org, "a coalition of listeners, artists, labels and webcasters" that opposed the proposed royalty rates. To focus attention on the consequences of the impending rate hike, many US Internet broadcasters participated in a "Day of Silence" on June 26, 2007. On that day, they shut off their audio streams or streamed ambient sound, sometimes interspersed with brief public service announcements voiced, written and produced by popular voiceover artist Dave Solomon. Notable participants included Rhapsody, Live365, MTV, Pandora, Digitally Imported and SHOUTcast.

Some broadcasters did not participate, such as Last.fm, that had just been purchased for US $280 million by CBS Music Group. According to a Last.fm employee, they were unable to participate because participation "may compromise ongoing license negotiations."

SoundExchange, representing supporters of the increase in royalty rates, pointed out the fact that the rates were flat from 1998 through 2005, without even being increased to reflect cost-of-living increases. They also declared that if internet radio is to build businesses from the product of recordings, the performers and owners of those recordings should receive fair compensation.

On May 1, 2007, SoundExchange came to an agreement with certain large webcasters regarding the minimum fees that were modified by the determination of the Copyright Royalty Board. While the CRB decision imposed a $500 per station or channel minimum fee for all webcasters, certain webcasters represented through DiMA negotiated a $50,000 "cap" on those fees with SoundExchange. However, DiMA and SoundExchange continue to negotiate over the per song, per listener fees.

SoundExchange has also offered alternative rates and terms to certain eligible small webcasters, that allows them to calculate their royalties as a percentage of their revenue or expenses, instead of at a per performance rate. To be eligible, a webcaster had to have revenues of less than US $1.25 million a year and stream less than 5 million "listener hours" a month (or an average of 6830 concurrent listeners). These restrictions would disqualify independent webcasters like AccuRadio,

Digitally Imported, Club977 and others from participating in the offer, and therefore many small commercial webcasters continue to negotiate a settlement with SoundExchange.

An August 16, 2008 *Washington Post* article reported that although Pandora was "one of the nation's most popular Web radio services, with about 1 million listeners daily...the burgeoning company may be on the verge of collapse" due to the structuring of performance royalty payment for webcasters. "Traditional radio, by contrast, pays no such fee. Satellite radio pays a fee but at a less onerous rate, at least by some measures." The article indicated that "other Web radio outfits" may be "doom[ed]" for the same reasons.

On September 30, 2008, the United States Congress passed "a bill that would put into effect any changes to the royalty rate to which [record labels and web casters] agree while lawmakers are out of session." Although royalty rates are expected to decrease, many webcasters nevertheless predict difficulties generating sufficient revenue to cover their royalty payments.

In January 2009, the US Copyright Royalty Board announced that "it will apply royalties to streaming net services based on revenue." Since then, websites like Pandora Radio, AccuRadio, Mog, 8tracks and even recently Google Music have changed the way people discover and listen to music.

The Webcaster Settlement Act of 2009 expired in January 2016, ending a 10-year period in which smaller online radio stations, Live365 among them, could pay reduced royalties to labels. On January 31, 2016, webcasters who are governed by rules adopted by the Copyright Royalty Board were required to pay to SoundExchange an annual, nonrefundable minimum fee of $500 for each channel and station. the fee for services with greater than 100 stations or channels being $50,000 annual.

Internet Television

Internet television (or online television) is the digital distribution of television content via the public Internet (which also carries other types of data), as opposed to dedicated terrestrial television via an aerial, cable television, and satellite television systems. It is also sometimes called web television, though this phrase is also used to describe the genre of TV shows broadcast only online.

Basic Elements

Internet television is a type of over-the-top content. The system that transmits content to the consumer has several elements:

- Content provider. This might be:

  o   An independent service, such as Netflix or Amazon Video, Google Play Movies, WhereverTV, myTV (Arabic), Viewster, or Qello (which specializes in concerts).

  o   A service owned by a traditional terrestrial, cable, or satellite provider, such as Sling TV (owned by Dish Network)

  o   A service owned by a traditional film or television network, television channel, or content conglomerate, such as BBC Three since 17 Jan 2016, CBSN, CNNGo, HBO Now, Now TV (UK) (owned by Sky), PlayStation Vue (owned by Sony), or Hulu (a joint venture)

- o A peer-to-peer video hosting service such as YouTube, Vimeo, or Crunchyroll

- o Combination services like TV UOL which combines a Brazilian Internet-only TV station with user-uploaded content, or Crackle, which combines content owned by Sony Pictures with user uploaded content

- o Audio-only services like Spotify, though not "Internet television" per se, are sometimes accessible through video-capable devices in the same way

- o Complete listings: List of Internet television providers, List of video hosting services

- The public Internet, used for transmission from the streaming servers to the consumer

- A receiver, which must have an Internet connection (typically by Wifi or Ethernet) and could be:

  - o A web browser running on a personal computer (typically controlled by computer mouse and keyboard) or mobile device, such as Firefox, Google Chrome, or Internet Explorer

  - o A mobile app running on a smartphone or tablet computer

  - o A dedicated digital media player, typically with remote control. These can take the form of a small box, or even a stick that plugs directly into an HDMI port. Examples include Roku, Amazon Fire, Apple TV, Google TV, Boxee, and WD TV. Sometimes these boxes allow streaming of content from the local network or storage drive, typically providing an indirect connection between a television and computer or USB stick

  - o A SmartTV which has Internet capability and built-in software accessed with the remote control

  - o A Video Game Console connected to the internet such as the Xbox One and PS4.

  - o A DVD player, Blu-ray player with Internet capabilities in addition to its primary function of playing content from physical discs

  - o A set-top box or digital video recorder provided by the cable or satellite company or an independent party like TiVo, which has Internet capabilities in addition to its primary function of receiving and recording programming from the non-Internet cable or satellite connection

- A display device, which could be:

  - o A television set or video projector linked to the receiver with a video connector (typically HDMI)

  - o A computer monitor

  - o The built-in display of a smartphone or tablet

Not all receivers can access all content providers. Most have web sites that allow viewing of content in a web browser, but sometimes this is not done due to digital rights management concerns. While a web browser has access to any web site, some consumers find it inconvenient to control with mouse and keyboard, inconvenient to connect a computer to their television, or confusing. Many providers have mobile apps dedicated to receive only their own content. Manufacturers of SmartTVs, boxes, sticks, and players must decide which providers to support, typically based either on popularity, common corporate ownership, or receiving payment from the provider.

Comparison with IPTV

As described above, "Internet television" is "over-the-top technology" (OTT). It is delivered through the open, unmanaged Internet, with the "last-mile" telecom company acting only as the Internet service provider. Both OTT and IPTV use the Internet protocol suite over a packet-switched network to transmit data, but IPTV operates in a closed system - a dedicated, managed network controlled by the local cable, satellite, telephone, or fiber company.

In its simplest form, IPTV simply replaces traditional circuit switched analog or digital television channels with digital channels which happen to use packet-switched transmission. In both the old and new systems, subscribers have set-top boxes or other customer-premises equipment that talks directly over company-owned or dedicated leased lines with central-office servers. Packets never travel over the public Internet, so the television provider can guarantee enough local bandwidth for each customer's needs.

The Internet Protocol is a cheap, standardized way to provide two-way communication and also address different data to different customers. This supports DVR-like features for time shifting television, for example to catch up on a TV show that was broadcast hours or days ago, or to replay the current TV show from its beginning. It also supports video on demand - browsing a catalog of videos (such as movies or syndicated television shows) which might be unrelated to the company's scheduled broadcasts.

IPTV has an ongoing standardization process (for example, at the European Telecommunications Standards Institute).

Comparison Tables

	IPTV	**Over-the-top technology**
Content provider	Local telecom	Studio, channel, or independent service
Transmission network	Local telecom - dedicated owned or leased network	Public Internet + local telecom
Receiver	Local telecom provides (set-top box)	Purchased by consumer (box, stick, TV, computer, or mobile)
Display device	Screen provided by consumer	Screen provided by consumer

	OTT (Over the Top Technology)	IPTV (Internet Protocol Television)
Examples	Popular Video on demand services like Sky Go, YouTube, Netflix, Amazon, YuppTV, Lovefilm, BBC iPlayer, Hulu, myTV, Now TV, WhereverTV, Emagine	Service Example includes U-verse (AT&T)
Protocol	Delivered using HTTP (TCP), a connected transport protocol. Emerging trends using adaptive streaming technologies like HLS (Apple), Smooth Streaming (Microsoft) and HDS (Adobe). Delivered content over UDP in combination with FEC	Traditional IPTV uses TS (transport stream) transmission technology. Delivers content over UDP in combination with FEC, connectionless protocol
Content Catalog	Widely used for freemium and economical VOD delivery models	Used primarily for premium content and real time content delivery like broadcasting TV
Routing Topology	Unicast (Based on HTTP) or Simulated Multicast (UDP/TCP)	Multicast, Unicast burst during channel change leading multicast join
Major Players	Huawei OTT solutions, Accenture, Piksel, OVP (Kaltura, Brightcove, Ooyala, Mobibase), CDN Players (Akamai, Level 3, Limelight, Octoshape, Tata Communications) and Content Aggregators	TSP and IPTV Platform vendors - Huawei, Accenture, Piksel, Microsoft Mediaroom (Ericsson), Alu, Cisco,ZTE
Key Challenges	Low quality, Non Premium Content No Live Broadcast, Unicast model	Expensive, Competition from Cable/ DTH industry, Bandwidth and Infrastructure
Key Benefits	Low cost, Flexibility of content consumption across devices	Interactive Service, Quality of Service and Quality of Experience

Technologies used for Internet Television

The Hybrid Broadcast Broadband TV (HbbTV) consortium of industry companies (such as SES, Humax, Philips, and ANT Software) is currently promoting and establishing an open European standard (called HbbTV) for hybrid set-top boxes for the reception of broadcast and broadband digital television and multimedia applications with a single-user interface.

Current providers of Internet television use various technologies to provide a service such as peer-to-peer (P2P) technologies, VoD systems, and live streaming. BBC iPlayer makes use of the Adobe Flash Player to provide streaming-video clips and other software provided by Adobe for its download service. CNBC, Bloomberg Television and Showtime use live-streaming services from BitGravity to stream live television to paid subscribers using the HTTP protocol. DRM (digital rights management) software is also incorporated into many Internet television services. Sky Go has software that is provided by Microsoft to prevent content being copied. Internet television is also cross platform, the Sky Player service has been expanded to the Xbox 360 on October 27 and to Windows Media Center and then to Windows 7 PCs on November 19. The BBC iPlayer is also available through Virgin Media's on-demand service and other platforms such as FetchTV and games consoles including the Wii and the PlayStation 3. Other Internet-television platforms include mobile platforms such as the iPhone and iPod Touch, Nokia N96, Sony Ericsson C905 and many other mobile devices.

Samsung TV has also announced their plans to provide streaming options including 3D Video on Demand through their Explore 3D service.

Stream Quality

Stream quality refers to the quality of the image and audio transferred from the servers of the distributor to the user's home screen.

Higher-quality video such as video in high definition (720p+) requires higher bandwidth and faster connection speeds. The generally accepted kbit/s download rate needed to stream high-definition video that has been encoded with H.264 is 3500 kbit/s, whereas standard-definition television can range from 500 to 1500 kbit/s depending on the resolution on screen.

In the UK, the BBC iPlayer deals with the largest amount of traffic yet it offers HD content along with SD content. As more people get broadband connections which can deal with streaming HD video over the Internet, the BBC iPlayer has tried to keep up with demand and pace. However, as streaming HD video takes around 1.5 gb of data per hour of video the BBC has had to invest a lot of money collected from License Fee payers to implement this on such a large scale.

For users which do not have the bandwidth to stream HD video or even high-SD video which requires 1500 kbit/s, the BBC iPlayer offers lower bitrate streams which in turn lead to lower video quality. This makes use of an adaptive bitrate stream so that if the user's bandwidth suddenly drops, iPlayer will lower its streaming rate to compensate.

This diagnostic tool offered on the BBC iPlayer site measures a user's streaming capabilities and bandwidth for free.

In last few years Channel 4 have started serving HD contents on its wide range of On Demand platform such as iOS App, Android App and Channel4.com website.

Although competitors in the UK such as Demand Five have not yet offered HD streaming, the technology to support it is fairly new and widespread HD streaming is not an impossibility. The availability of Channel 4 and Five content on YouTube is predicted to prove incredibly popular as series such as *Skins*, *Green Wing*, *The X Factor* and others become available in a simple, straightforward format on a website which already attracts millions of people every day.

Usage

Internet television is common in most US households as of the mid 2010s. About one in four new televisions being sold is now a smart TV. Considering the vast popularity of smart TVs and devices such as the Roku and Chromecast, much of the US public can watch television via the internet. Internet-only channels are now established enough to feature some Emmy-nominated shows, such as Netflix's *House of Cards*.

Many networks also distribute their shows the next day to streaming providers such as Hulu Some networks may use a proprietary system, such as the BBC utilizes their iPlayer format. This has resulted in bandwidth demands increasing to the point of causing issues for some networks. It was reported in February 2014 that Verizon is having issues coping with the demand placed on their network infrastructure. Until long term bandwidth issues are worked out and regulation such at net neutrality Internet Televisions push to HDTV may start to hinder growth.

Before 2006, most services used peer-to-peer (P2P) networking, in which users downloaded an application and data would be shared between the users rather than the service provider giving the now more commonly used streaming method. Now most service providers have moved away from the P2P systems and are now using the streaming media. The old P2P service was selected because the existing infrastructure could not handle the bandwidth necessary for centralized streaming distribution. Some consumers didn't like their upload bandwidth being consumed by their video player, which partially motivated the roll-out of centralized streaming distribution.

Launched in March 2012 in New York City (and subsequently stopped from broadcasting in June 2014), Aereo streamed network TV only to New York customers over the Internet. Broadcasters filed lawsuits against Aereo, because Aereo captured broadcast signals and streamed the content to Aereo's customers without paying broadcasters. In mid-July 2012, a federal judge sided with the Aereo start-up. Aereo planned to expand to every major metropolitan area by the end of 2013. The Supreme Court ruled against Aero June 24, 2014.

Market Competitors

Many providers of Internet television services exist including conventional television stations that have taken advantage of the Internet as a way to continue showing television shows after they have been broadcast often advertised as "on-demand" and "catch-up" services. Today, almost every major broadcaster around the world is operating an Internet television platform. Examples include the BBC, which introduced the BBC iPlayer on 25 June 2008 as an extension to its "RadioPlayer" and already existing streamed video-clip content, and Channel 4 that launched 4oD ("4 on Demand") (now All 4) in November 2006 allowing users to watch recently shown content. Most Internet television services allow users to view content free of charge; however, some content is for a fee.

Control

Controlling content on the Internet presents a challenge for most providers; to try to ensure that a user is allowed to view content such as content with age certificates, providers use methods such as parental controls that allows restrictions to be placed upon the use and access of certificated material. The BBC iPlayer makes use of a parental control system giving parents the option to "lock" content, meaning that a password would have to be used to access it. Flagging systems can be used to warn a user that content may be certified or that it is intended for viewing post-watershed. Honour systems are also used where users are asked for their dates of birth or age to verify if they are able to view certain content.

Archives

An archive is a collection of information and media much like a library or interactive-storage facility. It is a necessity for an on-demand media service to maintain archives so that users can watch content that has already been aired on standard-broadcast television. However, these archives can vary from a few weeks to months to years, depending on the curator and the type of content.

For example, the BBC iPlayer's shows are in general available for up to seven days after their original broadcast. This so-called "seven-day catch-up" model seems to become an industry standard for Internet television services in many countries around the world. However, some shows may only be available for shorter periods. Others, such as the BBC's Panorama, may be available for an extended period because of the show's documentary nature or its popularity.

In contrast, All 4, Channel 4's on-demand service offers many of its television shows that were originally aired years ago. An example of this is the comedy *The IT Crowd* where users can view the full series on the Internet player. The same is true for other hit Channel 4 comedies such as *The Inbetweeners* and *Black Books*.

The benefit of large archives, is that they bring in far more users who, in turn, watch more media, leading to a wider audience base and more advertising revenue. Large archives will also mean the user will spend more time on that website rather than a competitors, leading to starvation of demand for the competitors.

Having an extensive archive, however, can bring problems along with benefits. Large archives are expensive to maintain, server farms and mass storage is needed along with ample bandwidth to transmit it all. Vast archives can be hard to catalogue and sort so that it is accessible to users.

Broadcasting Rights

Broadcasting rights vary from country to country and even within provinces of countries. These rights govern the distribution of copyrighted content and media and allow the sole distribution of that content at any one time.

An example of content only being aired in certain countries is BBC iPlayer. The BBC checks a user's IP address to make sure that only users located in the UK can stream content from the BBC. The BBC only allows free use of their product for users within the UK as those users have paid for a television license that funds part of the BBC. This IP address check is not foolproof as the user may be accessing the BBC website through a VPN or proxy server.

Broadcasting rights can also be restricted to allowing a broadcaster rights to distribute that content for a limited time. Channel 4's online service All 4 can only stream shows created in the US by companies such as HBO for thirty days after they are aired on one of the Channel 4 group channels. This is to boost DVD sales for the companies who produce that media.

Some companies pay very large amounts for broadcasting rights with sports and US sitcoms usually fetching the highest price from UK-based broadcasters.

An increasing trend among major content producers in North America is the use of the TV Everywhere system. Especially for live content, the TV Everywhere system restricts viewership of a video feed to select Internet service providers, usually cable television companies that pay a retransmission consent or subscription fee to the content producer. This often has the negative effect of making the availability of content dependent upon the provider, with the consumer having little or no choice on whether they receive the product.

Profits and Costs

With the advent of broadband internet Connections multiple streaming providers have come onto the market in the last couple of years. The main providers are Netflix, Hulu and Amazon. Some of these providers such as Hulu adverstise and charge a monthly fee. Other such as netflix and amazon charge a monthly fee and have no commercials. Netflix is the largest provider with over 43 million members and growing. The rise of internet TV has resulted in Cable Companies losing customer to a new kind of customer called "Cord Cutters" these cord cutters are forming communities and proving a solid alternative to cable and satellite television. Most of the cable cutters are younger and have opted to not sign up for traditional cable service.

Overview of Platforms and Availability

Service	Supporting company/companies	Regional availability	Website-based	Windows application	Mac application	Linux application	iOS application	Android application	Console application	TV set application	Set Top Box application	Free
WhereverTV	WhereverTV, Al-Iraqiya, Al Jazeera – English, Al Maghribia, Al Mayadeen, Al Qurann Al Kareem TV, Al Sunnah Al Nabawiyah TV, Alalam News, Canal Algerie, ERT World, GO TelecomTV, iFilm-Arabic, Jordan TV, Mega Cosmos, 2M Maroc, Oman TV, Qatar TV, Reelkandi.tv, RIK Sat, Saudi Arabia TV 1, Skai TV, Star International, Sudan TV, Syria Drama, Syria Satellite Channel, TV Tunisia 1, Yemen TV	North America, South America, Europe, Australia, Worldwide/International	Yes	Yes	Yes	No	Yes	Yes	Yes	Samsung, Sony, Panasonic, Philips, Vizio	Google TV, AppleTV (via Airplay), Boxee, Roku, etc.	No
BBC iPlayer	BBC	UK	Yes	Yes	Yes	Yes	Yes	Yes	Wii, PS3, Xbox 360	Samsung, Sony, Panasonic, Philips	Virgin Media On Demand, Freesat, Roku	Yes
NBC	NBC		Yes	No	No	No	Yes	Yes	PS3, Xbox 360			Yes
Tivibu	Argela	TR	Yes	Yes	Yes		Yes	Argela Android Player	Pending	None	Ttnet on Demand	No
Sky Go	Sky	UK & Ireland	Yes	Yes	Yes		Yes	Yes	Xbox 360			No
ITV Hub	ITV	UK	Yes	Yes	Yes	Yes	Yes	Yes	PS3		Virgin Media On Demand	Yes
ABC iview	Australian Broadcasting Corporation	Australia	Yes				iPad		PS3, Xbox 360	Samsung, Sony		Yes
All 4	Channel 4	UK & Ireland	Yes	Yes	Yes		Yes	Yes	PS3, Xbox 360		Virgin Media On Demand	Yes
SeeSaw	Arqiva	UK	Yes	Yes	Yes							No

Hulu	FOX, NBC Universal, ABC,...	US & Japan	Yes	Yes	Yes	Yes	Yes		PS3, Xbox 360	Samsung, Vizio	Roku	No
RTÉ Player	RTÉ	Ireland	Yes				Yes	Yes				Yes
TG4 Beo	TG4	Ireland and World-wide/ Interna-tional	Yes									Yes
TV3 Catch Up	TV3	Ireland	Yes				Yes					Yes
Global Video	Global	Canada	Yes				Yes					No
Global Video	SBNTV1, The Sumlin Broadcasting Network, Classic Soul Channel.....	US	Yes	Yes	Yes	Yes	Yes		PS3, Xbox 360	Samsung, Vizio		Yes
myTV	OSN, Rotana Group, SNA Corp.....	North America, Canada, South America, New Zealand, Australia	No	Not Yet	Not Yet	No	Yes	Yes	Not Yet	Samsung Smart TV, LG Smart TV, Google TV	Western Digital, Boxee Box, Netgear NTV 300, Google TV devices, Samsung and Android tablets	No
PTCL Smart TV App	PTCL	Pakistan	Yes	Yes	No	No	Yes	Yes	No	None	Stand-alone PTCL Smart Settop Box	No

Smart TV

A smart TV, sometimes referred to as connected TV or hybrid TV, is a television set or set-top box with integrated Internet and interactive "Web 2.0" features. Smart TV is a technological convergence between computers and flatscreen television sets and set-top boxes. Besides the traditional functions of television sets and set-top boxes provided through traditional broadcasting media, these devices can also provide Internet TV, online interactive media, over-the-top content (OTT), as well as on-demand streaming media, and home networking access.

Smart TV should not be confused with Internet TV, IPTV or with Web TV. Internet TV refers to receiving television content over the Internet instead of traditional systems (terrestrial, cable and satellite) (although Internet itself is received by these methods). Internet Protocol television

(IPTV) is one of the Internet television technology standards for use by television broadcasters. Web television is a term used for programs created by a wide variety of companies and individuals for broadcast on Internet TV.

A smart TV displaying content from a museum website; unlike traditional TVs, a smart TV enables the viewer to interact with icons or images on the screen. For example, on a museum website, viewers can "click" on items depicted onscreen to learn more about them.

In smart TVs, the operating system is preloaded or is available through the set-top box. The software applications or "apps" can be preloaded into the device, or updated or installed on demand via an app store or app marketplace, in a similar manner to how the apps are integrated in modern smartphones.

The technology that enables smart TVs is also incorporated in external devices such as set-top boxes and some Blu-ray players, game consoles, digital media players, hotel television systems and smartphones and other network-connected interactive devices that utilize television-type display outputs. These devices allow viewers to search, find and play videos, movies, TV shows, photos and other content from the Web, on a cable TV channel, on a satellite TV channel, or on a local storage drive.

Background

A first patent was published in 1994 (and extended the following year) for an "intelligent" television system, linked with data processing systems, by means of a digital or analog network. Apart from being linked to data networks, one key point is its ability to automatically download necessary software routines, according to a user's demand, and process their needs. The mass acceptance of digital television in late 2000s and early 2010s greatly improved smart TVs. Major TV manufacturers have announced production of smart TVs only, for their middle-end to high-end TVs in 2015. Smart TVs are expected to become the dominant form of television by the late 2010s. At the beginning of 2016, Nielsen reported that 29 percent of those with incomes over $75,000 a year had a smart TV.

Definition

A *smart TV* device is either a television set with integrated Internet capabilities or a set-top box for television that offers more advanced computing ability and connectivity than a contemporary basic television set. Smart TVs may be thought of as an information appliance or the computer system from a handheld computer integrated within a television set unit, as such smart TV often allows the user to install and run more advanced applications or plugins/addons based on a specific platform. Smart TVs run complete operating system or mobile operating system software providing a platform for application developers.

Smart TVs on display

Smart TV platforms or middleware have a public Software development kit (SDK) and/or Native development kit (NDK) for apps so that third-party developers can develop applications for it, and an app store so that the end-users can install and uninstall apps themselves. The public SDK enables third-party companies and other interactive application developers to "write" applications once and see them run successfully on any device that supports the smart TV platform or middleware architecture which it was written for, no matter who the hardware manufacturer.

Smart TVs deliver content (such as photos, movies and music) from other computers or network attached storage devices on a network using either a Digital Living Network Alliance / Universal Plug and Play media server or similar service program like Windows Media Player or Network-attached storage (NAS), or via iTunes. It also provides access to Internet-based services including traditional broadcast TV channels, catch-up services, video-on-demand (VOD), electronic program guide, interactive advertising, personalisation, voting, games, social networking, and other multimedia applications.

Functions

Smart TV devices also provide access to user-generated content (either stored on an external hard drive or in cloud storage) and to interactive services and Internet applications, such as YouTube, many using HTTP Live Streaming (also known as HLS) adaptive streaming. Smart TV devices facilitate the curation of traditional content by combining information from the Internet with content from TV Providers. Services offer users a means to track and receive reminders about shows or sporting events, as well as the ability to change channels for immediate viewing. Some devices feature additional interactive organic user interface / natural user interface technologies for navigation controls and other human interaction with a Smart TV, with such as second screen companion devices, spatial gestures input like with Xbox Kinect, and even for speech recognition for natural language user interface.

Technology

Platforms

Smart TV technology and software is still evolving, with both proprietary and open source software frameworks already available. These can run applications (sometimes available via an 'app store' digital distribution platform), interactive on-demand media, personalized communications, and have social networking features.

Social Networking

Some smart TV platforms come prepackaged, or can be optionally extended, with social networking technology capabilities. The addition of social networking synchronization to smart TV and HTPC platforms may provide an interaction with both on-screen content and other viewers than is currently available to most televisions, while simultaneously providing a much more cinematic experience of the content than is currently available with most computers.

Advertising

Some smart TV platforms also support interactive advertising, addressable advertising with local advertising insertion and targeted advertising, and other advanced advertising features such as ad telescoping using VOD and DVR, enhanced TV for consumer call-to-action and audience measurement solutions for ad campaign effectiveness. The marketing and trading possibilities offered by Smart TVs are sometimes summarized by the term t-commerce. Taken together, this bidirectional data flow means that smart TVs can be and are used for clandestine observation of the owners. Even in sets that are not configured off-the-shelf to do so, default security measures are often weak and will allow hackers to easily break into the TV.

Security and Privacy

There is evidence that a smart TV is vulnerable to attacks. Some serious security bugs have been discovered, and some successful attempts to run malicious code to get unauthorized access were documented on video. There is evidence that it is possible to gain root access to the device, install malicious software, access and modify configuration information for a remote control, remotely access and modify files on TV and attached USB drives, access camera and microphone. There have also been concerns that hackers may be able to remotely turn on the microphone on a smart TV and be able to eavesdrop on private conversations.

Anticipating growing demand for an antivirus for a smart TV, some security software companies are already working with partners in digital TV field on the solution. At this moment it seems like there is only one antivirus for smart TVs available. Ocean Blue Software partnered with Sophos and developed first cloud based antimalware system "Neptune". Also antivirus company Avira has joined forces with digital TV testing company Labwise to work on the software that would protect against potential attacks. The privacy policy for Samsung's Smart TVs has been called Orwellian (a reference to George Orwell and the dystopian world of constant surveillance he depicted in *1984*), and compared to Telescreens because of eavesdropping concerns. Samsung introduced GAIA, a security system for smart TV. GAIA will be included in all 2016 smart TV line-up.

Restriction of Access

Internet websites can block smart TV access to content at will, or tailor the content that will be received by each platform. Google TV-enabled devices were blocked by NBC, ABC, CBS, and Hulu from accessing their Web content since the launch of Google TV in October 2010. Google TV devices were also blocked from accessing any programs offered by Viacom's subsidiaries.

Market Share

According to a report from the researcher NPD In-Stat, only about 12 million U.S. households have their Web-capable TVs connected to the Internet, although In-Stat estimates about 25 million U.S. TV households own a set with the built-in network capability. Also, In-Stat predicts that 100 million homes in North America and western Europe will own television sets that blend traditional programs with internet content by 2016.

References

- Hoeg, Wolfgang; Lauterbach, Thomas (2009). Digital audio broadcasting: principles and applications of DAB, DAB+ and DMB. Wiley. p. 26. ISBN 978-0-470-51037-7.

- Savetz, K., Randall, N., and Lepage, Y., "MBONE: Multicasting Tomorrow's Internet" (in the Musical Events section: "Severe Tire Damage was the first live band on the Internet. On June 24, 1993"), John Wiley, 1996, ISBN 1-56884-723-8

- Dominguez, Robert (February 18, 2014). "'House of Cards' season 2 sees surge of Netflix viewers over first season". NY Daily News. Retrieved July 2, 2016.

- Niemietz; et al. "Not so Smart: On Smart TV Apps" (PDF). International Workshop on Secure Internet of Things. Retrieved 15 September 2015.

- "Streaming the London Olympic Games with the "Go Live Package" from iStreamPlanet and Haivision | iStreamPlanet". www.istreamplanet.com. Retrieved 2015-11-11.

- Stockment, Andrew (December 2009). "Internet Radio: The Case for a Technology Neutral Royalty Standard". Virginia Law Review. Retrieved October 6, 2013.

- Broache, Anne (April 26, 2007). "Lawmakers propose reversal of Net radio fee increases". CNet News. Archived from the original on January 19, 2013. Retrieved March 14, 2010.

- Narang, Nitin. "Concept Series : What is the Difference between OTT and IPTV". Researcher on TV technology. Media Entertainment Info. Retrieved 4 September 2013.

- Jeremy Toeman 41 (October 20, 2010). "Why Connected TVs Will Be About the Content, Not the Apps". Mashable.com. Retrieved January 17, 2012.

- Chacksfield, Marc (May 12, 2010). "Intel: Smart TV revolution 'biggest since move to colour' – The wonders of widgets?". Techradar.com. Retrieved January 17, 2012.

- Previous post Next post (September 7, 2010). "Android Holds the Key to Samsung's Smart TV Plans". Wired. Retrieved January 17, 2012.

- "Thuuz Android App for Google TV Gives DISH Customers Instant Alerts of Most Exciting Moments in Sports". Bloomberg. January 8, 2012. Retrieved July 12, 2012.

- Narcisse, Evan (2011-12-08). "Wave Hello: Microsoft's Requiring Kinect Functionality for All Future Apps Built for Xbox 360". Kotaku.com. Retrieved 2012-03-12.

- "Opinion: Will Google's Smart TV Finally Bring Apps and Web Browsing To The Living Room?". Socialtimes.com. May 17, 2010. Retrieved January 17, 2012.

9

Mobile Media: A Comprehensive Study

The cellphone has made possible the mobility of media in which a consumer is able to access media on mobile devices and this has helped change the field of information and communication. This chapter explores the various technologies that have made information and media portable. The content deals extensively with topics like multimedia messaging service (MMS) and multimedia database. It will give a detailed explanation of mobile media technologies.

Mobile Media

Mobility and portability of media, or as Paul Levinson calls it in his book *Cellphone*, "the media-in-motion business" has been a process in the works ever since the "first time someone thought to write on a tablet that could be lifted and hauled – rather than on a cave wall, a cliff face, a monument that usually was stuck in place, more or less forever". For a time, mobile media devices such as mobile phones and PDA's were the primary source of portable media from which we could obtain information and communicate with one another. More recently, the smartphone (which has combined many features of the cell phone with the PDA) has rendered the PDA obsolete. The growth of new mobile media as a true force in society was marked by smartphone sales outpacing personal computer sales in 2011.

While mobile phone independent technologies and functions may be new and innovative (in relation to changes and improvements in media capabilities in respect to their function what they can do when and where and what they look like, in regard to their size and shape) the need and desire to access and use media devices regardless of where we are in the world has been around for centuries. Indeed Paul Levinson remarks in regard to telephonic communication that it was "intelligence and inventiveness" applied to our need to communicate regardless of where we may be, led logically and eventually to telephones that we carry in our pockets". Levinson in his book goes on to state that the book, transistor radio, Kodak camera are also bearers of portable information. And that it is thanks to the printing press that information became available to a mass audience, the reduction in size and portability of the camera allowed people to capture what they saw no matter where they were and the Internet meant that people could talk to anyone and use on demand information.

Smartphones consume much of our daily lives. These devices and their corresponding media technologies, particularly cloud-based technologies, play an increasingly important role in the everyday lives of millions of people world wide. Media can be downloaded onto the device by podcasting or can be streamed over the internet.

Multimedia Messaging Service

Multimedia Messaging Service (MMS) is a standard way to send messages that include multimedia content to and from mobile phones over a cellular network. Users and providers may refer to such a message as a PXT, a picture message, or a multimedia message. The MMS standard extends the core SMS (Short Message Service) capability, allowing the exchange of text messages greater than 160 characters in length. Unlike text-only SMS, MMS can deliver a variety of media, including up to forty seconds of video, one image, a slideshow of multiple images, or audio.

The most common use involves sending photographs from camera-equipped handsets. Media companies have utilized MMS on a commercial basis as a method of delivering news and entertainment content, and retailers have deployed it as a tool for delivering scannable coupon codes, product images, videos, and other information.

The 3GPP and WAP groups fostered the development of the MMS standard, which is now continued by the Open Mobile Alliance (OMA).

History

Multimedia messaging services were first developed as a captive technology which enabled service providers to "collect a fee every time anyone snaps a photo."

Early MMS deployments were plagued by technical issues and frequent consumer disappointments. In recent years, MMS deployment by major technology companies have solved many of the early challenges through handset detection, content optimization, and increased throughput.

China was one of the early markets to make MMS a major commercial success, partly as the penetration rate of personal computers was modest but MMS-capable camera phones spread rapidly. The chairman and CEO of China Mobile said at the GSM Association Mobile Asia Congress in 2009 that MMS in China was now a mature service on par with SMS text messaging.

Europe's most advanced MMS market has been Norway, and in 2008, the Norwegian MMS usage level passed 84% of all mobile phone subscribers. Norwegian mobile subscribers sent on average one MMS per week.

Between 2010 and 2013, MMS traffic in the U.S. increased by 70% from 57 billion to 96 billion messages sent. This is due in part to the wide adoption of smartphones.

Technical Description

MMS messages are delivered in a different way from SMS. The first step is for the sending device to encode the multimedia content in a fashion similar to sending a MIME message (MIME content formats are defined in the MMS Message Encapsulation specification). The message is then forwarded to the carrier's MMS store and forward server, known as the MMSC (Multimedia Messaging Service Centre). If the receiver is on a carrier different from the sender, then the MMSC acts as a relay, and forwards the message to the MMSC of the recipient's carrier using the internet.

Once the recipient's MMSC has received a message, it first determines whether the receiver's handset is "MMS capable", that it supports the standards for receiving MMS. If so, the content is extracted and sent to a temporary storage server with an HTTP front-end. An SMS "control message" containing the URL of the content is then sent to the recipient's handset to trigger the receiver's WAP browser to open and receive the content from the embedded URL. Several other messages are exchanged to indicate the status of the delivery attempt. Before delivering content, some MMSCs also include a conversion service that will attempt to modify the multimedia content into a format suitable for the receiver. This is known as "content adaptation".

If the receiver's handset is not MMS capable, the message is usually delivered to a web-based service from where the content can be viewed from a normal internet browser. The URL for the content is usually sent to the receiver's phone in a normal text message. This behavior is usually known as a "legacy experience" since content can still be received by a phone number, even if the phone itself does not support MMS.

The method for determining whether a handset is MMS capable is not specified by the standards. A database is usually maintained by the operator, and in it each mobile phone number is marked as being associated with a legacy handset or not. This method is unreliable, however, because customers can independently change their handsets, and many of these databases are not updated dynamically.

MMS does not utilize operator-maintained "data" plans to distribute multimedia content, which is only used if the operator clicks links inside the message.

E-mail and web-based gateways to the MMS system are common. On the reception side, the content servers can typically receive service requests both from WAP and normal HTTP browsers, so delivery via the web is simple. For sending from external sources to handsets, most carriers allow a MIME encoded message to be sent to the receiver's phone number using a special e-mail address combining the recipient's public phone number and a special domain name, which is typically carrier-specific.

Challenges

There are some interesting challenges with MMS that do not exist with SMS:

Handset configuration can cause problems sending and receiving MMS messages.

- Content adaptation: Multimedia content created by one brand of MMS phone may not be entirely compatible with the capabilities of the recipient's MMS phone. In the MMS architecture, the recipient MMSC is responsible for providing for *content adaptation* (e.g., image resizing, audio codec transcoding, etc.), if this feature is enabled by the mobile network operator. When content adaptation is supported by a network operator, its MMS subscribers enjoy compatibility with a larger network of MMS users than would otherwise be available.

- Distribution lists: Current MMS specifications do not include distribution lists nor methods by which large numbers of recipients can be conveniently addressed, particularly by content providers, called *Value-added service providers* (VASPs) in 3GPP. Since most SMSC vendors have adopted FTP as an ad-hoc method by which large distribution lists are transferred to the SMSC prior to being used in a bulk-messaging SMS submission, it is expected that MMSC vendors will also adopt FTP.

- Bulk messaging: The flow of *peer-to-peer* MMS messaging involves several over-the-air transactions that become inefficient when MMS is used to send messages to large numbers of subscribers, as is typically the case for VASPs. For example, when one MMS message is submitted to a very large number of recipients, it is possible to receive a *delivery report* and *read-reply report* for each and every recipient. Future MMS specification work is likely to optimize and reduce the transactional overhead for the bulk-messaging case.

- Handset Configuration: Unlike SMS, MMS requires a number of handset parameters to be set. Poor handset configuration is often blamed as the first point of failure for many users. Service settings are sometimes preconfigured on the handset, but mobile operators are now looking at new device management technologies as a means of delivering the necessary settings for data services (MMS, WAP, etc.) via over-the-air programming (OTA).

- WAP Push: Few mobile network operators offer direct connectivity to their MMSCs for content providers. This has resulted in many content providers using WAP push as the only method available to deliver 'rich content' to mobile handsets. WAP push enables 'rich content' to be delivered to a handset by specifying the URL (via binary SMS) of a pre-compiled MMS, hosted on a content provider's Web server. A consequence is that the receiver who pays WAP per kb or minute (as opposed to a flat monthly fee) pays for receiving the MMS, as opposed to only paying for sending one, and also paying a different rate.

Although the standard does not specify a maximum size for a message, 300 kB is the current recommended size used by networks due to some limitations on the WAP gateway side.

Interfaces

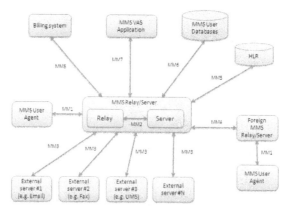

MMSC Reference Architecture

- MM1: the 3GPP interface between MMS User Agent and MMS Center (MMSC, the combination of the MMS Relay & Server)

- MM2: the 3GPP interface between MMS Relay and MMS Server

- MM3: the 3GPP interface between MMSC and external servers

- MM4: the 3GPP interface between different MMSCs

- MM5: the 3GPP interface between MMSC and HLR

- MM6: the 3GPP interface between MMSC and user databases

- MM7: the 3GPP interface between MMS VAS applications and MMSC

- MM8: the 3GPP interface between MMSC and the billing systems

- MM9: the 3GPP interface between MMSC and an online charging system

- MM10: the 3GPP interface between MMSC and a message service control function

- MM11: the 3GPP interface between MMSC and an external transcoder

Multimedia Database

A Multimedia database (MMDB) is a collection of related multimedia data. The multimedia data include one or more primary media data types such as text, images, graphic objects (including drawings, sketches and illustrations) animation sequences, audio and video.

A Multimedia Database Management System (MMDBMS) is a framework that manages different types of data potentially represented in a wide diversity of formats on a wide array of media sources. It provides support for multimedia data types, and facilitate for creation, storage, access, query and control of a multimedia database.

Contents of MMDB

A Multimedia Database (MMDB) hosts one or more multimedia data types (i.e. text, images, graphic objects, audio, video, animation sequences. These data types are broadly categorized into *three classes*:

- Static media (time-independent: image and graphic object).

- Dynamic media (time-dependent: audio, video and animation).

- Dimensional media(3D game and computer aided drafting programs).

Comparison of Multimedia Data Types

Medium	Elements	Time-dependence
Text	Printable characters	No
Graphic	Vectors, regions	No

Image	Pixels	No
Audio	Sound, Volume	Yes
Video	Raster images, graphics	Yes

Additionally, a Multimedia Database (MMDB) needs to manage additional information pertaining to the actual multimedia data. The information is about the following:

- Media data: the actual data representing an object.

- Media format data: information about the format of the media data after it goes through the acquisition, processing, and encoding phases.

- Media keyword data: the keyword descriptions, usually relating to the generation of the media data.

- Media feature data: content dependent data such as contain information about the distribution of colours, the kinds of textures and the different shapes present in an image.

The last three types are called metadata as they describe several different aspects of the media data. The media keyword data and media feature data are used as indices for searching purpose. The media format data is used to present the retrieved information.

Requirements of Multimedia Databases

Like the traditional databases, Multimedia databases should address the following requirements:

- Integration

    o Data items do not need to be duplicated for different programs invocations

- Data independence

    o Separate the database and the management from the application programs

- Concurrency control

    o Allows concurrent transactions

- Persistence

    o Data objects can be saved and re-used by different transactions and program invocations

- Privacy

    o Access and authorization control

- Integrity control

    o Ensures database consistency between transactions

- Recovery

     o   Failures of transactions should not affect the persistent data storage

- Query support

     o   Allows easy querying of multimedia data

Multimedia databases should have the ability to uniformly query data (media data, textual data) represented in different formats and have the ability to simultaneously query different media sources and conduct classical database operations across them. *(Query support)*

They should have the ability to retrieve media objects from a local storage device in a good manner. *(Storage support)*

They should have the ability to take the response generated by a query and develop a presentation of that response in terms of audio-visual media and have the ability to deliver this presentation. *(Presentation and delivery support)*

Issues and Challenges

- Multimedia data consists of a variety of media formats or file representations including TIFF, BMP, PPT, IVUE, FPX, JPEG, MPEG, AVI, MID, WAV, DOC, GIF, EPS, PNG, etc. Because of restrictions on the conversion from one format to the other, the use of the data in a specific format has been limited as well. Usually, the data size of multimedia is large such as video; therefore, multimedia data often require a large storage.

- Multimedia database consume a lot of processing time, as well as bandwidth.

- Some multimedia data types such as video, audio, and animation sequences have temporal requirements that have implications on their storage, manipulation and presentation, but images, video and graphics data have spatial constraints in terms of their content.

Application Areas

Examples of multimedia database application areas:

- Digital Libraries
- News-on-Demand
- Video-on-Demand
- Music database
- Geographic Information Systems (GIS)
- Telemedicine

References

- Yu, Chien; Teri Brandenburg (February 2011). "Multimedia database applications: issues and concerns for classroom teaching" (PDF) 3 (1): 2. Retrieved May 28, 2014.

- Adjeroh, Donald; Nwosu, Kingsley (1997). "Multimedia Database Management - Requirements and Issues" (PDF). IEEE Multimedia 4 (3): 1. Retrieved 28 May 2014.

10

Allied Fields of Multimedia

The chapter explores topics like the multimedia computer, multimedia database, multimedia telephony and IP multimedia subsystem. These allied fields of multimedia have transformed media and communication strategies and techniques. Improvement of technology have bridged the gap between separate locations. This chapter provides a plethora of interdisciplinary topics for better comprehension of multimedia.

Multimedia Computer

A multimedia computer is a computer that is optimized for high multimedia performance.

Early home computers lacked the power and storage necessary for true multimedia. The games for these systems, along with the demo scene were able to achieve high sophistication and technical polish using only simple, blocky graphics and digitally generated sound. The Amiga 1000 from Commodore International has been called the first multimedia computer. Its groundbreaking animation, graphics and sound technologies enabled multimedia content to flourish. Famous demos such as the Boing Ball and Juggler showed off the Amiga's abilities. Later the Atari ST series and Apple Macintosh II extended the concept; the Atari integrated a MIDI port and was the first computer under US$1000 to have 1 megabyte of RAM which is a realistic minimum for multimedia content and the Macintosh was the first computer able to display true photorealistic graphics as well as integrating a CD-ROM drive, whose high capacity was essential for delivering multimedia content in the pre-Internet era.

Multimedia capabilities were not common on IBM PC compatibles until the advent of Windows 3.0 and the MPC standards in the early 1990s. The original PCs were devised as "serious" business machines and colorful graphics and powerful sound abilities weren't a priority. The few games available suffered from slow video hardware, PC speaker sound and limited color palette when compared to its contemporaries. But as PCs penetrated the home market in the late 1980s, a thriving industry arose to equip PCs to take advantage of the latest sound, graphics and animation technologies. Creative's SoundBlaster series of sound cards, as well as video cards from ATi, nVidia and Matrox soon became standard equipment for most PCs sold.

Most PCs today have good multimedia features. They have dual- or single-core CPUs clocked at 3.0 GHz or faster, at least 1GB of RAM, a 128 MB or higher video card and TV Tuner card. Popular graphics cards include Nvidia Gforce or ATI Radeon. The Intel Viiv platform, and Microsoft Windows XP Media Center Edition are some of today's products aimed at multimedia computing.

More recently, high-performance devices have become more compact, and multimedia computer capabilities are found in mobile devices such as the Apple iPhone and Nokia Nseries, featuring DVD-like video quality, megapixel class cameras, fully capable browser, music and video players, podcasting, blogging, as well as e-mail, instant messaging, presence and internet call (VoIP) functionality. Multiradios help to offer broadband wireless connectivity, including for instance WCDMA/HSDPA and WLAN/Wifi. Devices are also increasingly equipped with GPS receivers and maps applications, providing new capabilities for location-aware services. The Nseries devices are also expandable, allowing for the addition of multiple applications and multimedia content

Multimedia Database

A Multimedia database (MMDB) is a collection of related multimedia data. The multimedia data include one or more primary media data types such as text, images, graphic objects (including drawings, sketches and illustrations) animation sequences, audio and video.

A Multimedia Database Management System (MMDBMS) is a framework that manages different types of data potentially represented in a wide diversity of formats on a wide array of media sources. It provides support for multimedia data types, and facilitate for creation, storage, access, query and control of a multimedia database.

Contents of MMDB

A Multimedia Database (MMDB) hosts one or more multimedia data types (i.e. text, images, graphic objects, audio, video, animation sequences. These data types are broadly categorized into *three classes*:

- Static media (time-independent: image and graphic object).

- Dynamic media (time-dependent: audio, video and animation).

- Dimensional media(3D game and computer aided drafting programs).

Comparison of Multimedia Data Types

Medium	Elements	Time-dependence
Text	Printable characters	No
Graphic	Vectors, regions	No
Image	Pixels	No
Audio	Sound, Volume	Yes
Video	Raster images, graphics	Yes

Additionally, a Multimedia Database (MMDB) needs to manage additional information pertaining to the actual multimedia data. The information is about the following:

- Media data: the actual data representing an object.

- Media format data: information about the format of the media data after it goes through the acquisition, processing, and encoding phases.

- Media keyword data: the keyword descriptions, usually relating to the generation of the media data.

- Media feature data: content dependent data such as contain information about the distribution of colours, the kinds of textures and the different shapes present in an image.

The last three types are called metadata as they describe several different aspects of the media data. The media keyword data and media feature data are used as indices for searching purpose. The media format data is used to present the retrieved information.

Requirements of Multimedia Databases

Like the traditional databases, Multimedia databases should address the following requirements:

- Integration

  o Data items do not need to be duplicated for different programs invocations

- Data independence

  o Separate the database and the management from the application programs

- Concurrency control

  o Allows concurrent transactions

- Persistence

  o Data objects can be saved and re-used by different transactions and program invocations

- Privacy

  o Access and authorization control

- Integrity control

  o Ensures database consistency between transactions

- Recovery

  o Failures of transactions should not affect the persistent data storage

- Query support

  o Allows easy querying of multimedia data

Multimedia databases should have the ability to uniformly query data (media data, textual data) represented in different formats and have the ability to simultaneously query different media sources and conduct classical database operations across them. *(Query support)*

They should have the ability to retrieve media objects from a local storage device in a good manner. *(Storage support)*

They should have the ability to take the response generated by a query and develop a presentation of that response in terms of audio-visual media and have the ability to deliver this presentation. *(Presentation and delivery support)*

Issues and Challenges

- Multimedia data consists of a variety of media formats or file representations including TIFF, BMP, PPT, IVUE, FPX, JPEG, MPEG, AVI, MID, WAV, DOC, GIF, EPS, PNG, etc. Because of restrictions on the conversion from one format to the other, the use of the data in a specific format has been limited as well. Usually, the data size of multimedia is large such as video; therefore, multimedia data often require a large storage.

- Multimedia database consume a lot of processing time, as well as bandwidth.

- Some multimedia data types such as video, audio, and animation sequences have temporal requirements that have implications on their storage, manipulation and presentation, but images, video and graphics data have spatial constraints in terms of their content.

Application Areas

Examples of multimedia database application areas:

- Digital Libraries

- News-on-Demand

- Video-on-Demand

- Music database

- Geographic Information Systems (GIS)

- Telemedicine

Multimedia PC

The Multimedia PC (MPC) was a recommended configuration for a personal computer (PC) with a CD-ROM drive. The standard was set and named by the "Multimedia PC Marketing Council", which was a working group of the Software Publishers Association (SPA, now the Software and

Information Industry Association). The MPMC comprised companies including Microsoft, Creative Labs, Dell, Gateway, and Fujitsu. Any PC with the required standards could be called an "MPC" by licensing the use of the logo from the SPA.

CD-ROM drives were just coming to market in 1990, and it was difficult to concisely communicate to a consumer all the hardware requirements for using "multimedia software", which mostly meant "displaying video synced with audio on a PC via a CD-ROM drive". The MPC standard was supposed to communicate this concisely, so a consumer buying hardware or software could simply look for the MPC logo and be assured of compatibility.

The MPC program had mixed results primarily because of the vast number of PCs sold under different brands, and once Windows became ubiquitous on PCs, specifying minimum or recommended Windows versions and features was often clearer to consumers than the MPC nomenclature. As the standardized term failed to catch on, and as the Software Publishers Association turned away from consumer software in the late 1990s, interest in the MPC standard vanished. The problem of software labeling continues, especially in the field of computer games, where a multitude of 3D video cards has been manufactured with an extremely wide range of capabilities, and no common industry labeling standard to let consumers know whether their card is powerful enough to let them play a particular game.

MPC Level 1

The first MPC minimum standard, set in 1991, was:

- 16 MHz 386SX CPU

- 2 MB RAM

- 30 MB hard disk

- 256-color, 640×480 VGA video card

- 1× (single speed) CD-ROM drive using no more than 40% of CPU to read, with < 1 second seek time

- Sound card (Creative Sound Blaster recommended as closest available to standard at the time) outputting 22 kHz, 8-bit sound; and inputting 11 kHz, 8-bit sound

- Windows 3.0 with Multimedia Extensions.

MPC Level 2

In 1993, an MPC Level 2 minimum standard was announced:

- 25 MHz 486SX CPU

- 4 MB RAM

- 160 MB hard disk

- 16-bit color, 640×480 VGA video card

- 2× (double speed) CD-ROM drive using no more than 40% of CPU to read at 1x, with < 400 ms seek time

- Sound card outputting 44 kHz, 16-bit CD quality sound.

- Windows 3.0 with Multimedia Extensions, or Windows 3.1.

MPC Level 3

In 1996, MPC Level 3 was announced:

- 75 MHz Pentium CPU

- 8 MB RAM

- 540 MB hard disk

- Video system that can show 352×240 at 30 frames per second, 16-bit color

- MPEG-1 hardware or software video playback

- 4× CD-ROM drive using no more than 40% of CPU to read, with < 250 ms seek time

- Sound card outputting 44 kHz, 16-bit CD quality sound

- Windows 3.11 or Windows 95

Multimedia Telephony

The 3GPP/NGN IP Multimedia Subsystem (IMS) multimedia telephony service (MMTel) is a global standard based on the IMS, offering converged, fixed and mobile real-time multimedia communication using the media capabilities such as voice, real-time video, text, file transfer and sharing of pictures, audio and video clips. With MMTel, users have the capability to add and drop media during a session. You can start with chat, add voice (for instance Mobile VoIP), add another caller, add video, share media and transfer files, and drop any of these without losing or having to end the session. MMTel is one of the registered ICSI (IMS Communication Service Identifier) feature tags.

The MMTel standard is a joint project between the 3GPP and ETSI/TISPAN standardization bodies. The MMTel standard is today the only global standard that defines an evolved telephony service that enables real-time multimedia communication with the characteristics of a telephony service over both fixed broadband, fixed narrowband and mobile access types. MMTel also provides a standardized network-to-network interface (NNI). This allow operators to interconnect their networks which in turn enables users belonging to different operators to communicate with each other, using the full set of media capabilities and supplementary services defined within the MMTel service definition.

One of the main differences with the MMTel standard is that, in contrast of legacy circuit switched telephony services, IP transport is used over the mobile access. This means that the mobile access technologies that are in main focus for MMTel are access types such as high-speed packet access (HSPA), 3GPP long-term evolution (LTE) and EDGE Evolution that all are developed with efficient IP transport in mind.

MMTel allows a single SIP session to control virtually all MMTel supplementary services and MMTel media. All available media components can easily be accessed or activated within the session. Employing a single session for all media parts means that no additional sessions need to be set up to activate video, to add new users, or to start transferring a file. Even though it is possible to manage single-session user scenarios with several sessions – for instance, using a circuit-switched voice service that is complemented with a packet-switched video session, a messaging service or both – there are some concrete benefits to MMTel's single-session approach. A single SIP session in an all-IP environment benefits conferencing; in particular, lip synchronization, which is quite complex when the voice part is carried over a circuit-switched service and the video part is carried over a packet-switched service. In fixed-mobile convergence scenarios, the single-session approach enables all media parts of the multimedia communication solution to interoperate.

IP Multimedia Subsystem

The IP Multimedia Subsystem or IP Multimedia Core Network Subsystem (IMS) is an architectural framework for delivering IP multimedia services. Historically, mobile phones have provided voice call services over a switched-circuit-style network, rather than strictly over an IP packet-switched network. Alternative methods of delivering voice or other multimedia services over IP have become available on smartphones (e.g. VoIP or Skype), but they have not become standardized across the industry. IMS is an architectural framework to provide such standardization.

IMS was originally designed by the wireless standards body 3rd Generation Partnership Project (3GPP), as a part of the vision for evolving mobile networks beyond GSM. Its original formulation (3GPP Rel-5) represented an approach to delivering "Internet services" over GPRS. This vision was later updated by 3GPP, 3GPP2 and ETSI TISPAN by requiring support of networks other than GPRS, such as Wireless LAN, CDMA2000 and fixed lines.

To ease the integration with the Internet, IMS uses IETF protocols wherever possible, e.g., SIP (Session Initiation Protocol). According to the 3GPP, IMS is not intended to standardize applications, but rather to aid the access of multimedia and voice applications from wireless and wireline terminals, i.e., to create a form of fixed-mobile convergence (FMC). This is done by having a horizontal control layer that isolates the access network from the service layer. From a logical architecture perspective, services need not have their own control functions, as the control layer is a common horizontal layer. However, in implementation this does not necessarily map into greater reduced cost and complexity.

Alternative and overlapping technologies for access and provisioning of services across wired and wireless networks include combinations of Generic Access Network, soft switches and "naked" SIP.

Since it is becoming increasingly easier to access content and contacts using mechanisms outside the control of traditional wireless/fixed operators, the interest of IMS is being challenged.

Examples of global standards based on IMS are MMTel which is the basis for Voice over LTE (VoLTE) and Rich Communication Services (RCS) which is also known as joyn or Advanced Messaging.

History

- IMS was originally defined by an industry forum called 3G.IP, formed in 1999. 3G.IP developed the initial IMS architecture, which was brought to the 3rd Generation Partnership Project (3GPP), as part of their standardization work for 3G mobile phone systems in UMTS networks. It first appeared in Release 5 (evolution from 2G to 3G networks), when SIP-based multimedia was added. Support for the older GSM and GPRS networks was also provided.

- 3GPP2 (a different organization from 3GPP) based their CDMA2000 Multimedia Domain (MMD) on 3GPP IMS, adding support for CDMA2000.

- 3GPP release 6 added interworking with WLAN, inter-operability between IMS using different IP-connectivity networks, routing group identities, multiple registration and forking, presence, speech recognition and speech-enabled services (Push to talk).

- 3GPP release 7 added support for fixed networks by working together with TISPAN release R1.1, the function of AGCF (access gateway control function) and PES (PSTN emulation service) are introduced to the wire-line network for the sake of inheritance of services which can be provided in PSTN network. AGCF works as a bridge interconnecting the IMS networks and the Megaco/H.248 networks. Megaco/H.248 networks offers the possibility to connect terminals of the old legacy networks to the new generation of networks based on IP networks. AGCF acts a SIP User agent towards the IMS and performs the role of P-CSCF. SIP User Agent functionality is included in the AGCF, and not on the customer device but in the network itself. Also added voice call continuity between circuit switching and packet switching domain (VCC), fixed broadband connection to the IMS, interworking with non-IMS networks, policy and charging control (PCC), emergency sessions.

- 3GPP release 8 added support for LTE / SAE, multimedia session continuity, enhanced emergency sessions and IMS centralized services.

- 3GPP release 9 added support for IMS emergency calls over GPRS and EPS, enhancements to multimedia telephony, IMS media plane security, enhancements to services centralization and continuity.

- 3GPP release 10 added support for inter device transfer, enhancements to the single radio voice call continuity (SRVCC), enhancements to IMS emergency sessions.

- 3GPP release 11 added USSD simulation service, network-provided location information for IMS, SMS submit and delivery without MSISDN in IMS, and overload control.

Architecture

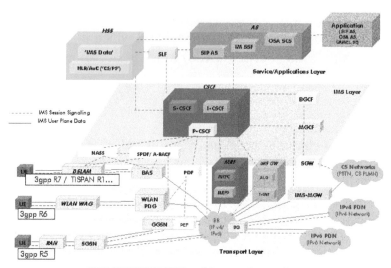

3GPP / TISPAN IMS architectural overview

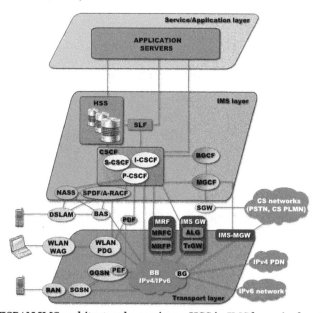

3GPP / TISPAN IMS architectural overview – HSS in IMS layer (as by standard)

Each of the functions in the diagram is explained below.

The IP multimedia core network subsystem is a collection of different functions, linked by standardized interfaces, which grouped form one IMS administrative network. A function is not a node (hardware box): An implementer is free to combine two functions in one node, or to split a single function into two or more nodes. Each node can also be present multiple times in a single network, for dimensioning, load balancing or organizational issues.

Access Network

The user can connect to IMS in various ways, most of which use the standard IP. IMS terminals (such as mobile phones, personal digital assistants (PDAs) and computers) can register directly on

IMS, even when they are roaming in another network or country (the visited network). The only requirement is that they can use IP and run SIP user agents. Fixed access (e.g., Digital Subscriber Line (DSL), cable modems, Ethernet), mobile access (e.g. W-CDMA, CDMA2000, GSM, GPRS) and wireless access (e.g., WLAN, WiMAX) are all supported. Other phone systems like plain old telephone service (POTS—the old analogue telephones), H.323 and non IMS-compatible systems, are supported through gateways.

Core Network

HSS – Home subscriber server:The *home subscriber server* (HSS), or *user profile server function* (UPSF), is a master user database that supports the IMS network entities that actually handle calls. It contains the subscription-related information (subscriber profiles), performs authentication and authorization of the user, and can provide information about the subscriber's location and IP information. It is similar to the GSM home location register (HLR) and Authentication centre (AuC).

A *subscriber location function* (SLF) is needed to map user addresses when multiple HSSs are used.

User identities:Various identities may be associated with IMS: IP multimedia private identity (IMPI), IP multimedia public identity (IMPU), globally routable user agent URI (GRUU), wildcarded public user identity. Both IMPI and IMPU are not phone numbers or other series of digits, but uniform resource identifier (URIs), that can be digits (a Tel URI, such as *tel:+1-555-123-4567*) or alphanumeric identifiers (a SIP URI, such as *sip:john.doe@example.com"*).

IP Multimedia Private Identity:The *IP Multimedia Private Identity* (IMPI) is a unique permanently allocated global identity assigned by the home network operator, and is used, for example, for Registration, Authorization, Administration, and Accounting purposes. Every IMS user shall have one IMPI.

IP Multimedia Public Identity:The *IP Multimedia Public Identity* (IMPU) is used by any user for requesting communications to other users (e.g. this might be included on a business card). There can be multiple IMPU per IMPI. The IMPU can also be shared with another phone, so that both can be reached with the same identity (for example, a single phone-number for an entire family).

Globally Routable User Agent URI:*Globally Routable User Agent URI* (GRUU) is an identity that identifies a unique combination of IMPU and UE instance. There are two types of GRUU: Public-GRUU (P-GRUU) and Temporary GRUU (T-GRUU).

- P-GRUU reveal the IMPU and are very long lived.

- T-GRUU do not reveal the IMPU and are valid until the contact is explicitly de-registered or the current registration expires

Wildcarded Public User Identity:A *wildcarded Public User Identity* expresses a set of IMPU grouped together.

The HSS subscriber database contains the IMPU, IMPI, IMSI, MSISDN, subscriber service profiles, service triggers, and other information.

CSCF – Call Session Control Function

Several roles of SIP servers or proxies, collectively called Call Session Control Function (CSCF), are used to process SIP signalling packets in the IMS.

- A *Proxy-CSCF* (P-CSCF) is a SIP proxy that is the first point of contact for the IMS terminal. It can be located either in the visited network (in full IMS networks) or in the home network (when the visited network is not IMS compliant yet). Some networks may use a Session Border Controller (SBC) for this function. The P-CSCF is at its core a specialized SBC for the User–network interface which not only protects the network, but also the IMS terminal. The use of an additional SBC between the IMS terminal and the P-CSCF is unnecessary and infeasible due to the signaling being encrypted on this leg. The terminal discovers its P-CSCF with either DHCP, or it may be configured (e.g. during initial provisioning or via a 3GPP IMS Management Object (MO)) or in the ISIM or assigned in the PDP Context (in General Packet Radio Service (GPRS)).

    o It is assigned to an IMS terminal before registration, and does not change for the duration of the registration.

    o It sits on the path of all signalling, and can inspect every signal; the IMS terminal must ignore any other unencrypted signalling.

    o It provides subscriber authentication and may establish an IPsec or TLS security association with the IMS terminal. This prevents spoofing attacks and replay attacks and protects the privacy of the subscriber.

    o It inspects the signaling and ensures that the IMS terminals do not misbehave (e.g. change normal signaling routes, do not obey home network's routing policy).

    o It can compress and decompress SIP messages using SigComp, which reduces the round-trip over slow radio links.

    o It may include a Policy Decision Function (PDF), which authorizes media plane resources e.g., quality of service (QoS) over the media plane. It is used for policy control, bandwidth management, etc. The PDF can also be a separate function.

    o It also generates charging records.

- An *Interrogating-CSCF* (I-CSCF) is another SIP function located at the edge of an administrative domain. Its IP address is published in the Domain Name System (DNS) of the domain (using NAPTR and SRV type of DNS records), so that remote servers can find it, and use it as a forwarding point (e.g., registering) for SIP packets to this domain.

    o it queries the HSS to retrieve the address of the S-CSCF and assign it to a user performing SIP registration

    o it also forwards SIP request or response to the S-CSCF

    o Up to Release 6 it can also be used to hide the internal network from the outside world (encrypting parts of the SIP message), in which case it's called a *Topology*

Hiding Inter-network Gateway (THIG). From Release 7 onwards this "entry point" function is removed from the I-CSCF and is now part of the *Interconnection Border Control Function* (IBCF). The IBCF is used as gateway to external networks, and provides NAT and firewall functions (pinholing). The IBCF is practically a Session Border Controller specialized for the NNI.

- A *Serving-CSCF* (S-CSCF) is the central node of the signalling plane. It is a SIP server, but performs session control too. It is always located in the home network. It uses Diameter Cx and Dx interfaces to the HSS to download user profiles and upload user-to-S-CSCF associations (the user profile is only cached locally for processing reasons only and is not changed). All necessary subscriber profile information is loaded from the HSS.

    o it handles SIP registrations, which allows it to bind the user location (e.g., the IP address of the terminal) and the SIP address

    o it sits on the path of all signaling messages of the locally registered users, and can inspect every message

    o it decides to which application server(s) the SIP message will be forwarded, in order to provide their services

    o it provides routing services, typically using Electronic Numbering (ENUM) lookups

    o it enforces the policy of the network operator

    o there can be multiple S-CSCFs in the network for load distribution and high availability reasons. It's the HSS that assigns the S-CSCF to a user, when it's queried by the I-CSCF. There are multiple options for this purpose, including a mandatory/optional capabilities to be matched between subscribers and S-CSCFs.

Application Servers

SIP Application servers (AS) host and execute services, and interface with the S-CSCF using SIP. An example of an application server that is being developed in 3GPP is the Voice call continuity Function (VCC Server). Depending on the actual service, the AS can operate in SIP proxy mode, SIP UA (user agent) mode or SIP B2BUA mode. An AS can be located in the home network or in an external third-party network. If located in the home network, it can query the HSS with the Diameter Sh or Si interfaces (for a SIP-AS).

- SIP AS: Host and execute IMS specific services

- *IP Multimedia Service Switching Function* (IM-SSF): Interfaces SIP to CAP to communicate with CAMEL Application Servers

- OSA service capability server (OSA SCS) : Interfaces SIP to the OSA framework;

Functional Model

The AS-ILCM and AS-OLCM store transaction state, and may optionally store session state depending on the specific service being executed. The AS-ILCM interfaces to the S-CSCF (ILCM) for an incoming leg and the AS-OLCM interfaces to the S-CSCF (OLCM) for an outgoing leg. Application Logic provides the service(s) and interacts between the AS-ILCM and AS-OLCM.

Public Service Identity

Public Service Identities (PSI) are identities that identify services, which are hosted by application servers. As user identities, PSI takes the form of either a SIP or Tel URI. PSIs are stored in the HSS either as a distinct PSI or as a wildcarded PSI:

- a distinct PSI contains the PSI that is used in routing

- a wildcarded PSI represents a collection of PSIs.

Media Servers

The *Media Resource Function* (MRF) provides media related functions such as media manipulation (e.g. voice stream mixing) and playing of tones and announcements.

Each MRF is further divided into a *media resource function controller* (MRFC) and a *media resource function processor* (MRFP).

- The MRFC is a signalling plane node that interprets information coming from an AS and S-CSCF to control the MRFP

- The MRFP is a media plane node used to mix, source or process media streams. It can also manage access right to shared resources.

The *Media Resource Broker* (MRB) is a functional entity that is responsible for both collection of appropriate published MRF information and supplying of appropriate MRF information to consuming entities such as the AS. MRB can be used in two modes:

- Query mode: AS queries the MRB for media and sets up the call using the response of MRB

- In-Line Mode: AS sends a SIP INVITE to the MRB. The MRB sets up the call

Breakout Gateway

A *Breakout Gateway Control Function* (BGCF) is a SIP proxy which processes requests for routing from an S-CSCF when the S-CSCF has determined that the session cannot be routed using DNS or ENUM/DNS. It includes routing functionality based on telephone numbers.

PSTN Gateways

A PSTN/CS gateway interfaces with PSTN circuit switched (CS) networks. For signalling, CS networks use ISDN User Part (ISUP) (or BICC) over Message Transfer Part (MTP), while IMS uses SIP over IP. For media, CS networks use Pulse-code modulation (PCM), while IMS uses Real-time Transport Protocol (RTP).

- A signalling gateway (SGW) interfaces with the signalling plane of the CS. It transforms lower layer protocols as Stream Control Transmission Protocol (SCTP, an IP protocol) into

Message Transfer Part (MTP, an Signalling System 7 (SS7) protocol), to pass ISDN User Part (ISUP) from the MGCF to the CS network.

- A *media gateway controller function* (MGCF) is a SIP endpoint that does call control protocol conversion between SIP and ISUP/BICC and interfaces with the SGW over SCTP. It also controls the resources in a *Media Gateway* (MGW) across an H.248 interface.

- A *media gateway* (MGW) interfaces with the media plane of the CS network, by converting between RTP and PCM. It can also transcode when the codecs don't match (e.g., IMS might use AMR, PSTN might use G.711).

Media Resources

Media Resources are those components that operate on the media plane and are under the control of IMS core functions. Specifically, *Media Server* (MS) and *Media gateway* (MGW)

NGN Interconnection

There are two types of next-generation networking interconnection:

- *Service-oriented interconnection* (SoIx): The physical and logical linking of NGN domains that allows carriers and service providers to offer services over NGN (i.e., IMS and PES) platforms with control, signalling (i.e., session based), which provides defined levels of interoperability. For instance, this is the case of "carrier grade" voice and/or multimedia services over IP interconnection. "Defined levels of interoperability" are dependent upon the service or the QoS or the Security, etc.

- *Connectivity-oriented interconnection* (CoIx): The physical and logical linking of carriers and service providers based on simple IP connectivity irrespective of the levels of interoperability. For example, an IP interconnection of this type is not aware of the specific end to end service and, as a consequence, service specific network performance, QoS and security requirements are not necessarily assured. This definition does not exclude that some services may provide a defined level of interoperability. However, only SoIx fully satisfies NGN interoperability requirements.

An NGN interconnection mode can be direct or indirect. Direct interconnection refers to the interconnection between two network domains without any intermediate network domain. Indirect interconnection at one layer refers to the interconnection between two network domains with one or more intermediate network domain(s) acting as transit networks. The intermediate network domain(s) provide(s) transit functionality to the two other network domains. Different interconnection modes may be used for carrying service layer signalling and media traffic.

Charging

Offline charging is applied to users who pay for their services periodically (e.g., at the end of the month). Online charging, also known as credit-based charging, is used for prepaid services, or real-time credit control of postpaid services. Both may be applied to the same session.

Charging function addresses are addresses distributed to each IMS entities and provide a common location for each entity to send charging information. *charging data function* (CDF) addresses are used for offline billing and *Online Charging Function* (OCF) for online billing.

- Offline Charging : All the SIP network entities (P-CSCF, I-CSCF, S-CSCF, BGCF, MRFC, MGCF, AS) involved in the session use the Diameter Rf interface to send accounting information to a CDF located in the same domain. The CDF will collect all this information, and build a *call detail record* (CDR), which is sent to the billing system (BS) of the domain. Each session carries an *IMS Charging Identifier* (ICID) as a unique identifier generated by the first IMS entity involved in a SIP transaction and used for the correlation with CDRs. *Inter Operator Identifier* (IOI) is a globally unique identifier shared between sending and receiving networks. Each domain has its own charging network. Billing systems in different domains will also exchange information, so that roaming charges can be applied.

- Online charging : The S-CSCF talks to a *IMS gateway function* (IMS-GWF) which looks like a regular SIP application server. The IMS-GWF can signal the S-CSCF to terminate the session when the user runs out of credits during a session. The AS and MRFC use the Diameter Ro interface towards an OCF.

  o When *immediate event charging* (IEC) is used, a number of credit units is immediately deducted from the user's account by the ECF and the MRFC or AS is then authorized to provide the service. The service is not authorized when not enough credit units are available.

  o When *event charging with unit reservation* (ECUR) is used, the ECF (event charging function) first reserves a number of credit units in the user's account and then authorizes the MRFC or the AS. After the service is over, the number of spent credit units is reported and deducted from the account; the reserved credit units are then cleared.

IMS-based PES Architecture

IMS-based PES (PSTN Emulation System) provides IP networks services to analog devices. IMS-based PES allows non-IMS devices to appear to IMS as normal SIP users. Analog terminal using standard analog interfaces can connect to IMS-based PES in two ways -

- Via A-MGW (Access Media Gateway) that is linked and controlled by AGCF. AGCF is placed within the Operators network and controls multiple A-MGW. A-MGW and AGCF communicate using H.248.1 (Megaco) over the P1 reference point. POTS phone connect to A-MGW over the z interface. The signalling is converted to H.248 in the A-MGW and passed to AGCF. AGCF interprets the H.248 signal and other inputs from the A-MGW to format H.248 messages into appropriate SIP messages. AGCF presents itself as P-CSCF to the S-CSCF and passes generated SIP messages to S-CSCF or to IP border via IBCF (Interconnection Border Control Function). Service presented to S-CSCF in SIP messages trigger PES AS. AGCF has also certain service independent logic, for example on receipt of off-hook event from A-MGW, the AGCF requests the A-MGW to play dial tone.

- Via VGW (VoIP-Gateway) or SIP Gateway/Adapter on customer premises. POTS phones via VOIP Gateway connect to P-CSCF directly. Operators mostly use session border controllers between VoIP gateways and P-CSCFs for security and to hide network topology. VoIP gateway link to IMS using SIP over Gm reference point. The conversion from POTS service over the z interface to SIP occurs in the customer premises VoIP gateway. POTS signaling is converted to SIP and passed on to P-CSCF. VGW acts as SIP user agent and appears to P-CSCF as SIP terminal.

Both A-MGW and VGW are unaware of the services. They only relay call control signalling to and from the PSTN terminal. Session control and handling is done by IMS components.

Interfaces Description

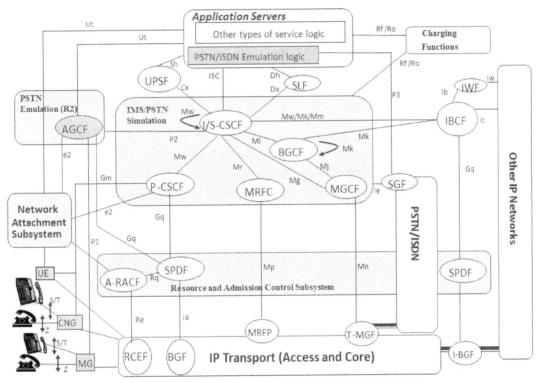

TISPAN IMS architecture with interfaces

Interface name	IMS entities	Description	Protocol	Technical specification
Cr	MRFC, AS	Used by MRFC to fetch documents (e.g. scripts, announcement files, and other resources) from an AS. Also used for media control related commands.	TCP/SCTP channels	
Cx	(I-CSCF, S-CSCF), HSS	Used to send subscriber data to the S-CSCF; including filter criteria and their priority. Also used to furnish CDF and/or OCF addresses.	Diameter	TS29.229, TS29.212

Dh	AS (SIP AS, OSA, IM-SSF) <-> SLF	Used by AS to find the HSS holding the user profile information in a multi-HSS environment. DH_SLF_ QUERY indicates an IMPU and DX_SLF_RESP return the HSS name.	Diameter	
Dx	(I-CSCF or S-CSCF) <-> SLF	Used by I-CSCF or S-CSCF to find a correct HSS in a multi-HSS environment. DX_SLF_QUERY indicates an IMPU and DX_SLF_ RESP return the HSS name.	Diameter	TS29.229, TS29.212
Gm	UE, P-CSCF	Used to exchange messages between SIP user equipment (UE) or Voip gateway and P-CSCF	SIP	
Go	PDF, GGSN	Allows operators to control QoS in a user plane and exchange charging correlation information between IMS and GPRS network	COPS (Rel5), diameter (Rel6+)	
Gq	P-CSCF, PDF	Used to exchange policy decisions-related information between P-CSCF and PDF	Diameter	
Gx	PCEF, PCRF	Used to exchange policy decisions-related information between PCEF and PCRF	Diameter	TS29.211, TS29.212
Gy	PCEF, OCS	Used for online flow-based bearer charging. Functionally equivalent to Ro interface	Diameter	TS23.203, TS32.299
ISC	S-CSCF <-> AS	Reference point between S-CSCF and AS. Main functions are to : • Notify the AS of the registered IMPU, registration state and UE capabilities • Supply the AS with information to allow it to execute multiple services • Convey charging function addresses	SIP	

Ici	IBCFs	Used to exchange messages between an IBCF and another IBCF belonging to a different IMS network.	SIP	
Izi	TrGWs	Used to forward media streams from a TrGW to another TrGW belonging to a different IMS network.	RTP	
Ma	I-CSCF <-> AS	Main functions are to: • Forward SIP requests which are destined to a public service identity hosted by the AS • Originate a session on behalf of a user or public service identity, if the AS has no knowledge of a S-CSCF assigned to that user or public service identity • Convey charging function addresses	SIP	
Mg	MGCF -> I,S-CSCF	ISUP signalling to SIP signalling and forwards SIP signalling to I-CSCF	SIP	
Mi	S-CSCF -> BGCF	Used to exchange messages between S-CSCF and BGCF	SIP	
Mj	BGCF -> MGCF	Used for the interworking with the PSTN/CS domain, when the BGCF has determined that a breakout should occur in the same IMS network to send SIP message from BGCF to MGCF	SIP	
Mk	BGCF -> BGCF	Used for the interworking with the PSTN/CS domain, when the BGCF has determined that a breakout should occur in another IMS network to send SIP message from BGCF to the BGCF in the other network	SIP	
Mm	I-CSCF, S-CSCF, external IP network	Used for exchanging messages between IMS and external IP networks	SIP	

Mn	MGCF, IM-MGW	Allows control of user-plane resources	H.248	
Mp	MRFC, MRFP	Allows an MRFC to control media stream resources provided by an MRFP.	H.248	
Mr Mr'	S-CSCF, MRFC AS, MRFC	Used to exchange information between S-CSCF and MRFC Used to exchange session controls between AS and MRFC	Application server sends SIP message to MRFC to play tone and announcement. This SIP message contains sufficient information to play tone and announcement or provide information to MRFC, so that it can ask more information from application server through Cr Interface.	SIP
Mw	P-CSCF, I-CSCF, S-CSCF, AGCF	Used to exchange messages between CSCFs. AGCF appears as a P-CSCF to the other CSCFs	SIP	
Mx	BGCF/ CSCF, IBCF	Used for the interworking with another IMS network, when the BGCF has determined that a breakout should occur in the other IMS network to send SIP message from BGCF to the IBCF in the other network	SIP	
P1	AGCF, A-MGW	Used for call control services by AGCF to control H.248 A-MGW and residential gateways	H.248	
P2	AGCF, CSCF	Reference point between AGCF and CSCF.	SIP	
Rc	MRB, AS	Used by the AS to request that media resources be assigned to a call when using MRB in-line mode or in query mode	SIP, in query mode (not specified)	
Rf	P-CSCF, I-CSCF, S-CSCF, BGCF, MRFC, MGCF, AS	Used to exchange offline charging information with CDF	Diameter	TS32.299
Ro	AS, MRFC, S-CSCF	Used to exchange online charging information with OCF	Diameter	TS32.299

Rx	P-CSCF, PCRF	Used to exchange policy and charging related information between P-CSCF and PCRF Replacement for the Gq reference point.	Diameter	TS29.214
Sh	AS (SIP AS, OSA SCS), HSS	Used to exchange User Profile information (e.g., user-related data, group lists, user-service-related information or user location information or charging function addresses (used when the AS has not received the third-party REGISTER for a user)) between an AS (SIP AS or OSA SCS) and HSS. Also allow AS to activate/deactivate filter criteria stored in the HSS on a per-subscriber basis	Diameter	
Si	IM-SSF, HSS	Transports CAMEL subscription information, including triggers for use by CAMEL-based application services information.	MAP	
Sr	MRFC, AS	Used by MRFC to fetch documents (scripts and other resources) from an AS	HTTP	
Ut	UE and SIP AS (SIP AS, OSA SCS, IM-SSF) PES AS and AGCF	Facilitates the management of subscriber information related to services and settings	HTTP(s), XCAP	
z	POTS, Analog phones and VoIP gateways	Conversion of POTS services to SIP messages		

Session Handling

One of the most important features of IMS, that of allowing for a SIP application to be dynamically and differentially (based on the user's profile) triggered, is implemented as a filter-and-redirect signalling mechanism in the S-CSCF.

The S-CSCF might apply filter criteria to determine the need to forward SIP requests to AS. It is important to note that services for the originating party will be applied in the originating network, while the services for the terminating party will be applied in the terminating network, all in the respective S-CSCFs.

Initial Filter Criteria

An initial filter criteria (iFC) is an XML-based format used for describing control logic. iFCs represent a provisioned subscription of a user to an application. They are stored in the HSS as part of the IMS Subscription Profile and are downloaded to the S-CSCF upon user registration (for registered users) or on processing demand (for services, acting as unregistered users). iFCs are valid throughout the registration lifetime or until the User Profile is changed.

The iFC is composed of:

- Priority - determines the order of checking the trigger.

- Trigger point - logical condition(s) which is verified against initial dialog creating SIP requests or stand-alone SIP requests.

- Application server URI - specifies the application server to be forwarded to when the trigger point matches.

There are two types of iFCs:

- Shared - When provisioning, only a reference number (the shared iFC number) is assigned to the subscriber. During registration, only the number is sent to the CSCF, not the entire XML description. The complete XML will have previously been stored on the CSCF.

- Non-shared - when provisioning, the entire XML description of the iFC is assigned to the subscriber. During registration, the entire XML description is sent to the CSCF.

Security Aspects of Early IMS and Non-3GPP Systems

It is envisaged that security defined in TS 33.203 may not be available for a while especially because of the lack of USIM/ISIM interfaces and prevalence of devices that support IPv4. For this situation, to provide some protection against the most significant threats, 3GPP defines some security mechanisms, which are informally known as "early IMS security," in TR33.978. This mechanism relies on the authentication performed during the network attachment procedures, which binds between the user's profile and its IP address. This mechanism is also weak because the signaling is not protected on the user–network interface.

CableLabs in PacketCable 2.0, which adopted also the IMS architecture but has no USIM/ISIM capabilities in their terminals, published deltas to the 3GPP specifications where the Digest-MD5 is a valid authentication option. Later on, TISPAN also did a similar effort given their fixed networks scopes, although the procedures are different. To compensate for the lack of IPsec capabilities, TLS has been added as an option for securing the Gm interface. Later 3GPP Releases have included the Digest-MD5 method, towards a Common-IMS platform, yet in its own and again different approach. Although all 3 variants of Digest-MD5 authentication have the same functionality and are the same from the IMS terminal's perspective, the implementations on the Cx interface between the S-CSCF and the HSS are different.

References

- Yu, Chien; Teri Brandenburg (February 2011). "Multimedia database applications: issues and concerns for classroom teaching" (PDF). 3 (1): 2. Retrieved May 28, 2014.

- Adjeroh, Donald; Nwosu, Kingsley (1997). "Multimedia Database Management - Requirements and Issues" (PDF). IEEE Multimedia. 4 (3): 1. Retrieved 28 May 2014.

- Alexander Harrowell, Staff Writer (October 2006), A Pointless Multimedia Subsystem?, Mobile Communications International, archived from the original on September 2010.

11

Multimedia Softwares

This chapter gives a detailed account of the various kinds of software related to multimedia like mobile soft device, media player (software), 4K video downloader, multimedia framework etc. This text introduces the reader to each of these tools. This chapter is an overview of the subject matter incorporating all the major aspects of multimedia software.

Multimedia Framework

A multimedia framework is a software framework that handles media on a computer and through a network. A good multimedia framework offers an intuitive API and a modular architecture to easily add support for new audio, video and container formats and transmission protocols. It is meant to be used by applications such as media players and audio or video editors, but can also be used to build videoconferencing applications, media converters and other multimedia tools.

In contrast to function libraries, a multimedia framework provides a run time environment for the media processing. Ideally such an environment provides execution contexts for the media processing blocks separated from the application using the framework. The separation supports the independent processing of multimedia data in a timely manner. These separate contexts can be implemented as threads.

Media Player (Software)

MPlayer, an example of a cross-platform media player

A media player is a computer program for playing multimedia files like videos movies and music. Media players display standard media control icons known from physical devices such as tape recorders and CD players, such as play (▶), pause (❚❚), fastforward, backforward, and stop (■) buttons.

Mainstream operating systems have at least one built-in media player. For example, Windows comes with Windows Media Player while OS X comes with QuickTime Player. Linux distributions may also come with a media players, such as SMPlayer, Amarok, Audacious, Banshee, MPlayer, Rhythmbox, Totem, VLC, and xine.

Functionality Focus

Clementine v1.2, an audio player with a media library and online radio

Different media players may have different goals and feature sets. *Video players* are a group of media players that have their features geared more towards playing digital video. For example, Windows DVD Player exclusively plays DVD-Video discs and nothing else. Media Player Classic can play individual audio and video files but many of its features such as color correction, picture sharpening, zooming, set of hotkeys, DVB support and subtitle support are only useful for video material such as films and cartoons. *Audio players*, on the other hand, specialize in digital audio. For example, AIMP exclusively plays audio formats. MediaMonkey can play both audio and video format but many of its features including media library, lyric discovery, music visualization, online radio, audiobook indexing and tag editing are geared toward consumption of audio material. In addition, watching video files on it can be a trying feat. General-purpose media players also do exist. For example, Windows Media Player has exclusive features for both audio and video material, although it cannot match the feature set of Media Player Classic and MediaMonkey combined.

3D Video Players

3D video players are used to play 2D video in 3D format. A high-quality three-dimensional video presentation requires that each frame of a motion picture be embedded with information on the depth of objects present in the scene. This process involves shooting the video with special equipment from two distinct perspectives or modelling and rendering each frame as a collection of objects composed of 3D vertices and textures, much like in any modern video game, to achieve special effects. Tedious and costly, this method is only used in a small fraction of movies produced worldwide, while most movies remain in the form of traditional 2D images. It is, however, possible to give an otherwise two-dimensional picture the appearance of depth. Using a technique known as anaglyph processing a "flat" picture can be transformed so as to give an illusion of depth when viewed through anaglyph glasses (usually red-cyan). An image viewed through anaglyph glasses appears to have both protruding and deeply embedded objects in it, at the expense of somewhat distorted colours. The method itself is old enough, dating back to mid-19th century, but it is only with recent advances in computer technology that it has become possible to apply this kind of transformation to a series of frames in a motion picture reasonably fast or even in real time, i.e. as the video is being played back. Several implementations exist in the form of 3D video players, that render conventional 2D video in anaglyph 3D, as well as in the form of 3D video converters, that transform video into stereoscopic anaglyph and transcode it for playback with regular software or hardware video players.

Home Theater PC

A home theater PC or media center computer is a convergence device that combines some or all the capabilities of a personal computer with a software application that supports video, photo, audio playback, and sometimes video recording functionality. Although computers with some of these capabilities were available from the late 1980s, the "Home Theater PC" term first appeared in mainstream press in 1996. Since 2007, other types of consumer electronics, including gaming systems and dedicated media devices have crossed over to manage video and music content. The term "media center" also refers to specialized computer programs designed to run on standard personal computers.

Mobile Soft Device

Mobile soft device or MSD is a mobile communication service software package that executes on mobile devices such as smartphones and tablets. An MSD is commonly implemented as a smartphone app.

A mobile soft device is integrated with the core mobile network and its voice call, SMS and MMS services in the same way as a normal mobile phone (with an installed SIM card). Therefore, an MSD uses the mobile voice call, SMS and 3GPP MMS services as an integrated part of the overall service provided to the end user.

As a result, an MSD makes it possible to establish a real-time communication link between two end points even if neither end point is connected to the Internet. In contrast, other smartphone communication apps, such as OTT services, often require both sides to be connected to the Internet in order to establish a real-time communication connection between the two end points.

A further result of the mobile network integration is that a mobile soft device does not require both end points to have an MSD installed in the mobile device in order to fully use voice, SMS and multimedia services. In contrast, an OTT mobile communication app often requires that both end points have the same app installed.

An MSD can thus be used to establish a real-time communication with any other mobile device, anytime and anywhere. This would not be possible with an ordinary OTT smartphone communication app.

The MSD software program executes on mobile hardware devices, such as smartphones or tablets, on top of the mobile device operating system, for example Apple iOS, Google Android or Windows Mobile. The MSD does not need to be installed onto a device with a physical SIM, which is traditionally used to identify and authenticate the particular mobile hardware device and the particular user. An MSD has a virtual SIM card function implemented by software and is therefore not dependent on a physical SIM card to authenticate the mobile user.

An MSD can be used by a mobile network operator or an MVNO to provide OTT services similar to Skype, Viber and WhatsApp (in March 2013), with the added benefit of using the integration with the core mobile network to provide these services anytime and anywhere. In addition, the MSD can provide completely new services as it has access to mobile subscriber data and other mobile network infrastructure, something traditional OTT services generally do not have.

In the special case of voice calls, text messaging and 3GPP MMS, the MSD can be viewed as a mobile soft phone in contrast to a hardware phone device. The cost for a mobile operator to reach new customers, or to distribute physical mobile phones and SIM cards, is usually high. As the MSD is typically distributed over app stores at virtually no cost to the mobile operator, the MSD concept is expected to reshape the mobile industry.

MSD and VoLTE

MSD also has significant relevance for 3GPP IMS in general and Voice-over-LTE VoLTE. VoLTE is generally expected to provide an IP voice quality that is superior to other voice services over Internet. As the MSD is a software application executing on top of a mobile hardware device operating system, the MSD can be used to introduce VoLTE services even before the hardware device itself has VoLTE support. By moving the voice services from the mobile legacy net LTE, the mobile operator can consolidate the network technologies by phasing out 2G (and even 3G) networks and having all services carried over 4G and LTE networks even before the device industry has caught up with VoLTE support. Such a network technology consolidation will have a significant impact on the mobile network operations cost.

4K Video Downloader

4K Video's Downloader is a multi-platform software for downloading video and audio from popular websites like YouTube, Vimeo, Dailymotion or Facebook. It supports the following output formats: MP4, MKV, OGG Theora, MP3, M4A.

Features

- Downloading playlists

- Downloading channels

- Downloading embedded subtitles and additional subtitles on various languages as .srt files

Supported Sites:

- YouTube
- Vimeo
- Facebook
- SoundCloud
- Flickr
- Dailymotion
- Metacafe

Video Quality Options

- 8K
- 4K
- High definition
- Standard definition
- Low definition

Video Formats:

- MP4, MKV, FLV, 3GP

Audio Formats:

- MP3, M4A, OGG

4K Video Downloader has been submitted to Steam GreenLight Community for voting and received around 1,500 votes.

Tabs

- Smart Mode allows user to download videos in one click; once format, quality and output directory are chosen, the application applies the settings to all further downloads.

- Preferences allows user..

1. Choosing the level of intensity

2. Choosing Speed limit

3. Adding the numeration to file names in playlists

4. Generating .m3u file for downloaded playlists

5. Adding the downloaded videos and audios directly to iTunes

6. Skipping duplicates in playlist

7. Adding embed subtitles in video if possible

8. Searching audio tags on the basis of track title

9. Playing sound when download is completed

10. Changing proxy to download blocked videos

Development

4K Video Downloader was originally developed in the programming language C++ with QT framework using such libraries as Boost, FFmpeg, OpenCV, OpenSSL, LAME, and PortAudio.

Price

4K Video Downloader is free for sole public videos, and playlists consisting of up to 25 videos from the supported sites. However, for downloading playlists larger than that you need to buy a licence key.

Permissions

All chapters in this book are published with permission under the Creative Commons Attribution Share Alike License or equivalent. Every chapter published in this book has been scrutinized by our experts. Their significance has been extensively debated. The topics covered herein carry significant information for a comprehensive understanding. They may even be implemented as practical applications or may be referred to as a beginning point for further studies.

We would like to thank the editorial team for lending their expertise to make the book truly unique. They have played a crucial role in the development of this book. Without their invaluable contributions this book wouldn't have been possible. They have made vital efforts to compile up to date information on the varied aspects of this subject to make this book a valuable addition to the collection of many professionals and students.

This book was conceptualized with the vision of imparting up-to-date and integrated information in this field. To ensure the same, a matchless editorial board was set up. Every individual on the board went through rigorous rounds of assessment to prove their worth. After which they invested a large part of their time researching and compiling the most relevant data for our readers.

The editorial board has been involved in producing this book since its inception. They have spent rigorous hours researching and exploring the diverse topics which have resulted in the successful publishing of this book. They have passed on their knowledge of decades through this book. To expedite this challenging task, the publisher supported the team at every step. A small team of assistant editors was also appointed to further simplify the editing procedure and attain best results for the readers.

Apart from the editorial board, the designing team has also invested a significant amount of their time in understanding the subject and creating the most relevant covers. They scrutinized every image to scout for the most suitable representation of the subject and create an appropriate cover for the book.

The publishing team has been an ardent support to the editorial, designing and production team. Their endless efforts to recruit the best for this project, has resulted in the accomplishment of this book. They are a veteran in the field of academics and their pool of knowledge is as vast as their experience in printing. Their expertise and guidance has proved useful at every step. Their uncompromising quality standards have made this book an exceptional effort. Their encouragement from time to time has been an inspiration for everyone.

The publisher and the editorial board hope that this book will prove to be a valuable piece of knowledge for students, practitioners and scholars across the globe.

Index

CPSIA information can be obtained
at www.ICGtesting.com
Printed in the USA
BVHW02*0447020218
506942BV00003B/37/P

9 781635 491913